Praise for This Book

"An appealing and original work, this book evokes to the reader, by its very title, Mark Twain's *Connecticut Yankee in King Arthur's Court*. Reflecting on my post-WWII small-town German childhood and young adulthood in Berlin, I recognize in reading this diary specific cultural differences and the more general distinction between an American innocence, with fresh, at times revelatory, perceptions of an older world with its repressive traditions, fatally not changing for the better at the time of the diarist's journey.

Some fifty years later, my own academic studies in sociology and political theory brought me to America and were completed at Stanford with a PhD in educational philosophy. From that experience and perspective, I appreciate the challenges faced by an unworldly University of Chicago PhD candidate from Texas in 1928, setting out bravely on a journey of exploration and discovery, motivated to understand foreign peoples and customs, the values and struggles of their time. Motivated above all to learn!

What Joseph S. Werlin saw and learned informed his life well beyond his academic objectives, and it informs the present reader of his diary about both history and culture and the 'Texas greenhorn' himself. Extracts of the perceptive, searching, at times astonishing, letters he sent to folks back home in 1928, together with other documents compiled by Joella Werlin, a loving daughter dedicated both to her father and to scholarship, makes this a work of unusual and vivid interest. A riveting reading experience, shedding light on a gathering darkness that was to spread beyond Europe over the world."

— Margret Buchmann, PhD
Retired professor of education and Senior Researcher,
Institute for Research on Teaching, Michigan State University

"Personally, I couldn't put the book down. It seems to have something for every history buff: Russia, Germany, Mexico, Judaism, anti-Semitism, the Depression of the 1930s, academic life under the constraints of political turmoil. The correspondence between the writer and his fiancée adds additional validity to the historical side of things and is imbued with warmth and passion.

For obvious reasons, I found Joseph Werlin's time in Russia the most interesting and relevant segments in the diary for my own background and teaching career. I thought he captured very well the dark and tumultuous years of post-NEP Moscow: the squalor, the housing crisis in the city, the misery of communal living, the pitiful state of the citizens, the introduction of cooperatives, the treatment of the Russian Jews. He projects effectively the image of the country ravished by the October Revolution. He is familiar with the names and policies of the key Soviet personalities, and though a Texan in the land of the Bolsheviks, he can see through the pretense and lack of genuine policy. I also stumbled into a whole web of unexpected connections to the icons of that time, with Trotsky and Frida Kahlo somehow making their way into the narrative!

Joseph Werlin said, 'It will not be easy for me to forget my first impression of Moscow.' It will be equally hard for me to forget my impressions of reading his diary!"

— Dr. Rima Greenhill
Stanford Humanities Center Fellow (2019-20) and Senior Lecturer in Russian Language
Department of Slavic Languages and Literatures, Stanford University

"As Joseph Werlin, still a graduate student, is traveling in Europe, and in time, towards his future marriage, his family, his career as a professor, there are traveling with him our ever-contemporary historical questions. About nations, or about humans we meet in consulates and trains, in universities and apartments. About our borders between people. Or about your borders of governing for your own good, or the good of many. About our tribal stories. About your identity, or your prejudice. About anti-Semitism. About the Wandering Jew in Berlin, Warsaw, Moscow, Chicago. Or the wandering borders of our understanding. . . .

One of the history lessons gets its finishing shape from a snapshot in front of the Monument to the Heroes of the Warsaw Ghetto Uprising. Like Joseph Werlin, with an endless passion for life, for details of beauty and wonder, Joella Werlin captures 'a picture of a small Asian child pushing her pink doll buggy in front of the fallen hero, now bloodied by autumn leaves.'

Like a good journey, the book takes us where we need to be — beyond what we already know."

— Anna Grudzien, Oxford DPhil
Writer in English and in Polish

"I was engrossed by this remarkable letter-diary as soon as I opened the book. Twenty-seven-year-old Joseph Werlin had such openness to experience, such an eye for detail, such intellectual clarity, and such earnest humility that I liked him immediately and envied the fiancée who, in 1928, received Werlin's riveting, caring, and candid accounts of living in Berlin and Moscow."

— Peggy McIntosh, PhD
Founder, National SEED Project on Inclusive Curriculum, Wellesley Centers for Women
Author, *On Privilege, Fraudulence, and Teaching as Learning* (Routledge, 2019)

"The book is so fascinating that I read it from cover to cover in just one day.

Joseph Sidney Werlin visited Weimar Germany and Soviet Russia in 1928 to better understand the origins of the Bolshevik revolution, a subject of his doctoral dissertation at the University of Chicago. What he saw was a continent in transition, with a vibrant Jewish life and democratic politics in Germany, a militarized society and culture in Poland, and radical social reforms in Russia. His intelligence and curiosity, professional training, and personal background as a second-generation Jewish American made him a keen observer and commentator on the political and social changes in Europe before Stalinism and Nazism. *A Texas Greenhorn in Berlin and Moscow, 1928* brings his experience and reflections, originally entrusted to the diary and letters to his fiancée, to a broad audience.

Lovingly prepared by his daughter and featuring unique personal documents and archival materials, this book invites its readers to join Joseph Werlin on a fascinating intellectual journey to see Europe and America at the moment when the roaring twenties were about to give way to a decade of radicalism and depression."

— Alexey Golubev, PhD
Assistant professor of Russian history
University of Houston

"Beautiful writing combined with dynamic times and such insights makes this fantastic reading."

— Gloria Grimson Mighell
Retired educator and student of Russian language and literature

A Texas Greenhorn in Berlin and Moscow, 1928

A Texas Greenhorn in Berlin and Moscow, 1928

Travel Diary of Joseph S. Werlin
and History Lessons from My Father

Joseph S. Werlin
and Joella Werlin

Copyright © 2020 Joella Werlin

All rights reserved. No part of this publication may be reproduced, stored in a retrieval system or transmitted, in any form or by any means, without prior permission of the publisher or, in the case of photocopying or other reprographic copying, a license from Access Copyright, the Canadian Copyright Licensing Agency, www.accesscopyright.ca, 1-800-893-5777, info@accesscopyright.ca.

Names: Werlin, Joseph S., author. | Werlin, Joella, author.
Title: A Texas Greenhorn in Berlin and Moscow, 1928 : travel diary of Joseph S. Werlin and history lessons from my father / Joseph S. Werlin and Joella Werlin.
Description: Includes bibliographical references. | Vancouver, BC: Granville Island Publishing, 2019.
Identifiers: ISBN 9781989467107 (pbk.) | 9781989467114 (ebook)
Subjects: LCSH Werlin, Joseph S.—Travel. | Historians—United States—Biography. | Jews, Russian—United States—Biography. | Russia—Historiography. | Depressions—1929—United States—Personal narratives. | Berlin (Germany)—Description and travel. | Berlin (Germany)—History. | Moscow (Russia)—Description and travel. | Moscow (Russia)—History. | BISAC BIOGRAPHY & AUTOBIOGRAPHY / Personal Memoirs | TRAVEL / Special Interest / Literary
Classification: LCC DK27.W47 2019 | DDC 947.08/092—dc23

Editor: Joella Werlin
Book designers: Omar Gallegos and Jakob Vala
Copyeditor: Rebecca Coates

Page 176: Photo of Kant statue by Feng Mo Long

Front cover: Joseph S. Werlin at the *Völkerschlachtdenkmal* (Monument to the Battle of the Nations), Leipzig, June 24, 1928

Granville Island Publishing Ltd.
212 – 1656 Duranleau St. Granville Island
Vancouver, BC, Canada V6H 3S4

604-688-0320 / 1-877-688-0320
info@granvilleislandpublishing.com
www.granvilleislandpublishing.com

Printed in Canada on recycled paper

*To Joseph's Rose,
Rosella Horowitz Werlin,
love of his life, career journalist,
and partner in all endeavors*

I see now how insufficient and wasteful of time and opportunity I have been. Yet I think it can justly be ascribed to the mistakes all "greenhorns" make, and that if I had to do it over, I would do much better.

— Joseph Werlin,
Berlin, July 31, 1928
Letter to Rose

Joseph S. Werlin and Rosella Horowitz Werlin
PhD diploma conferral, University of Chicago, June 1931

Contents

Preface	xi
Acknowledgements	xiii
Foreword	xix
Travel Diary	1
Correspondence	149
Afterword	211
As Life Turned Out	235
Biographical Note	255
A Daughter's Tribute	265
Sources and Resources	270

Preface

THE HEART OF THIS VOLUME is Joseph Werlin's 1928 diary, replicated here from a 1982 typescript his widow had copied from crumbling pages her sister initially typed up in 1928. Letters, photos, documents, and text have been added to illuminate the story.

The Acknowledgments section lays the foundation for all that follows, introducing characters who were with Joe on this journey in one sense or another.

The Foreword explains the author's motivation for his travels and his original intent in starting a diary while aboard ship from Galveston, Texas, to Le Havre. As the reader will learn, the author's purpose in keeping a diary changes during his months in Berlin and, finally, Moscow.

Following the Diary, "Correspondence" consists largely of extracts of letters from Joe to Rose, followed by three important letters exchanged between Joseph Werlin and his PhD thesis advisor at the University of Chicago. The introduction to this section explains that the extracts were selected primarily to amplify experiences and impressions that Joe reports in the Diary. But the reader will grasp that these selections mostly conceal what Joe's letters are really about: they are courtship letters of a man deeply in love and anxious to impress his Rose with the wonders of his adventures in a world where she might be his companion!

The Afterword principally covers the years 1929–1934, when Joe and Rosella (as she is known after their marriage) are living in Chicago. Joe is completing his doctorate and struggling desperately — literally — for a job and professional opportunities. This is a period of hard truths and crushed dreams, brought on by the Great Depression and darkening times.

The final section, "As Life Turned Out," tells that story in brief, taking a different trajectory than Joe anticipated. His was nonetheless a remarkable life, richly informed by this year of particular interest, 1928.

"Biographical Notes" offers a summary of Joseph Werlin's personal history, written by his widow for various purposes after his death in May 1964. I have added other details pertinent to this story.

"A Daughter's Tribute" recalls my opportunity in 1990 to visit sites my father wrote about in 1928.

— Joella Werlin
December 2018

Acknowledgements

How the past perishes is how the future becomes.

— Alfred North Whitehead

THEY ARE ALL GONE NOW — mentors, family, and friends who inspired and supported Joseph Werlin's personal and professional ambitions. However, many individuals cited in the Diary and letters, most of whom my siblings and I never knew, have endured in family legend. Some are so alive they seemed to tell the story to me as I tried to reconstruct it beyond the pages of the Diary.

Rose — Rosella Horowitz Werlin — our mother, is in every page. No part of this story could have been told without her. Joe wrote the Diary for her, irrespective of his other motivations. She was his muse, his confidante, his greatest promoter. She saved their letters. Literally, she saved the Diary.

There are two clusters of individuals who figure in Joe's story in 1928 or in the immediate years thereafter: Joe and Rosella's families and Joe's University of Chicago circle of friends and advisors.

Among family, Joe most sought to please his self-educated but learned father, Jacob Baer Werlin. Although the generational and cultural divide was troublesome for both of them, father and son respected one another as equals. Penned comments on the cover of a reprinted journal article Joe authored in 1939, "The Pathology of Hyper-Nationalism" (*Southwestern Social Science Quarterly*, vol. XX), offers harsh insight: "To Dad, who is responsible for it all — Jos. S. Werlin 1/14/40." Jacob Werlin's response: "For Son J.S. Am happy to assume the responsibility of it all. But your conclusions must remain your own. Dad . . . Werlin 1/21/40." (Jacob's penciled comments stop less than halfway into the 11-page article. It appears he felt his son was naive to offer any illusions of hope emerging from Germany and Eastern Europe.)

Within Rose's family, her sister Shirley Horowitz was especially honored. Shirley, who had access to an office typewriter, deciphered Joe's handwriting and typed up the diary pages as Rose delivered them to her. Shirley must be credited for the form in which the Diary was preserved. Joe recognized her commitment on his behalf and warmly conveyed his gratitude. Shirley married but died childless. Her Werlin nephews and niece adored her, drawn to her by her youthful style, her sense of humor, and her indulgence of us.

No letters to Joe from Rose's father, Rabbi Henry Horowitz, survive. But Joe often expresses appreciation for his encouragement, and no doubt for his approval. Judgment and approval twisted into a heavy, often knotty, thread throughout family ties.

Joe and Rose's letters frequently mention Rabbi Henry Cohen, PhD, of Galveston, Texas. A national leader in the Reform movement, he was recognized for his work on behalf of immigrants and for a more humane prison system. He was a kind of father figure for Rose, who served him as secretary, publicist, and writer. He became an advocate for Joe, subsidizing his passage by ship to and from Europe and helping financially during lean Chicago years.

Dr. Ray K. Daily recognized and advanced Joe's academic career, publicly and behind the scenes. She promoted his appointment to the founding faculty of the University of Houston. Having graduated from University of Texas Medical School at Galveston in 1913, she was an early champion for women's rights and became a fearless advocate for progressive civic and educational causes.

Members of Joe's University of Chicago circle were especially important during the years between 1928 and 1934, although almost all the names known appear only in correspondence. Samuel Northrup Harper, foremost Russian scholar and policy specialist of the early twentieth century, whose reputation drew Joseph to the university and who became his thesis advisor, endures in Joe's reminiscences about his travails at the university. This book includes letters to and from Dr. Harper in 1928, preserved in the university's special collections. Joe cites his communication with Dr. Harper in letters to Rose, expressing appreciation for his encouragement. Later interaction was more ambiguous and disappointing, a development which begs for broader explanation. (Speculation is pursued in the Afterword.)

At least five University of Chicago friends are mentioned in Joe's 1928 letters to Rose, and two others of high significance in later correspondence of 1932–1933. In 1928, Joe encountered two Chicago friends by coincidence, attending lectures or waiting to register at the University of Berlin: John Morrison, son of a professor at the University of Chicago, and Albert Robbins. Al Robbins warrants special note, as many years later, in the early 1950s, Joe was able to reconnect with him in London. Robbins became a noted international lawyer, practicing as a barrister and as a member of the American bar. Their friendship deepened through Joe's arrangement for him to obtain a visiting position on the law faculty of the University of Houston and through the Robbins family's generous hospitality towards all three Werlin children during our studies in England.

Another Chicago colleague, also under direction by Dr. Harper in the History Department, slipped out of sight after Joe met up with him in Moscow. That mysterious friend, Chao-Ting Chi — Chi, as Joe refers to him — was born into a wealthy family in China. He had high-ranking associations in Russia and helped Joe make useful connections. It isn't clear whether Chi ever returned to Chicago after leaving Moscow for a visit home with his bride, or whether Rose actually met him. But his subsequent disappearance from contact caused ongoing speculation and regret.

The hero among Joe's University of Chicago colleagues during his trying years of graduate study was, without question, Frederick L. Schuman, though his name does not appear in the 1928 correspondence. By the fall of that year, he had already been awarded a faculty position in the Political Science Department. Very early in his career he focused intently on political movements in Germany and the USSR, and Joe's experiences in both places drew them closer together. When Joe was unable to obtain any significant financial support from the History Department to continue his doctoral studies, Schuman created opportunities for him. Significantly, in 1932 he obtained a research grant for Joe — then a PhD but still unemployed — to assemble the bibliography for his first book on the rise of Nazi Germany.

In 1979 Rosella and I visited Professor Schuman in Portland, Oregon, where he had retired and was then a widower. She brought him three letters he had written to Joe in 1933, the photocopies of which I read. I was stunned to read in particular a long letter he sent from Bozen (Bolzano), dated May 23, 1933, his eyewitness account of Germany gripped by "a violent (and seemingly chronic) attack of national insanity." I transcribed it for inclusion in this book, where it appears in the Afterword. I am pleased to learn that the original letters were added to the Frederick L. Schuman archives at Williams College, where he was a distinguished faculty member for more than thirty years.

Professor Ferdinand Schevill, of the University of Chicago, is mentioned only once in passing in Joe and Rose's correspondence. It seems Joe never actually studied with him, but they became acquainted on campus at some point between 1931 and 1933. Evidence of the warmth of their friendship and his influence on my father, especially in his appreciation of classical European history, endured in conversation in our household and in words on a signed and framed photograph, which he kept in his office throughout his life.

Finally, I acknowledge three other significant individuals in this story: Joe and Rosella's children, only two of whom survive. Herbert Holland Werlin, their "Depression baby," was born in Chicago on May 23, 1932. Herb followed our father's footsteps to the University of Chicago for his bachelor's degree. He earned a doctorate in political science from the University of California, Berkeley, with a focus on Africa. His interests turned to public administration. In addition to his scholarly bent, Herb shared our father's pleasure in reading poetry out loud. Our father did not live to read Herb's two published books, *Governing an African City: A Study of Nairobi* (Holmes & Meier, 1974) and *Mysteries of Development: Studies Using Political Elasticity Theory* (University Press of America, 1998). Herb died from cancer on January 25, 2014.

Ernest Pyle Werlin — yes, named by Rosella for the famous World War II journalist — was a welcomed baby boomer, born in June 1944 to "aged parents," as they were regarded at the time. Ernie was a prize history student; dinner table conversations between father and son about modern history were their shared hobby and passion. Ernie was not quite 20 when our father died, having just finished his freshman year at the University of Texas. Our parents' financial hardships prompted him to pursue a more lucrative career than what we jokingly called "the family business," leading him to graduate study in economics and business as a Woodrow Wilson Scholar at the University of Michigan, and on to Wall Street. He was devoted to our mother, taking inspiration from her tenacity and grit in fighting battles for her husband and children, carrying forth as a freelance journalist and winning journalism awards, and after our father's death, supporting herself as a public schoolteacher. Now retired, Ernie writes a biweekly opinion column on financial issues for the *Sarasota Herald-Tribune* and, with exhaustive preparation, has offered modern history courses for seniors. He has encouraged and supported this book project in myriad ways, not least by his formidable command of historical context and his insights into our father's concerns during the decade after my elder brother and I had left Texas.

I, the middle child, was born in January 1938. I followed Herb to Oxford for graduate study, as Ernie did later on a Rotary scholarship. We were pursuing a dream our parents had for us, perhaps ignited by our father's dear friend Albert Robbins. Our father was determined that we each know the summit of educational experience through Oxford's unique tutorial system. After earning a BA in European history from Connecticut College, I studied social anthropology at Oxford, a pursuit inspired by my father. A handsome University of Oxford "Diploma in Anthropology" hangs above my desk, but a related career path eluded me.

My contributions to this book must also be acknowledged because Joe and Rosella would have had it no other way. I cannot be at all sure that I have reported their views or experiences accurately as I have tried to reconstruct and understand them. But I have done so with love and gratitude. I bear their names.

— Joella Werlin
December 2018

The diary has become a sort of register not merely of my external experiences but my internal reactions and thoughts. I believe that in later life I shall at times return to it with interest as a record of my impressions and standards of judgment at my present age.

— Joseph Werlin
June 14, 1928

Joseph Werlin
Leipzig, June 24, 1928

Foreword

Your good opinion gives me a lot of pleasure and is causing me to take the diary more seriously. This you may rely on: that I endeavor to be painfully exact and truthful in my descriptions or accounts . . . I simply am determined not to be a shoddy, rambling thinker. One of my chief desires is to avoid anything that smacks of demagoguery.

— Letter to Rose
March 15, 1928

JOSEPH WERLIN WAS 27 YEARS OLD, a graduate student at the University of Chicago, when he set out from Galveston, Texas, on the travels about which this account is written. The purpose for his journey in January to August of 1928 was to study documents pertaining to the founding period of Russian social democracy, the focus of his proposed doctoral thesis. The most promising materials, including newspapers and scholarly sources, were in the archives of the University of Berlin, where he spent most of his months abroad. He departed the United States understanding that in Russia "official historians" had expunged records and sanitized documents to reflect the currently approved narrative. Obtaining a visa for entry into the USSR was an uncertain prospect in any case. Remarkably, he succeeded. The Moscow experience concludes the Diary, with an added report on the Reichstag elections in May 1928.

This is not a diary in the usual sense, a daily record of events and thoughts for one's own keeping. The Diary was written with a specific audience in mind: Rose (whom Joe had met the previous summer), his parents, her parents, and other family members who lived in Houston and Galveston. After all, the arid soil of Pearland, Texas, had not yet totally washed off the feet of the impoverished university student, now on an unimaginable expedition to "the old country." Although without any love lost for their former homeland in the area around Kiev, his family nonetheless was curious to learn what changes had been brought about by the Revolution. His parents and their friends were also able to connect Joe with relatives who lived in Moscow.

Joe's handwritten diary pages weren't saved. Rose initiated a better plan for circulating the content: she passed on the pages as she received them to her sister Shirley, who in turn made a master copy on an office typewriter. Judging from Joe's letters of the period, his handwriting, while carefully formed, was often difficult to decipher. One must truly appreciate the challenge of Shirley's task — not least to interpret foreign words and concepts — and her patience and care in carrying out this labor of love. Shirley also made a ribbon copy, which was circulated among the family. The typewritten pages were assembled into two loose-leaf ring binders. This 1928 version of the Diary survives, although the pages and binders are crumbling. In 1982, Rosella had the Diary retyped on an electric typewriter. That copy, with spelling and other corrections, is the basis of the text reproduced here. However, in resetting the typed version for this volume, many more errors (especially geographical locations and German words and expressions) and uncertainties in textual meaning became obvious. Every effort has been made to recapture the author's intent.

In the beginning, Joe saw his diary as a way to share his observations and to impress the girl with whom he was in love. Joe reserved intimate thoughts for long, romantically passionate letters meant only for Rose's eyes. But as time went on, with Rose's encouragement, the Diary became more serious, more objective and journalistic. Joe and Rose actively discussed possibilities for offering parts of the Diary to suitable publications.

By the time Joe was granted permission to enter the USSR, he was nearing the close of his allotted time for his studies in Europe. But he was excited for the opportunity. He understood that the three-week excursion to Moscow, in April 1928, would be of paramount importance for achieving his objectives and enhancing his credibility as a teacher and public speaker. Even without prior assurance, he hoped to deepen his research through direct contact, if possible, with participants in the events on which his thesis would be focused, and to examine records that might be made available to him.

Joe's diary entries apparently ended with his travel to Moscow, and judging by his letters to Rose, episodes he meant to be included were not clearly identified. In part, his correspondence was constrained by a hand injury that especially troubled him when he was traveling. Joe sent Rose the long section on Moscow only after he had returned to Berlin, explaining in his letters that he was concerned about Russian censorship. He believed his Moscow impressions might have potential interest for publications in Houston if he wrote up that experience to stand alone. The final entry, a report on the May 20, 1928, elections in Germany, is different in tone and purpose. It appears this was added later, a duplicate of an article he submitted to *Current Affairs Magazine*, a publication of the *New York Times*. A *Times* editor respectfully responded that they might have been interested but his report had arrived too late for their purposes.

Portions of Joe's letters to Rose often offer personal observations or amplify experiences he withheld from the Diary. Extracts from their correspondence (with further explanations about my rationale for choosing the selections) follow the Diary. The telling of Joseph Werlin's story continues through the "Correspondence" section and succeeding sections.

These remarks, however, must conclude with a mystery: it appears that Joseph Werlin never looked at the Diary as it was finally assembled in 1928! How might we know that, and why not?

Joe's children can assure you that their father would never let stand a document bearing his name that contained misspellings and transcription errors, as did Shirley's lovingly produced typescript (e.g., "Habenzollern" for Hohenzollern). He was obsessive about correctness in many respects, occasionally causing unintended hurt, as when he returned to his teenage children their laboriously written letters and essays marked up with grammatical and spelling corrections. If he had looked even once at the 1928 Diary, his pencil marks would show all over it! But the pages are absolutely pristine.

Why did he never look at the typewritten Diary? His outlook had to shift dramatically after he returned to Houston at the beginning of September 1928. Given Rose's promotion of her suitor, no doubt he was a local celebrity for a while, impressing audiences with his experiences in a far-off land very few knew much about. He was an engaging personality and didn't need the Diary to refresh his memories. But he was broke, and without savings. He focused his energy on the small commercial printing business he had set up with his father, personalizing and selling Christmas cards (an unspoken cause of tension with the rabbi's daughter!). He also was distracted by constant planning and activity for the wedding Rose grandly publicized, staged at the Galvez Hotel in Galveston on December 23, 1928. Beyond the holiday excitement, he had very serious worries about sources of income for continuing his studies at the University of Chicago, about the uncertainty of his academic standing, and about whether he had met course requirements and would be prepared to sit for qualifying exams.

And then, 1929 was around the corner. No one of that generation needs to be reminded what happened in 1929! No life was left unchanged.

Travel Diary, 1928
Joseph S. Werlin

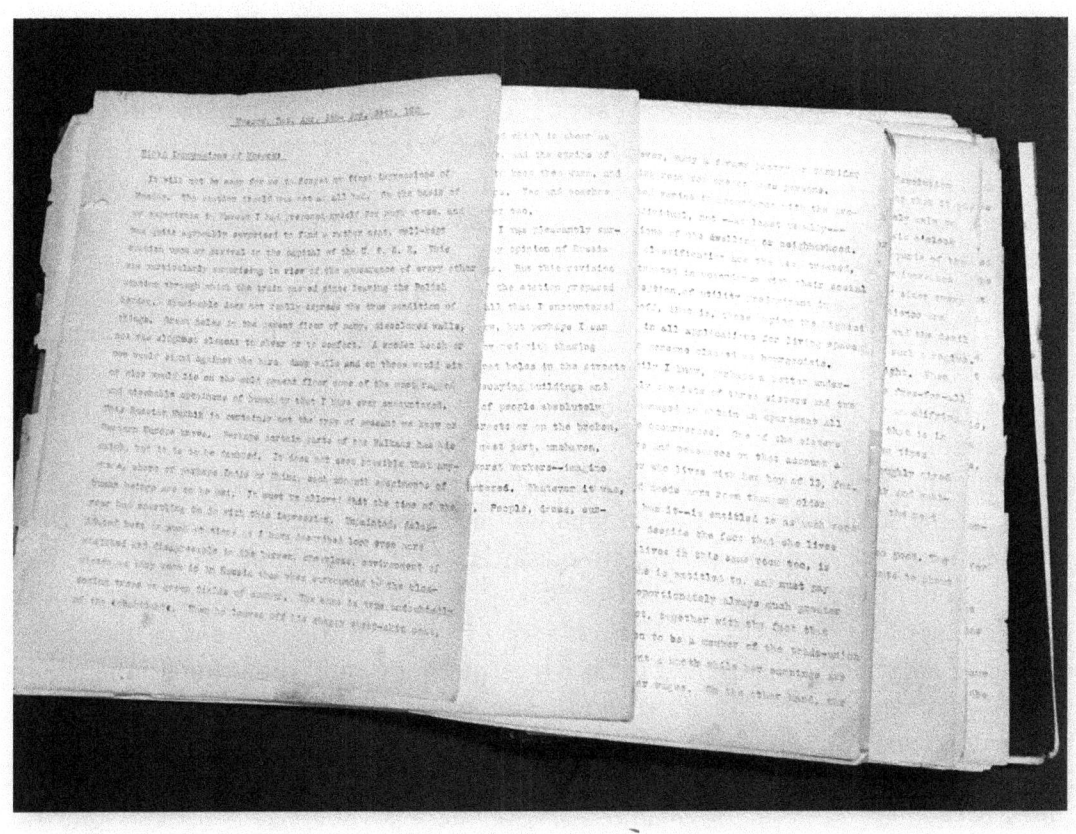

The 1928 transcription of Werlin's handwritten diary

Wednesday, January 11, 1928. Aboard the De La Salle, 8:30 p.m.

Sitting in the *salon de musique* all alone. As I write, the radio is pouring forth sweet music from Houston: "Rose Marie," "Me and My Shadow," etc.

The *De La Salle* is flowing through inky darkness; only a soft swish of the waters about the hull and a slight trembling of the ship to indicate that we are moving.

Time is passing rapidly, strange to say. I am beginning to think that the 18 or 19 days will pass rapidly between studying, conversation, musing, observing, and in performing the daily functions of eating, sleeping, and dressing.

An almost deserted ship; only three first-class passengers, nine third-class, and one *amphibian*. I'm the amphibian, neither fish nor fowl. I've got a first-class cabin and have all the privileges of first class yet must eat with the third class. Lucky for the company, it carries a large freight cargo, else it would go bankrupt. Only two more first-class passengers are expected at New Orleans, which means that any prospect of a hilarious time is unlikely. It is just as well; I can study more. I shall have the reading rooms (i.e., the music room) all to myself.

The passengers are all without especially striking characteristics. There is a young Irish-looking woman with a baby and an English woman with ruddy nose traveling third class, and about seven men. One is totally blind, a silver-haired, fat, German-appearing man.

The supper meal was unquestionably plain, but good: boiled beef with kidney beans, fried potatoes, nuts for dessert, and coffee. One can tell this is a French boat if from no other evidence than the abundance of wine served at the table: *vin ordinaire*. Our blind man evidently felt that his sense of direction already had been totally destroyed and a glass of wine more or less wouldn't make any difference, for he drained large glassful after large glassful of the liquid.

I've struck up a friendship which promises to be close with the deck steward, a Frenchman who for two years lived in Pittsburgh. He speaks English fluently and is ready with proffers of information and assistance. The one drawback is that he smells heavily of whiskey. Asked me if Mr. and Mrs. Horowitz who accompanied me to the ship were my parents and expressed gladness to learn that a certain young lady was my "sweetheart."

The two women of the first class have just come into the salon to disturb my tranquility. One has just ordered that her breakfast be brought to her room and told her acquaintance that "this is being civilized. American breakfasts are so ghastly plain."

Enough — I must turn to my reading. I've just finished an hour of Russian.

Thursday, January 12, 1928. On board the De La Salle, 1:55 p.m.

Hurrah! We're about to enter the Mississippi. The pilot has just come aboard. The mouth of the river isn't visible yet, but it won't be long now. The color of the sea has undergone an entire change from the blue or blue-green that it usually is to a very muddy color produced by the huge volume of silt and debris from the Mississippi. We are expecting to dock about 10:30 p.m. — quite fine; didn't anticipate getting to New Orleans before the morning.

The weather and the ocean have so far been fine. Soon after leaving Galveston I began experiencing an internal disquietude which, to my utter disgust, I believed was impending *mal de mer*. My manly pride was touched to the quick to think that already, only two hours from port, the sea almost without a ripple and the sky serene, I was being overtaken by seasickness. I lay down in my bunk awaiting the worst. To my surprise, nothing happened.

I had probably mistaken the first slight sensations of dizziness for the genuine thing. Besides, I was very tired from having stayed up so late the night before. This was proven to me by the fact that I slept without a pause from 10:30 last night until 7:30 this morning, despite the newness of my bunk and general surroundings.

The *De La Salle* is riding the waves wonderfully; there is hardly a tremble felt. I am told she is a remarkably easy-riding boat and will continue to perform this way all through the trip. If this should prove true, then the terrors of the sea that I anticipated will be groundless, but I think it will not. After all, we're in the Gulf of Mexico, not the Atlantic, and in the back part of the Gulf, at that. We cannot be sailing very far from the coast, though far enough to render it invisible.

Hurrah! We've just entered one of the mouths of the Mississippi. I didn't dream, five minutes ago when I began this writing, that the river would be reached so soon. The channel we are using seems about three blocks wide; irregular strips of land, some fairly wide, others narrow, but all covered with small lakes, separate us from the neighboring channels. Ah, some white cabins are coming to view. Wonder who lives in them? We are just now passing by a long series of cabins grouped on the right bank. Wonder what the inhabitants do for their living? Can't be farming; there is no sign of cultivation, and these houses are too good for fishermen. Ah, I believe I know: it's a government reservation to patrol and guard the river, perhaps against smugglers, perhaps against some future enemy.

I made three new acquaintanceships today, with Bunze, O'Connor, and Martin (I believe that's his name). Bunze should prove invaluable to me. He's an undersized consumptive-looking young fellow, about 24 years of age, German in nationality. He is returning to Bohemia after a 20-month stay in America, but only for the purpose of securing influence which will enable him to come within the immigration quota for his country and thus be able to reside permanently in America. It is imperative that he does so, for he married an American girl, who is now about to become a mother. To take his wife back to the old country and struggle for a living there is undesirable; to stay in America, he cannot; he is in a predicament. The temptation to stay in America is all the greater owing to the fact that he has secured a responsible job with a Hollywood movie concern — he's from Los Angeles. Since German is his native tongue, he's a real find for me. Already I have talked in German to him continuously, and tomorrow I shall write him a composition in German which he will correct.

O'Connor is also from Los Angeles: a fat, old man, deputy-marshal in the Los Angeles Municipal Court. He is one of the three first-class passengers. Last night he got drunk and talked so loud that the whole forepart of the promenade deck could hear him. A fine servant of the government he is. Told me how humorous it was to sit by quietly as liquor was served to the passengers while the boat was still at the dock in Galveston, and then at a psychological moment, to show his badge and watch them change color. But, of course, he didn't do anything. He knows all about the Hickman case* and told me many stories of graft and corruption in the local administration of Los Angeles.

Martin, I know little of, except that this is his 22nd trip on the ocean, that he has a wife living in Luxembourg whom he is now going to visit, and he is not yet an American citizen though he has lived in the States off and on for 25 years.

Enough for today; the writer's cramp has overtaken me.

Friday, January 13, 1928. On board the De La Salle at New Orleans, 9:30 p.m.

Tired as can be due to having stayed up so late last night but cannot sleep. The winches, hauling up cotton bales from the dock and dumping them into the holds, are making too much noise for that. In addition, the ship's officers are pulling a party in the dining

---

* The 1927 abduction and murder of 12-year-old Marion Parker by William Edward Hickman in Los Angeles was widely reported.

salon and have gotten two of the crew to play, one an accordion and the other a bass violin, the noise from which makes it impossible for my senses to sink into somnolence. I have a strange urge to dance with the others, but must refrain; it's a private party.

The Lord only knows when we'll leave New Orleans. I doubt if it will be before the morning. She should have finished loading at the dock by 5:00 p.m. and then have moved on to another wharf to take on still additional cargo, yet here it is, 9:30 p.m., and still not finished at this dock. The ship is taking on 6,500 bales of cotton at this point and it's a slow job. Four sets of winches are working, but they can only take on three bales apiece at one time.

Went to bed at 2:00 this morning and arose at 6:00 in order to get to a hotel to call Rose before she left for work. Was so tired that I came back to the ship within three hours. Bought a few things that I needed and saw a little of the business section in the course of my shopping. This is my third time in New Orleans, so the city is no novelty to me. The most dilapidated houses; the crookedest, narrowest streets; the oldest buildings — that's New Orleans. People call it "quaint." Perhaps it is, but I can't appreciate it, though it is true that I have seen only a small portion of it — the wharf section and the downtown district.

Two new passengers, first-class, have come aboard. I have seen one, a light-brown-haired woman, middle-aged, who smokes cigarettes and pretends to read *Mother India*, the book that aroused so much criticism among the native intellectual circles of India. A family of five joined the third-class group: mother, father, mother of one of the parents, and a little boy and little girl. They look Italian, though they speak French fluently.

The mother is a striking Italian type of the lower class. Put jet earrings in her ears and a tambourine in her hands and you would have the familiar gypsy or Italian dancing type. Next to them at the table sat the frowsy-haired, rather pretty young Danish mother (the one who Rose thought was Irish) and her pretty little boy. The contrast between the little boy and the little girl belonging to the Italian mother was remarkable. Each is a very handsome and very perfect representative of two European types — the Nordic and the Mediterranean. One has straight, golden hair, a pink skin, light blue eyes, and an air of restrained mirth; the other has jet-black eyes and curly hair, olive skin, and a face that is alive with vivacity and sensitiveness to all external impression and internal emotions.

Already, my Jewish consciousness has been stung. I'd be spared a lot of humiliation did people take me for Jewish, but not doing so, they speak their minds freely. To my chagrin the two defamers have both been American — one, the fat immigration officer who came on at Galveston with a load of deportees (15), and the other, the old man, the vice-marshal from Los Angeles Municipal Court. Usually, you can do nothing. A man has the right to say openly, "I hate Jews and I don't mind anyone knowing about it, either," or to crack jokes at the expense of our tribe. Besides, they usually are talking to their friends, not to me, and I become an unintentional listener.

Saturday, January 14, 1928. Aboard the De La Salle, 9:30 p.m.

We are now at the mouth of the Mississippi. The ship has stopped and is waiting for the pilot boat in order to get rid of the pilot. The fog is intense. On the horizon, lightning is flashing angrily, taking the form of semi-circular bands of red flames. Bad weather seems ahead of us. The lighthouse to our right is groaning like a bull. The river pilot has this moment left the ship and we are now waiting for the bar pilot to take us across the Rubicon, into the Gulf.

The paucity of passengers is appalling. The heavy mist all about us and the comparative quietness of the ship reminds me of the line "a phantom ship in a phantom sea."

In the music room with me are two of the three ladies of the first class, playing bridge with the purser (or *commissaire*, to use the French equivalent). I feel a bit guilty in refusing to make the fourth party. I dislike bridge, for one thing; for another, I'm a poor player; for another, I wanted to do a little studying tonight; and for a fourth thing, I'm afraid if I once start, I'll be considered wanting in the qualities of a gentleman should the occasion arise again and should I refuse. Since bridge is to be the chief diversion for the next 15 days, one can realize its peril to my studies should I ever allow myself to be considered a bridge player. In the smoking room sits the third lady of the first-class list, playing poker with O'Connor, Bunze, and Martin, the Luxembourger. She's one of these masculine types of women — smokes and drinks bar liquor straight, despite the fact that she is mother of a son 35 years of age (I believe that is his age).

I'm discovering that there is little to Bunze. In him, I already see certain characteristics that distinguish him and his type from a representative American. For instance, in his attitude toward the immigration officer and to O'Connor, the Los Angeles Municipal Court deputy-marshal. He tries to curry favor with them, though he has practically no personal interest in doing so. He'll flatter them and humor them; he'll laugh at their jokes and get the good fellow to the point of dragging in his own wife in connection with some lewd remark. In him, I fancy I see the average European of the non-noble class, who for generations and generations has drunk in with his mother's milk respect for authority — fear of the official, no matter how petty his position. He has learned to cringe before the aristocrat and the government office; to accept his insults and abuse with a smile; to cringe and fawn and flatter, though in his heart hating him with the stored-up hate of centuries. It is so bred in the bones of the average European that one like Bunze, even though he is on the high seas, completely outside the power of the officials, even should the latter bear him no grudge, must yield to this habitual attitude. The native-born American is alien to this. He feels himself as good as the Law, yea, even above the Law, for he elected him; the official is made to serve him, not vice versa.

Sunday, January 15, 1928. Aboard the De La Salle, 9:20 p.m.

What an execrable series of delays have befallen us! For three days we procrastinated, and finally when things seemed to have righted themselves at last and the green water of the ocean took the place of the muddy Mississippi, this last misfortune overtook us. Fog and whatnot caused the pilot to lose his bearings; the ship slipped out of the channel, and here we are stuck fast in the mud bottom of the Mississippi, 60 or 70 miles below New Orleans yet several miles from the open sea — between heaven and earth, as it were. All day the crew has been churning, in a valiant effort to get the ship free. For a time, we thought its heroic efforts would be successful, but our opinion is giving way to despair. Nothing short of two or three powerful tugs can set us free, but the captain is reluctant to incur the heavy charges that such service would cost his company — at least, so I'm told. Thus, the monotonous status quo continues: the angry swirls of water about the churning propellers, the interminable clang of the bells on the buoy to our right, and the nerve-wracking sound from the lighthouse on the port side, which resembles about exactly that emitted by a cow in heat calling for its mate. The crews will all be gathered in Europe by the time we arrive. I'm sure I'd have a long beard by that time and could pass as a genuine Russian, did I stop shaving now.

If there were any excitement aboard, it wouldn't be so bad, but I see nothing in sight except, perhaps, the confinement of the Syrian woman. I almost wish the child would come before the voyage ends, so monotonous are things becoming.

Mrs. Barns, the new arrival to the first-class group, promises to be a source of amusement. Her power of mimicking has caused us several laughs, and she has a ready store of jokes, which are entertaining.

Just finished Lenin's *Russian Traits*, which Rabbi Cohen lent me. Though written in 1854, its picture of the Russian cannot be out of date, for though tremendous institutional changes have taken place in Russia since then, the character of a people cannot be altered so readily. National characteristics are the products of a slow — painfully slow — action of historical forces over a period of literally centuries, so that 50 years cannot have greatly altered the psychology, habits, and standards of the Russian folk-mass, particu-larly in such fundamental items as honesty, fatalism, sloth, veracity, sexual morality, and anti-Semitism. The work is a terrible arraignment of the Russian people and so soundly written, couched in such a judicious and scientific form, that the conclusions cannot but command respect.

One trouble about calisthenics and physical exercise — at least it was in my case — is that the amount of food eaten due to the increase in appetite more than offsets the loss in avoirdupois due to the exercise. My appetite has grown by leaps and bounds, apparently, since coming aboard the ship. Rose has implanted in me such a wholesome fear of obesity that my present worry is whether the scales will show me with a gain or a loss when I arrive in Europe.

Monday, January 16, 1928. Aboard the De La Salle, 9:30 p.m.

Somewhere in the Gulf of Mexico. Well, well, we're off at last. Sometime after 11:00 last night, the *De La Salle* worked its tired self back into the channel, and when I awoke this morning a glad sight greeted me in the shape of the most inviting green waters of the Gulf and a most striking sunrise — the horizon was flooded with a fiery flame of red, which soon afterward, however, disappeared into the ocean. A more beautiful day than the present one can hardly be imagined. It was a pleasure simply to be alive, and I felt extra good. A half hour's brisk exercise on deck, followed by a warm bath and a cold shower, put me in excellent spirits. If things continue this way, I shall have nothing but happy memories to leave with. But I fear it is unlikely — the Atlantic is not the Gulf. At noon, our position was about 27° north and 86° west. The route we will follow, I am told, is due north after leaving Key West and until we get past Cape Hatteras, then north and northeast, which eventually will bring us in the lanes usually traversed by steamers sailing directly from New York to Paris, or vice versa.

Put in a few good hours of studying today, so far. Two of the crew are putting on a sort of concert just now in the music room where I am sitting, and this of course is not exactly conducive to quiet meditation over the positive statements which Bukharin makes in his *Historical Materialism*, which I began reading this morning. I agree with the deck steward's "It's rotten." His job in part consists of entertaining the guests. True, there are but three ladies in the first class, but duty is duty, and so he arranges for a dance in the music room, but the ladies have failed him. I'm itching to dance and would dance with a female rhinoceros if given the chance, but the ladies are shy and have taken refuge in a game of bridge. Not that I exactly blame them. Mrs. Barnes is 55 or 60, tall and fat; Mrs. Carpentair is a regular gray-haired schoolmarm; while Miss Davis, though relatively young, about 29 or so, is fat and short. Was there ever such poor material under such otherwise glorious and opportune circumstances? I know someone who should be thankful it is as it is!

At present, all the first-class passengers — to the grand total of five — together with Bunze and Martin of the second class, the captain, the chief engineer, and the purser, are in the smoking room playing cards or dice, the last being indulged in by the captain and the chief engineer. Funny-looking men for such responsible positions, judged by our standards. The engineer is a glutton for liquor; the flesh under his eyes is so puffed out that one scarcely perceives his eyes. The captain is a stocky, heavy-necked and heavy-jawed man. The steward tells me he is a fine officer. Disdained to ask for assistance in getting his ship loose and spent ten hours on the bridge directing operations without coming down to supper.

The phonograph is making me homesick. *Carmen* and *Romeo and Juliet*, both in French, make me think of my sweetheart. Just got a compliment for her from the steward. Showed him her picture and in his broken English, he said, "Pretty! Ah, pretty. She is beautiful. Is she a movie actress?"

Wednesday, January 18, 1928. Aboard the De La Salle, 9:45 p.m. (Tuesday missed)

Already the 18th, one whole week since I left Galveston!

Time is flying by much more rapidly than I had anticipated. Between the hours of arising and making one's toilette and lunch call, there is hardly a perceptible passage of time. The afternoon passes almost as quickly, and before one's fully aware of the fact, the night has come and gone. One phenomenon has struck me and that is the lack of consciousness of any divisions of time other than daylight and darkness. For instance, on land one is oftentimes acutely conscious that a particular day is Sunday or Monday, or a holiday. Sunday in particular has distinctive characteristics. One feels it in his bones, as it were, that Sunday is present; the very atmosphere seems to indicate it. But at sea it is not so; all is one. Time loses all meaning, becomes an infinite ocean, like space, or like the sea; its separate streams have merged in one.

Space, too, plays tricks on you at sea. The estimation of distance on land is relatively easy, owing to the presence of objects at fairly short distance from one another, or to the obstructions of the horizon. At sea, there is no such obstruction and one is called upon to exercise a faculty which, unless he has been to sea before, he has never used. For example, I tried to guess the distance between ourselves and a neighboring ship and fell far short of the mark, as I later learned from the fact that it took us a much longer time to catch up with it than would have been the case if my estimation had been correct.

Things are becoming more interesting. The steward has initiated us into several deck games, which help pass time very pleasantly. I forget the name of two of them, but a third is 'deck tennis,' in which a net is used, lines marked off, and the scoring is done exactly as in real tennis. The difference lies in the fact that rope rings are used, and the hand, instead of the racket, does the playing. Tomorrow morning I am to be awakened at 6:30 in order to take some strenuous exercise with the steward.

We passed the Florida coast late yesterday afternoon and have since been traveling northward along the Atlantic seaboard. We shall probably continue this route for another day or two, thereafter striking a northeasterly direction. The sea was a trifle rough yesterday owing to a moderate wind, but today it was almost without a ripple. The view was simply enchanting. Imagine a calm lake of huge dimensions, resting serenely under a hot sun in a cloudless sky, with a ship or two gliding along so smoothly as to seem suspended between sky and water, and you will have a slight idea of the indescribable beauty of my marine environment. But this, to my sorrow, will not last. A different story will be told within a day or two as we go past Hatteras and plow our way into the boundless Atlantic.

Thursday, January 19, 1928. Aboard the De La Salle, 9:30 p.m.

She's a-blowing hard now! Quite a change in the sea from yesterday. As I write, my cabin, including myself, goes now down, now up. Wonder that I'm not seasick. I thought this morning that I was at last seized upon, but to my intense delight, it proved only a fancy. But tomorrow may tell a different story if this howling wind gains some force. The sea has been running quite high all day, increasing in agitation as the night came on. There are no stars or moon to light up the water, but in the darkness I can make out huge, rolling waves, which, however, move in regular and rather lazy series. It is starting to rain; I can hear the patter of the drops on the deck. The wind is also increasing in intensity. Wonder what tomorrow will bring!

This is a remarkably easy-riding boat, so everyone tells me. It must be the truth, for its rolling or pitching is hardly perceptible — at least not until just now. As I stood on the promenade deck just a few minutes ago, looking outward on the sea, I couldn't help but reflect on the situation: like some dogged traveler making his way across a seemingly endless series of hills, refusing to be daunted by their height or number, the *De La Salle* plods its weary way from trough to crest and from crest to trough, contemptuous of their resistance and undismayed by their threats. The sea itself appears like a good-natured monster which is in no hurry to devour its victim and in the meantime is having fun with it. Yet, somehow, one cannot help but have faith in the victim, seditiously puny and weak though it may seem in comparison with its gigantic foe. It gives one an impression of sturdiness and dependability, a confidence that it is able to take care of itself. It does nothing in a sensational way, just methodically and deliberately plunges into a mountain of water before it and comes out again, entirely dry and without a sign of weariness. A gallant ship, truly. I am writing this in my cabin. The other passengers, together with the chief officers of the crew, are as usual in the smoking room playing cards. There is a great temptation to join them, but this tyrant Books is inexorable in his demands upon me. My socialistic vocabulary is being restored rapidly, and the old facility in juggling socialistic and communistic commonplaces is returning. It is well that it is; it will make my task of the next year or two easier.

Back to my Russian! Oh, Lord, when will this weary labor of thy servant cease?

Saturday, January 21, 1928. Aboard De La Salle, 8:00 p.m. (Friday skipped)

I begin this daily recital but am not at all sanguine of being able to conclude it. For one thing, it's rather uncomfortable, to say the least, to write from positions that rapidly alternate from a steep plane that inclines downward to one that inclines exactly opposite; for another, I may have to make a hurried exit to the rail, or what corresponds to it. For the monster has tired of playing and for the past two days has been hurling all his unmitigated wrath against us. All the elements are in league with him — the wind, the rain, the snow. Our brave boat meets every onslaught fearlessly and victoriously, but is being sorely pounded nevertheless. It is first on one side, then on the other; now it is elevated high above the water, now hurled with terrific force into a growling abyss of water which closes over it, only to disgorge it as it fights its way valiantly to the top again. For two days now this cruel punishment has continued! Heaven alone knows when it will cease.

I am still numbered among the living, technically so, at any rate, but at times today I heard my turn called. At moments, the voice, though low, was persistent, and I lay down in my bed fully expecting to receive the call, but each time I was given a respite. How many times today have I rushed to the washbasin expecting the death rattle, the eruption of the internal *vitalitas* (call it what you will), only to be mistaken, and frequently disappointedly so, I assure the world.

Hurrah! Hurrah! I just this minute received another call and rushed to the washroom — and succeeded. I feel a thousand times better, too! How long this present feeling of tranquility will last I cannot prophesize, but I certainly feel better just now. My head is clearer and my hand more sure.

The music room where I am at present is pitching like a Texas bronco. All the chairs and tables are cleated down to the floor so that there is no movement of the furniture, but there's plenty of creaking and cracking and straining of walls and windows and blinds just the same. A terrible sea is running, though the wind seems to have died down somewhat. It is fortunate indeed that the ship is so heavily loaded with cargo, otherwise, the rolling and pitching would be far more violent.

Two of the four first-class passengers are completely under: Miss Davis, the fat little schoolmarm from Taylor, Texas, and Mrs. Carpentair, the regular gray-haired lady of the same profession. Miss Davis made gallant efforts to resist *mal de mer* yesterday. She walked the deck and bent over the rail and tried, but all to no avail, poor thing. My sympathy goes out to her and Mrs. Carpentair. Only two of the nine third-classers have succumbed, the Syrian father and mother. The latter is *enceinte* [pregnant], as I have already mentioned, and I hope her sickness won't hurt the infant, which may come to light before the voyage is ended. If the last turns out, it will be her second child born at sea.

Some people are inexplicable. Their two kids, one four and the other two, already drive them almost to distraction — at least they would most people — and yet they go ahead and wish another on themselves! Bright, intelligent people, too. Spent almost all morning yesterday talking to them. The husband was educated in the French schools in Syria and in Egypt. Got further schooling in an English institution. He prepared himself for a law career but was persuaded by his father to try his luck in America. Twice he returned to his native land, and this makes his third and probably last trip, for he is thinking of giving up America entirely. Says he doesn't want his children brought up there, that children in America grow up to be immoral, materialistic, shallow, and without any respect for parents or conventions. Both he and his wife are really very intelligent persons, and I learned considerably from them of Syria and the Near East generally.

Saturday night! How different and how inferior my present environment to that which I have been used to these last three months. Oh, for a certain home in Galveston and a certain girl!

Monday, January 23, 1928. Aboard the De La Salle, 10:00 p.m. (Sunday skipped)

Getting closer to our destination — about 1,800 nautical miles farther. At noon our position was 42°40' north at 53°50' west longitude. I retain a little knowledge of navigation from my navy days and this helps me check the position, course, and speed of the ship, which is shown daily on a chart hanging outside the *salle à manger*. The ocean has an entirely changed appearance from Saturday night, when I last wrote of my experiences. Surprising thing, too, is that in addition to the relative tranquility of the sea, the weather has gotten warmer, though we are steaming northward with each passing hour. This is due to the fact that we are now in the midst of the Gulf Stream and have gotten away from the cold currents emanating from Newfoundland and the Arctic regions — at least, such is the explanation that I have adopted. Yes, the last two days have smacked of Elysian quietness when compared to the three preceding days.

I believe I can now congratulate myself without being premature on having made a trans-Atlantic trip in January with only a few hours of discomfort approaching seasickness. I came out much better than I had expected. I would go further just now and take stock of the generality of my feelings with respect to my present trip, but inasmuch as there are seven or eight more days of traveling to do and anything may occur during this period, I should perhaps defer the account until the voyage has come to an end.

I've managed to do some studying and reading while aboard the *De La Salle* — five or six hours a day, anyway. The novelty of the surroundings, the day or two stay at New Orleans, the two days of indisposition due to the roughness of the sea, and the frequent interference with the quietness of the music room where I do my reading account for the considerable shortage in the total hours which I might otherwise have devoted to my books.

Mrs. Barnes told me something of the romantic way in which she met her husband: how they first met aboard a ship which both were taking to Europe, how he was a serious student – a junior at Harvard – and she a flighty, silly girl, how he 'fell' for her at once. They were married soon after she returned from Europe, and he purchased a newspaper but was subsequently 'frozen out' by Hearst and is now publisher of a small country newspaper in New York. Lastly, she told me that they were divorced five years ago, the 'other woman' hounding him so much that he could refuse her no longer. Queer woman, that! Smokes like a fiend, tells smutty stories, has great power of imitating the mannerisms and sounds of people and animals, is moderately jolly, holds rather unorthodox views on many things, and has a whole list of distinguished people whom she refers to as friends or acquaintances. Has four or five houses on Nantucket Island, the rent of which support her comfortably. This is her 20th or 23rd trip across the ocean. Asserts she saves money by traveling. Has two sons, one "who is doing fine," the other being "worthless." "What that boy didn't cost me! Expelled or flunked out of a half-dozen schools, etc." She has lent me *Mother India*, the sensational book recently written by Katherine May. It is most uncomfortable reading. I believe her picture of India is mainly true, difficult as it is to accept. To think that in this day and age such horrid conditions exist!

Tuesday, January 24, 1928. Aboard the De La Salle, 9:30 p.m.

The weather continues to remain good. Whitecaps are visible, but on the whole the sea is subdued. Hope it continues this way until we dock at Havre. Almost two weeks on the water; it will be a pleasure to see land again. I feel the anxiety to see land couldn't have been much greater with Columbus than with me. After all, we shall be on the water if not quite as long in actuality, relatively – considering the greater speed in which distances are covered today from what they were in Columbus's day – just as long. I'm hungering for a sight of English coast and the cliffs of Normandy.

Speaking of Normandy reminds me to say something of my deck steward, Pegron, who is from there. He is a rather good-looking man, more British than French in appearance (his grandfather was an Englishman), almost 30 years of age. Has a wife and two children living in Havre. He is quite an actor, and his account of his home life was no less touching than amusing. What a time the respectable Frenchman must have to make both ends meet! Pegron gets only 150 francs a month (six American dollars) from the company; what other income he has comes from passengers' tips. Since there are only five first-class passengers aboard this time, you can imagine his plight. Told me of his debt to the landlord of 400 francs, which he must pay upon his arrival, through a tragic, comical, imaginative description of his encounter with the landlord. His home life from his own word-picture is charming: a little garden, two pigeons, two rabbits, one chicken, and a large German police dog which he got from his father. The cottage is a tiny three-room affair: two rooms downstairs and one up. No bath, of course. The ablutions are done periodically and apparently collectively, that is, on the same occasion by the whole family, in a wash tub placed in the kitchen. It was comical to watch him go through the motions of scrubbing his wife's back as she sat in the tub. His broken English and French vivaciousness lent further humor to the description. Conditions must be very hard in France now. Most people probably have a job of some kind, but it is a hand-to-mouth existence. A good bookkeeper gets 800 to 900 francs a month ($32–$36). Allowing for the lowered cost of living, it can't represent more than $75 to $80 in American money. Just think of supporting a family on that! Most wives work, and the number of children is kept down to a minimum.

The steward likes to draw me out respecting my affair of the heart. Showed him Rose's picture and he went into raptures. Reminds me continually about sending a message to my sweetheart.

I've given up trying to speak French to the crew. It interferes too much with my progress in the other languages. To study two languages simultaneously is bad enough; three is well-nigh impossible.

Thursday, January 26, 1928. Aboard the De La Salle

Getting nearer to our destination, but still five or six days away. These last days are becoming hard to bear. The passengers are getting loud in their complaints. Most of them were promised by the agents that they would reach Havre on the 26th for certain; if the ship arrives by the first, they will be lucky. Though the sea has pacified for the last three or four days, the *De La Salle* is losing speed instead of gaining. The reason is not clear, though each passenger has his own pet theory. One says that it is due to the desire of the captain to save coal by going slower, thus to make up for the loss sustained in the 12 hours' attempt to free the ship while we got stuck in the bottom of the Mississippi. Another says it is in order that the ship officers, in a list of underhand dealing, might pocket the money represented by the coal saved, and so forth. I fail to see it this way. How would going slower save coal? All the boilers do not seem to be operating. Perhaps one or two are damaged, this accounting for the retarded speed.

The doctor-passenger is particularly exasperated. He has a wife in England on the point of death, he says. He had cabled her that he would arrive on the 26th, having been positively assured this would be the case by the New Orleans French Line representative. None of his relatives will know what to think, and besides, he is consumed with anxiety over the condition of his wife, the exact state of which he does not, of course, know at present. Were not the tragic phase of it apparent, it would be comical to observe his restlessness and to hear him, presumably a tight-lipped, dignified professional man, curse the crew and ship. He's not alone, however. All of us are getting restless. We manifest our feelings in many ways: growling about the food, the service, the slowness of the boat. Each passenger is in turn analyzed and his or her peculiarities made much of. Everyone has forgotten what a nice, steady boat this is and how tasty the food and excellent the accommodations, considering the lowness of the price. Card-playing or reading or talking is becoming boresome; the ocean or the sky no longer invite inspection – in short, we're becoming terribly bored. I say 'we'; perhaps I should exclude myself, at least from the category of the greatest complainers. Not that I won't be overjoyed to set foot on *terra firma* again, not that I haven't lifted my voice in complaint also, but on the whole I am taking this situation quite tranquilly. I suppose it's due to the unconscious sense of gratefulness that I feel to the ship's company for my gratis passage. Another reason is that from the start I contemplated arriving not before the 29th, so a delay of two days does not seem like a snail's pace.

Not feeling good just now. Have a terrible cold. Has been flowing unchecked for the past two days.

Speaking of food, am starved for sweets. The third class gets no pastries of any kind, no pies or cakes, no ice cream or chocolate or cocoa. Bought a pound of Hershey's in New Orleans, but soon used it up. The ship's bartender sells some sweets, but they are terribly expensive and somehow not just what I crave.

The sea is becoming monotonous. Fifteen days in contact with it is apparently sufficient, at least for such prosaic people as myself. Yet I wonder if even a poet wouldn't tire of watching the eternal and endless succession of waves with hardly a variation in their action or effects, except that every now and then one rises higher than the others, or the propellers produce a little more foam which hisses angrily about the sides. Occasionally, entertainment is gotten in watching a sunset – though, with the exception of the evening when the sun stood out as a fiery red ball and sank beneath the horizon, I haven't witnessed one particularly noteworthy – or in watching the sunlight reflected in the foam about the ship when it occasionally takes the form of a solar spectrum, or in watching the seagulls. I marvel at the remarkable endurance power of these "[illegible] of the sea." To the very middle of the Atlantic, ten days' voyage from land, they have followed us. I am told that they fly from ship to ship, spending practically all their lives on the water. They are remarkably graceful birds, and one gets real pleasure in observing their graceful movements as they swoop and circle about the ship — now about the stern, now about the bow, up and down — without hardly a rest except for that which they momentarily take by settling on the water, only to be up and flying again as soon as the ship's stern has passed them.

Friday, January 27, 1928. Aboard De La Salle, 10:00 p.m.

Ten o'clock p.m.! One needn't look at his watch to know such is the time. The two musicians have just stopped playing, which can only mean that ten o'clock has struck. One plays an accordion, the other a bass violin. Most of the passengers remain entirely unmoved by the renderings, while I, plebian that I am, enjoy them after a fashion, though they become monotonous even for me occasionally. Frequently, my feet begin marking time to the music and I long to dance, but there is no one available. Just three women (excluding the third-classers), one of whom is the mother of a son 35 years of age, another gray-haired and on in years, the third of moderate age in comparison with the others but boundless in size and unalluring in appearance. Which but brings me the reflection of how groundless the fears of a certain person were.

Sat up to 1:30 this morning listening to Martin, the Luxembourger, and Bunze, the Bohemian, belabor the American and extol the European. Martin, except for yearly visits (oftener, occasionally) to the old country, has been living in the United States for 25 years and is a tailor by profession. Bunze came to America 18 months ago, married a Bohemian girl three months afterward, is now father of a child four or five months of age, and is returning to Czechoslovakia to see if he cannot come under the immigration quota and so be able to reside in America permanently. It was interesting to me to listen to an appraisal of Americans and America generally by Europeans, particularly such rather intelligent, if not overly educated representatives, and so I let them talk to their hearts' content. The fact that they had imbibed several glasses of cognac, beer, and other liquors, together with the entire desertion of the smoking room by all except ourselves, made them all the more loquacious. The net result of their criticisms may be briefly stated as follows:

1. The American girl/wife knows and cares nothing for housekeeping; is terribly extravagant; keeps the husband's nose to the grindstone; is merciless in her selfish exactions upon him, which go to benefit her own materialistic wants exclusively; and threatens him often with unfaithfulness if he doesn't 'come across,' and is usually unfaithful anyhow. She cares nothing for children and makes a poor mother.
2. The American girl is probably the finest-looking girl in the world, though somewhat flat-chested and too boyish. She is the best dressed. On the other hand, she has not the polish and breeding, on the average, of her European sister, in particular, the French girl.
3. The American boy is spoiled by money, disrespectful to his parents and elders, and immoral.
4. The American boy or man has not the solid qualities of the European man that make for dependable fathers for the family and the community.

How true these criticisms are, I can only know by further contact with Europe. I shall then be able to compare the two groups and assign places according to some agreed standard of measurement.

Sunday night, January 29, 1928. Aboard De La Salle, 11:00 p.m.

Two more days and my odyssey will have ended! How good it will feel to set foot on dry land again! The living sea is for some, but not for me. Imagine spending one's life on the ocean — it hurts me to even think of it. And I, eight years ago, dreamt of being an admiral one day! I am a social creature; I live only because others live around me. Solitude, the desert or the boundless sea, silent meditations in the depth of the forests or on the inaccessible crags of the mountains — no! It takes two types to enjoy permanent contact with the sea: the incorrigible nature lover — generally, therefore, a fanatic — and his opposite, the one lacking imagination almost entirely. Sailors are mostly of this latter sort, happy-go-lucky devils interested chiefly in satisfying friend-wants (hunger and sex), breathing in, as it were, love for the sea rather than consciously, hence artificially, arousing an affection in themselves for it.

This being the last Sunday, the ladies of the first class arranged a little program for the captain. Being only an amphibian (i.e., neither first class nor yet third), I was not invited and therefore learned of the success of the affair, as well as of its character, only through second hand. Lots of champagne was drunk. Miss Davis, who had never touched a drop before, was persuaded to take three or four glasses of liquor and was correspondingly hilarious. Dancing was indulged in, Mrs. Barnes and the chief engineer regaling the audience with a dance in which each held the other around the neck and did other scandalous things, etc. Mrs. Barnes was quite a philanthropist today, giving two kegs of beer to the crew and several bottles of champagne to honor the captain's dinner. Well, she can afford it — gets $1,000 a month alimony, I understand, draws $165 a month in dividends from shares in the American Tobacco Company, and gets $3,000 a year from her Nantucket houses, etc. Being of a frank disposition, she tells everyone all this. She was gorgeously dressed for tonight's occasion — wish I could describe ladies' apparel — and wore a diamond bracelet and one or two diamond rings. Though 55 or 60, she felt called upon to show me the ungrandmotherly brevity of the skirt of her dress. She's really quite a character. Very democratic and friendly and tries to get (after her own fashion) the most out of life.

Just passed a number of fishing smacks arranged in a longitudinal series. The deck steward yelled out *"Bateau de guerre!"* [battleship] and all of us rushed out to see. It was an imposing sight. They were all lighted up, the flagship at the head of the procession and the others strung along in the rear at rather equal distances. My imagination began to work and I thought to myself, How efficient and orderly everything is with military people. Then came the dull reality and my dreams were rudely shattered. Instead of stately ships with glistening white decks and burnished armor-plate shining by the light of the moon, they were nothing but prosaic fishing boats (here, too, I am guessing — they were too far off and the night too dark to make out anything more than the lights).

This is an example of the type of rumor that gains currency aboard a ship, and its accuracy. How many different versions of when we are to reach Havre haven't I heard, and of the speed we are making, the direction we are taking, and the size of the load we are carrying? Fifteen-odd people confined together for 20 full days in an area the size of one city lot; seeing never a new face but only water, water, water; hearing, smelling, seeing, tasting, touching always the identical things. Can one wonder then that every bit of news or information, as an incident, no matter how trivial and uninteresting, is zealously conveyed from mouth to mouth, and oftentimes back, and then back again, and that it should be distorted, magnified, or misunderstood in the process? How forcefully true, has it struck me, is the doctrine that man is made largely by his environment. One solid year of such existence and I believe the average person would be reduced to a simpleton.

Tomorrow afternoon we should sight the English coast. Hurrah! This is a rough part of the ocean we are in: short, choppy waves with plenty of whitecaps. The ship listed terribly to one side last night and has been rolling and pitching considerably, though I've had my baptism and feel myself a full-fledged citizen of the sea, entitled to all the immunities thereof. If nothing untoward occurs, our gallant ship will be at the harbor entrance of Le Havre by noon tomorrow. If we catch the high tide, we shall ride it in immediately; if not, we shall wait for its appearance and be docked by 4:00 p.m. Then *terra firma* again. Hurrah! Then Havre and Paris; yea, Paris!

I doubt if I can sleep tonight. I feel as excited as the little boy going on his first fishing trip. I feel like leaving word with the cabin steward to be sure and wake me early, out of fear that possibly I may oversleep. "Wake me early, wake me early, Mother dear, for tomorrow I'm to be Queen of the May."

One more luncheon and it will be all over with. Hurrah! My appetite has become cloyed. Twenty days of the same cooking has dulled my sense of taste. I suppose, to be fair, I must admit that the variety of food served, the type of cooking and the quality, considering this is third-class fare, was very satisfactory; yet the absence of pastries, good desserts, butter, milk, and eggs have prejudiced me against the kitchen. Last night, for the first time, they served cherry pie. I put away three pieces and only shame prevented me from calling for the only remaining piece on the service plate.

Monday, January 30, 1928. Aboard the De La Salle, 7:20 p.m.

What a gorgeous sky! What a wonderful sea! The moon, half-formed, looks coldly down upon the world. Banks of light clouds lie on the horizon as icebergs on a placid sea. On the port side, suspended in the blue-black firmament, hangs the great Bear, each of its seven members radiating a cold, clear light, like chiseled diamonds, while still further to the north, surrounded by a handful of stars, like a king sitting in council, is the North Star, rather glum and frigid in appearance. Below, as far as the eye can see, is the sea, its bosom heaving with gentle sighs and scintillating and sparkling with diamond points of light from a distant lighthouse. A cool, yet not cold, breeze strikes the check and rumples the hair. All is harmony, peace, and beauty with the universe.

At 2:00 p.m., the Scilly Islands came to view, the first bit of land encountered since we put out from New Orleans. A glad sight 'twas, surely! I felt like bursting forth into a poem of thanksgiving. Yea, like Columbus, to fall to my knees and give thanks to the Almighty for the favor He has shown to His servant. The Scilly Islands are not, however, inviting in appearance: a long, low-lying, jagged series of rocks. From our distance, the few structures we were able to make out looked like military prisons or forts perched high up on the crags, with the waves breaking violently against their stony cliffs.

Tuesday, January 31, 1928. Aboard the De La Salle, 10:00 a.m.

At last! There, ahead of us, lies Havre. One more hour. The sea is beautiful, marvelous, the water deep-green and its bosom severed with sails and boats of all descriptions. The sky is gorgeous blue. Apollo blazes forth — all's well with the world. There! There she stands, the cliffs of Normandy! Way ahead, obscured by mist, I can make them out. Normandy, gateway to sunny France, how beautiful! Havre, Rouen, Paris! Hurrah! How good it feels to be alive! First, I shall go to 89, Boulevard de Strasbourg to get a letter from my sweetheart, then on to Paris! Hip! Hip! Hurrah!

Sunday, February 5, 1928. 13 Cuxhavener Strasse, Berlin, 9:00 p.m.

Five days have gone by since I last wrote in my diary. I must go back and pick up the threads of my narrative. My last entry was made as the *De La Salle* was on the point of entering the harbor of Le Havre.

Le Havre from the side of the sea is very quaint and very pretty. The waterfront stands high out of the sea on a series of rugged cliffs. The harbor is medieval in arrangement, being flanked by stone walls along its entire length and guarded by two huge stone gateposts, which in time of siege or attack probably served as mooring stones for chains or cables to keep out the enemy.

The short ride from the quay to the railroad station was sufficient to confirm the first impression that Havre retained many traces of generations gone by: the crooked streets, the architecture of the buildings, the canals, the streetlamps, etc.

The four-hour ride by train to Paris was very delightful. The landscape is really charming: rolling hills, small patches of forests with the treetops nicely trimmed — at least they seemed to be — and layer after layer of meadowland, still retaining its greenness despite the season of the year. One fact immediately stood out: the thriftiness of the French. Hardly a vacant patch of ground could be seen anywhere. Even the small backyards of tenement houses had their greens. No hill or slope seems too steep to thwart the hard-working Frenchman.

Five o'clock and we came to Paris! Paris, the Mecca of all sightseers, the most cosmopolitan city in Europe, the cultural center of the world — what you will. My impression of it, however, was none too favorable. The Gare Saint-Lazare, where we arrived, was a very dilapidated building, and the neighboring streets and buildings were old, dirty, and far from aesthetic-looking. From the station, the Danish woman and I drove to the Gare du Nord, where we were to get the 10:00 a.m. train for Germany. The streets we passed over did not particularly destroy the first impression, and the last hour or two spent in walking half a dozen streets about the station also failed to shake the earlier reaction. However, I by no means wish to give this as my final and absolute judgment of the capital city of France. To judge a city by its railroad station environment would be a great mistake, as we so well know in America.

Whatever good might be said of Paris, one thing stands out supremely bad — the tipping system. I had been forewarned of this evil even before I left the ship, but the reality exceeded even the description. The system began to operate from the moment one set foot on the dock. Mrs. Plessner, the Danish woman, had four pieces of baggage. Four rascals each seized a piece, carried it to the bus, and demanded individual payment. When we got to the station, the bus driver, to our great surprise, asked each of us for a certain number of francs, depending on how many pieces of luggage were carried, and also for having taken us to the station. Now this was a dirty trick. The ship company is supposed to furnish free transportation from the dock to the train. It did have a truck waiting, but no one told us about it. The men at the dock probably work in cahoots with the private bus company and share in the booty.

When I got to Paris I learned that the possibilities and variety of ways which tips can be exacted were inexhaustible. Lucky for me I spent only four hours there, and most of this time under such circumstances that the opportunity to give *Trinkgeld* did not often present itself. However, I did not altogether escape. The man who carried my luggage to the taxi had to be paid handsomely; the taxicab man had to be paid three francs *alone,* plus the regular price; the company representative, for showing us to the station and giving us sundry help, had to be paid a handsome bonus; the waiter in the restaurant had to be paid 10 percent above the excessive cost of the meal; the girl who dispatched the cable for me (to Rose) had to be paid five francs (25¢); and the policeman who showed me the way to the cable office had to be given an equal sum.

If the costs of the tipping system came so high in merely going from train to train, just imagine what they must be to one who stays at a nice hotel and spends a week in Paris. The Parisians seemed to have lost all conscience and all sense of proportion in the matter of prices for foreigners. On the way to Berlin I met up with a fine-looking gentleman from Riga, one who spoke German, Russian, English, and French with seeming equal facility. He was forced to ride third class because of his experience in Paris — he, an old traveler who should know a thing or two. He showed me the bill he paid for three days at a Paris hotel of moderate size — 260 francs (something like that). They charged him nine francs (36¢) for two oranges and a banana (and France is a fruit country), 65 francs for some bacon and eggs, etc. Nothing escapes the tipping system. You must even pay the girl who shows you to your seat in a movie.

I cannot see how such a system can avoid demoralizing the people. No one cares any longer to do anything because of zeal or pride in his labor. No such thing as real service can exist. The people become servile, cunning, tricky, and downright dishonest. Right-thinking people in France should never have permitted such a nefarious system to come into being. It must have had the direct encouragement, and now the strong support, of the employers in order that they might avoid paying a living wage and shunt the burden onto the public.

Monday, February 6, 1928

Once arrived in Paris, the small group of third-class passengers who had remained together ever since the ship had docked at Havre took stock of their plans and reached the inevitable conclusion that they must break up. Bunze, who was going to Prague, had to wait over until the next day. Martin's train for Luxembourg was leaving that evening from the Gare de Lyon. Miss Kennedy, the Englishwoman, was stopping in Paris for a time. Albert, the Italian fisherman from Galveston, was also leaving sometime in the evening for Italy, but from a different station than the rest of us. Of the original group — with the exception of the Syrian family, who left us at Havre, where they were taking a train for Marseilles, thence by boat to Syria (by the way, the expected confinement of the mother was delayed; perhaps Marseilles will have the honor) — only three adhered together, and these for only another ten hours: the young Danish mother, Mrs. Plessner; her two-year-old son, Eric; and myself. Mrs. Plessner was on her way to Denmark and was going via Cologne and Hamburg. Since my itinerary also lay through Cologne, I decided to take her in hand. She was so helpless. She apparently had intelligence after a fashion, but she was so mouselike — quiet — and so readily dependent on others that she gave the impression of being more utterly destitute of self-assistance than was probably actually the case. Furthermore, she did not know a single word of the language, which only aggravated the situation. I, at least, could read, and though I could not understand 99 out of every 100 words spoken, I made up for the deficiency somewhat by keeping all my senses alert and watching the changing gestures and expressions of the people about me.

Perhaps I should interject at this point the statement that French seems an unusually difficult tongue to grasp by ear and to pronounce. This is due to several causes: the rapidity with which the French speak, the inconstancy of the pronunciation, the presence of so many silent letters, and so forth. To read it, however, comes easy — at least, so I found it. But to return to Mrs. Plessner. So, taking her and her cute son in tow and bidding a hearty goodbye to my fellow voyagers, after promising to drop Bunze and Martin a line now and then, I made my way to the Gare du Nord, from where our train left at ten o'clock that night. Accompanying us was a semi-official, a representative of the French lines — a sort of station hanger-on whose principal income seems to come from helping just such as we — who undertook to get us safely to our train, and a sickly-looking young fellow of whom more anon. We all piled into one taxicab — trunks, bags, people, and all (the baggage was loaded on top of the bus) — and proceeded to the station. We passed through a good many streets, but it was too dark and I was too interested in getting information from the agent for me to observe much of the city. Furthermore, we traversed what I should say was the downtown district, not the fashionable residence or business sections. Thus, I lost my first opportunity to see the so-called Wonder City of the World — I mean, of course, in any true sense of the word. At the station I paid the driver the accrued charges, plus the tip which the agent advised me to give. Then occurred a pretty scene — yet not so pretty. The size of the tip apparently did not please the driver and he let loose a volley of words, to which the agent gave prompt reply. For a moment or two the torrent continued, until finally the driver, feeling his cause lost, drove away muttering imprecations of various sorts. It was exactly like a scene from the movies or from several cartoons I have seen depicting Parisian life.

Mr. Russi, the agent, helped us buy our tickets, gave us the necessary instructions, and then took us to a cafe across from the station, where he ordered a meal to be served Mrs. Plessner and myself. Apparently it is in the nature of things to turn out better than one anticipates, for somehow, hit or miss, we got along. My French pronunciation is horrid, but I wrote down on paper the few things we needed and so made myself understood.

The three of us were famished, but between swallows I managed to look up and observe the people about me and the general surroundings.

The place was probably an ordinary cafe, nothing elaborate, with the tables set very close to one another and, in the proverbial French manner, both on the outside and inside. However, very few people sat outside; it was too cold. It was my first contact with real Parisians and therefore I observed the people about me with considerable curiosity. Not having seen other French people, I could make no comparisons or estimation as, for instance, with regard to their class, professions, native place, etc., but I did observe a few of the customs. For example, a lady was sitting at a table and a gentleman friend came in, kissed her heartily on one cheek then on the other, then proceeded to hold her hands, fondle her cheeks, peer deeply into her eyes, etc. It is apparently quite the custom for couples to arrange to meet in cafes instead of the man calling at the girl's home — however, this is quite common nowadays in the big cities of America. Water is conspicuous by its absence, and every table bears its load of bottles of wine and every other type of liquor. Water must be specifically asked for in France, and the same thing holds true in Germany. Wine is so cheap in France, and beer so cheap in Germany, that water is all but unknown for drinking purposes (incidentally, for bathing purposes also, as I shall later mention). How poorly I fit into the picture! What a strange creature who drinks neither wine in France nor beer in Germany!

As my Danish friend remarked, the people looked citified — in other words, blasé and bored. That is, some of them; others were laughing and carrying on in the proverbial gay manner of the French. A large number of the women smoked. My own stares were returned with interest and I was acutely conscious of the reason. The people must have thought to themselves, "What an odd-looking young couple. She and the baby are strikingly blonde, with light blue eyes and hair almost the color of sunlight, while he is so entirely different . . ." Nor was I particularly flattered at the association. Eric is a very handsome kid, but the mother, pretty after a certain fashion, is too lifeless, too mouselike, too much the timid, scared-looking country maid coming to the city for the first time. Actually, she wasn't at all countrified, but her quiet manner gave the impression too much to suit my vanity.

After the meal — a rather poor one, by the way, with a cost of 50 francs ($2), entirely too high — we walked around the neighboring streets for an hour or so, looking into the shop windows and observing prices, and then returned to the station. I sent a cable to Rose, paying the operator a five-franc tip and the policeman of the Information Bureau another five francs for showing me to the cable office, and then joined Mrs. Plessner. We had left our baggage in charge of the young, sickly-looking man who had accompanied us from the first station (Gare Saint-Lazare), and as he was on his way to Warsaw, or rather, to some small town in Poland, and was therefore taking the same train, I invited him to join us, which he did.

All of us being limited in resources, if not actually poor — that is, all but the stranger, who hardly had an extra franc to his name, as I later learned — we rode third class. Whoever hasn't been to Europe has yet to learn something with regard to traveling there. In France, three distinctions are made on the trains; in Germany, Poland, and probably elsewhere, four. Each distinction or class has its own special price and is distinguished from the other by a greater or less degree of comfort and type of appointment. Usually, at least I so gather, each class has its own separate car, though I have seen the same coach divided into first and second class. I know nothing as yet about the German trains, but in France I have observed this: the first class differs from the second class in that the seats are in the form of a well-upholstered sofa, with arms and back for each individual seat, and in the greater degree of ornamentation of the compartment; whereas the second class, though having wide, soft, sofa-like chairs, lacks the individual seats, the more elaborate lace headpieces, and the ornamentation of the first class. The third class is denuded of all artwork: the walls are bare. The seats are made of leather, and the backs of wood. Second class is just about twice the fare of third class, while first class is somewhat more than second, though how much more I do not know. That the distinction between the three grades is very real, I soon learned to my cost. Along with the third-class passengers, I had purchased a third-class ticket from Havre to Paris. Soon after the train left the station, I went into one of the second-class coaches to have a chat with Mrs. Barnes and Mr. O'Connor of the first-class group aboard the *De La Salle*. Bunze joined us later on and we spent the time chatting. Suddenly and unexpectedly, the conductor appeared and demanded tickets. Bunze and I showed him our third-class tickets and, in English, told him we were only visiting. He began yelling and stamping, and say what we would, he remained obdurate that we must pay the difference. Seeing there was no help for it, we did, and thus I got my first lesson in the complete distinction that exists between one class and another on French trains.

At Paris, we were told that in Germany the third-class cars are even better than in France, and since in the latter country, while to be sure they are very plain, third class is yet quite comfortable, we decided to go third class again. When we got on the train, however, we discovered that while the coach was clean, though plain and devoid of decoration, the seats were not as comfortable as the ones in the train from Havre to Paris. We soon learned that, this being a through train from France to Poland, the coaches were of the Polish type, hence the difference.

The people using this class comprise the best and the lowest. Next to our compartment — the coach is blocked off by partitions, or is in this train by the benches themselves, into separate compartments — was a very fine-looking French gentleman and his girlfriend (perhaps his wife). Hated very much to see him go, for they staged a shockingly open display of amorous feeling — one kiss followed by others in bewildering succession. (Of course, I averted my eyes.) On the next day, when we got into Germany, some of the very best people rode our class. Not that I would mind riding second or first class, but the money-savings is considerable, and besides, one comes in closer contact with the poorer classes, which is interesting to me.

I soon entered into a conversation with the sickly-looking man who accompanied us and learned his story. He was Jewish — this, our agent guide told me before — and had gone to Central America to find work. He had done rough work on a banana plantation in Honduras for the United Fruit Company, was advanced to a foremanship with pretty fair pay, but was so constantly sick with the tropical fever that the doctors warned him to leave the country if he didn't want to die. He headed for Cuba but could find no work. Nothing else remained for him but to go home. So, after a few years of bitter hardship in strange and inhospitable lands, he was returning to a land hardly less cheerless and uninteresting, even poorer in pocket and body than he had left it four years previously. My heart really went out to him. But, as he himself said [in Yiddish], *"Besser zu Materan sich zuchen eigne als zuchen Fremde."* ["Better to search again for one's mother at home than far away"?] Queer, isn't it, that the very first two people with whom I should have any lengthy conversations in Europe should both have been Jews, for the agent, Russi, was also a Jew, an Italian Jew, sharp as a whip and known to everyone in Paris, so my Polish friend informed me. The miracle is all the greater when I tell you that the first American who should accost me and show me about the streets turned out to be a Jew and that my landlady should also be a daughter of Israel. Coincidental, of course, yet interestingly strange just the same.

Sleeping was a simple matter, yet not so simple. It was simple to put a pillow which one has rented under one's head and stretch full length on the bench; it was quite another thing to fall asleep on a hard bench in a train moving and jolting and with strong electric lights beaming right down on you. Yet, it wasn't so bad. The experience of sleeping 20 days on a pitching, tossing ship stood me in good stead, and I did get four or five hours' continuous sleep.

At half past one in the morning, we were roused by Belgian customs officers wanting to inspect our luggage; we had arrived at the Belgian frontier, at Erquelinnes. At 7:20 a.m., we were again awakened, this time at Aix-la-Chappelle (Aachen), on the German frontier. It didn't take a seer to tell we were in Germany. The officials were already different — so entirely efficient. At Havre, the French officials hastily glanced at one of my bags, said nothing about my trunk, asked only if I had cigars or cigarettes, and let me go, the whole business not taking a half minute. The Belgian officials were hardly more circumspect, but the Germans showed an entirely different spirit. Not only did I have to display the contents of my bags, but I had to get off the train, go to the baggage room, open my trunk, and exhibit every drawer. Thus was the far-famed reputation of Germany for efficiency upheld, and thus did I know without the necessity of further proof that I was in the land of the Teuton and out of the Latin. Of course, this must be borne in mind: in going from America to France, I was going from a country of high prices to one of low prices; in traveling from France to Belgium, from one state of low prices to another equally low. In moving, however, from France to Germany, or Belgium to Germany, I was going, for one thing, from a land of low prices to one of relatively higher prices; for another, I was crossing countries separated from each other by a high tariff barrier. Nevertheless, this does not explain away the difference; the German official is really more disciplined and conscientious in the performance of his duties.

Monday, February 8, 1928. Germany

I had at last arrived in the country that was to be my residence for the next several months. An hour after we reached Aachen, the train pulled in at Cologne, and there I bid goodbye to my fellow voyager of 20 days' association. On the whole, I was quite glad to be rid of her; she was so absolutely dependent. Nothing like a certain person of the same sex whom I know. I kissed little Eric goodbye — poor kid, he had seen so much of me that he began calling me "Daddy" — shook Mrs. Plessner's hand warmly (no, I didn't kiss her), and spoke of possibly seeing her on the beach at Galveston sometime. (She intends moving to Galveston; she now lives in Houston. Her husband is a mate on one of the U.S. Shipping Board liners. She was returning to Denmark only for a visit and to show the grandparents their American grandson.)

I could only catch a glimpse of Cologne as the train sped by, but I did manage for the first time in my life to view the famous Rhine, that historic river where countless generations, peoples, and cultures come and go, the inspiration for good and evil, for commerce and war, for poetry and legend, as well as for blood and violence – "*Der Rhein, der Rhein, der schöne Rhein . . .*" – and found a quite ordinary-looking river, much like scores that we have in America. To be sure, I saw only a tiny section of it and probably a very unimpressive part. It is above Cologne – perhaps below it – where the Rhine comes into its full grandeur. There, with its high cliffs covered with verdure, the warm sun shining down from an azure-tinted sky onto the peaceful water, there, there is where Mother Rhine comes into its own! But, as I say, I haven't seen this; here, I only narrate what my eyes have viewed thus far. There was, however, something quite charming about the river, twisted and bent so that we were able to cross it several times after leaving Cologne. One other interesting thing I did see in passing through historic Cologne, and that was one of the great Gothic cathedrals for which Cologne, Mainz, Trevis, and other Rhineland cities are so famous. It was quite impossible to view it in anything like detail from the window of the moving train, yet I saw enough to greatly impress me and to make me feel that it was a truly noble structure, a worthy representative to symbolize man's highest genius at a certain stage in his historical evolution. Someday, I hope to be able to inspect these magnificent edifices at closer range and with plenty of leisure at my disposal.

Soon after leaving Cologne, we entered the Ruhr – the famous mining and steel and iron center of Germany, the home of the Krupp, Steiner, and other celebrated mammoth industrial organizations. The district was rendered particularly interesting by the decision of the peacemakers at Versailles, in 1919, to hold the Ruhr under the guardianship of Allied soldiers as a pledge of Germany's honorable intention to make amends for the harm she wantonly brought upon a world unaware – at least so they alleged. Today, no foreign military step is heard within her precincts; all is peace and order. Hardly a force is to be seen in the entire region, and were it not for the beautifully kept fields and the endless numbers of gigantic factories and industrial plants with their adjacent villages of fine stone houses and colored tile roofs, breathing cleanliness, order, thrift, and conservativeness, one might think that this quiet, peaceful region was deserted of human inhabitants. How spick and span, how neat, how orderly, how pretty are the German *Dörfchen*! Surely, the workers must live in these comfortable, clean stone houses, for I could see no others. The Ruhr industrialists have demonstrated what William Morris fought for in his own day, that beauty and light and cleanliness can be brought into the factory system; that the air and landscape needn't be choked with soot and cinders; that the workmen could have comfortable homes and little gardens and clean sunlight. True, I haven't talked to the workers, true, I have seen it all from a train window and closer contact may alter the picture, but this much must be allowed: the stamp of cleanliness, order, and substantiality is too indelible, too evident, to be denied.

Friday, February 9, 1928. Berlin

The advertising columns of certain German papers seem to do a brisk business in carrying want ads for spouses. Here are some good examples:

Seek for My Relative

40 years, exceptionally intelligent and good appearance, capable merchant, partner in a large gentlemen-clothing factory, and attractive income.

A Truly Handsome Lady

For the purpose of later marriage, age 20-26, with 40-50 thousand marks; 10 to 12,500 dowry, out of good house, discretion . . . Picture begged.

Seek for My Sister

In Leipzig, dark brown hair, gray eyes, unusually engaging, 33 years old.

A Life-Partner

My sister, an exceptionally educated person, refined character, musical (good pianist), besides that fine housekeeper, possesses a modern five-room house and 10,000 marks ($2,500). Gentlemen only of good circumstances and of good families, up to 45 years of age, need apply.

For My Niece

19 years, pretty blond girl, educated, with best character traits, of first family.

I Seek

In this way a *Lifemate*, from 30 to 40 years of age, in good position. Dowry 10,000 marks.

Chemist-Doctor
  Seeks a place, Saturday to be free.

Marriage
  Comes eventually into consideration . . .

Pharmacist
  32 years old, substantial, seeks marriage with woman of fortune or able to buy a pharmacy.

  Begging exists in Germany, though not with the prevalence that is generally thought in the States. Where it is found, it often takes on queer guises. This morning, the sounds of a melody strangely familiar came to my ears. Looking out of the window, I saw an elderly man, tidy and becoming of appearance, standing in the courtyard, singing in a low quavering voice. He was singing the one German song that I had learned in America, the famous "Lorelei" of Heinrich Heine, that sweetest of all German lyricists. Poor and cracked though his voice was, the words yet gave me some pleasure and I threw him some coins, for so he earned his bread. Strange to what ways men are reduced by poverty: a well-groomed old man who had clearly seen better days, reduced to the sorry business of singing in backyards for a few mendicant pfennig. But he fared better than others. The other day, two young men, cripples, World War victims undoubtedly, also appeared in the courtyard and lifted their voices in tuneful supplication — such vibrant, beer-toned voices of German freemen, raised, not as perhaps in former days to express inner exuberance or mayhap pride and love of *Vaterland*, but for a piece of bread — and they were unsuccessful.
  There are many less meritorious cases than these. A short while ago as I was sitting in beer halls hard by the University of Berlin, a rather odd-looking fellow at a neighboring table handed me a note on which he had just written in English, "Excuse me, sir, but I'm a poor student of philosophy. Can you give me some money?" How odd! Imagine an American university student reduced even to his last cent doing such a thing! Impossible, yet here was a German student sitting in a cafe, calmly drinking his beer, hence not reduced to a state of desperation, soliciting for alms. Not that this case is at all typical, yet it is another instance of the tricks which the last war has played with the moral character and self-respect of a good many Europeans.
  In France, this cheapening of character is going on at a much faster and more widespread rate because of the terrible hold which the tipping system has taken since the war. In the dire necessity

of making a living for themselves and their families, men, formerly self-contained and possessed of a sturdy pride, have become service creatures, lackeys, madly scrambling for tips, pennies wrung from the protesting hand of the public, most often from the foreigners. Imagine a system where men of families are paid $25 to $50 a month, the rest for existence purposes to come from ingenuity in wheedling out of the public a few extra pennies by knavery, servility, or buffoonery. Everywhere I went, I heard nothing but indignant protest among foreigners against this vicious incubus. The system makes for contempt, disgust, and irritation on the part of the visitor; for the absence of that healthy zeal and pleasure in one's work which makes for a contented working population and which makes that ineffable yet very real thing called in America 'service'; for trickery and chicanery; for a state of society where each man really becomes to every other man as a wolf, *homo homini lupus*. Yea, for revolution.

The German apparently discerned the unhappy consequence of such an order of things. At least the tipping system as known in France does not prevail. They solved the problem much more satisfactorily. In hotels, restaurants, and cabarets, 10 percent is openly added to the bill, this sum going to the personnel, while in other spheres tipping does not exist at all, or else is entirely optional with the generosity of the public. There are none of those injured looks, none of that open cursing if the tip isn't satisfactory that prevails in France, at least in Paris. The employers pay a compensation much nearer to a living wage than in France, and the nation is thus spared the humiliation and degradation of the *Trinkgeld* system.

But this is not to imply that conditions are rosy in Germany. An office worker or bookkeeper may get 180 to 250 marks a month ($40 to $60). Food and clothing and rent, it is true, are somewhat cheaper and perhaps one-third less than in America. Such a situation can only mean that such families must live deprived of everything except the barest necessities, and let it not be forgotten that there are between one and two million people out of work in Germany, who haven't even that much.

Saturday, February 10, 1928. Berlin

Berlin has a system of house numbering and a general street arrangement that is absolutely bewildering to the stranger, and even the Berliners themselves do not seem able to make heads or tails of it. Such a thing as a rectangular arrangement of streets on a large plan is totally unknown. Few streets have more than two or three intersections with others. The longest street in Berlin is only about a mile and a half long, and to this fact the honest burghers point with pride. There is no one direction for streets; every point on the compass is boxed with a small area. At every few blocks comes a *Platz* (a square). The shortness of each street makes for their unnecessary multiplication, which means, of course, more names to memorize. Another trouble is that so many streets have identical names. Thus there are four Kaiser-Friedrich Streets, four Kaiser-Wilhelm Streets, three Kant Streets, four Goethe Streets, four Friedrich Streets, and six First Streets. In addition, each important man or woman in German history usually has a *Platz* or *Allee* or *Chaussee* named after him, and the situation is made even more confusing by the close similarity of names. Thus there exist such streets as Friedrich, Friedrich-Ebert, Friedrich-Franz, Friedrich-Karl, Friedrichbummer, Friedrichfelder, Friedrichstrafever, Friedrichsruhe, Friedrich-Wilhelm, Kaiser-Friedrich, etc.

But worse than all in complicating this modern Cretan labyrinth is the system of street numbering. On one side of the street the numbers go up; on the other side, in the opposite order. One has absolutely no way of telling which side of the street bears the ascending number, which the descending, except if he memorizes the fact, for there is no uniformity whatever in the numbering. In two parallel streets, the numbering may begin at the north and on the right-hand side in one, and in the other at the south and on the left-hand side. There is no such thing, therefore, as telling, without actual investigation, how many squares you are from a desired point. For example, if you are in Chicago and you happen to be at 1020 S. Michigan Boulevard and you desire to go to, say, 2020 S. La Salle Street, you know you must go ten blocks south and two blocks west, or twelve blocks in all. This is entirely impossible in Berlin. Number 7 Unter den Linden may be three blocks from number 40 Unter den Linden, or it may be one; it may be on the same side of the street, or it may be on the opposite. A point on, say, Unter den Linden to a point on an intersecting street — this is doubly impossible. Things are further complicated by the fact that all business places and dwellings do not bear a visible number at all, and one can only guess which number is the one he wants.

The system of naming and numbering streets and houses is nothing more than a relic from medieval times, plus conservativeness and stubborn pride which refused to allow any changes. Berlin, like nearly all large cities, was built up by a process of absorbing its small neighbors. But every little town retained its customary and separate features for years thereafter. Since every patriotic German town had its Friedrich the Great, Goethe, Kant, and

Friedrich-Wilhelm, etc., bridge and street and square, every time one of them was brought into Berlin, a new Friedrich or Goethe or Whatnot Street was incorporated within the expanding city limits.

February 11, 1928. Berlin

The Order of the Scarred Cheek

I have just come from a restaurant. Near me had sat three young men, probably students, nothing particularly striking about them except the following phenomenon. One had two parallel gashes, or deep cuts, each about two inches long, on his right cheek and another gash, semi-circular in form, on his right temple, so close to his eye as to give it a slightly distorted appearance. All the wounds were red and raw-looking, as though recently made. Another of the youths had also two cuts on his right cheek, though not quite as bad-looking as those of his friend. Whether the last of the trio carried such curious markings too, I could not tell, for the right side of his face was turned away from me. Now did the sight of such ugly wounds, so strikingly similar, on the faces of two young men sitting together arouse my usually healthy curiosity? No, it did not, for the reason that I am in Berlin already 15 days, and hence the sight of mutilated faces, far from being uncommon or new to me, greets me at every few feet. For this is the badge or symbol of what I am pleased to call the Order of the Scarred Cheek. Thousands of men, usually of the better families, are members of this honorable 'society' and carry its markings on the face, usually in this shape, number, and general appearance. Thus, they may be deep or shallow grooves or cuts; semi-circular, diagonal, or straight; one or two or even half a dozen in number; on the cheek, chin, or forehead, though usually on the right cheek; with frilled or decorated edges; and may vary in color, usually depending on whether the cut was made recently or not, from about the hue of the ordinary old scar to a sort of livid or faded skin color.

Now this honorable order is not a new one in Germany. It has been in existence for decades and generations, but at no time does it appear to have been more flourishing, if we, the outsiders, are to judge by the number of its standard bearers. No young man in parts of Germany — by which I mean largely the sons of the well-to-do, upper classes, usually the ultra-patriotic and the aristocratic families — can really be said to have proven his worth or mettle until he possesses at least one such scar or marking. What the first scalp was to the young American Indian, the scar is to this type of young German, the difference being that the former had the forest for his environment and took the life of a tribal enemy, whereas the latter has the fencing room for his arena, fights with friends, is content with giving and receiving slashes on the face with naked sabers or broadswords, and is not particularly interested in killing his antagonist. The more hacked the face is, the greater is the glory. The young man has thereby shown his caliber and his warrior heritage; he has disdained suffering and danger; in him, the family and the German name has a worthy standard bearer. Honor is usually accorded him by his family — for the 'badge' of the order is usually a genealogical affair — and by his circle and friends, above all by the young female section thereof. In America, the sprains and bruises of the football field call forth the admiration of the girls. In Germany, it is a face where a cheek exhibits a number of gashes. Far from being repelled or sickened by such mutilations, which would put a medieval ascetic or a modern Hindu fakir to shame, the young women of this set seem overjoyed to have such surgical specimens as their lovers and husbands. Is it any wonder then that in the face of such temptation, such wounds are welcomed and deliberately sought? It has been even whispered to me — perhaps a bit maliciously — that many of them are self-inflicted. The young man, the whisper went, gets a slight scratch during a bout and in private widens and deepens it until it has become a permanent channel, forever testifying to the world just what sort of man this is.

And all this in the twentieth century and in Germany, the land supposedly representative of the highest degree of nationalism and civilization that mankind has yet reached. The theory that human nature has changed very little from the past may yet be there. As someone has wisely said, "History may not repeat itself, but it has some extraordinary and curious parallels."

February 13, 1928. Berlin

A great curiosity which possessed me, as it must also for many other Americans, was with regard to the postwar picture which Europe presents. What physical traces of war's devastating hand does it exhibit? What mental, moral, and economic effects has the same cruel hand wrought? And now that I am in Germany — Berlin — what do I see? Twelve days in the land is clearly not enough for this purpose. The action of the war is too widespread and at the same time too subtle, too crafty, to be able to point the finger and say accusingly, "This is what war has done!" This much is clear: all palpable, visible traces of the war have disappeared in Germany. Physically, of course, she did not feel the foot of the enemy, as did France or

Belgium. Economically — in the dress, living, and enjoyment of the people — great harm must have been done. Yet this is not as apparent as might be imagined by the average American. The Germans are a clean, thrifty people; a proud one also. By repairing, replacement, and conservation, houses and clothing are made to look respectable. No one lacks for a few marks: a government stipend goes out to every man without a job. It is usually a miserable pittance, yet it keeps open begging off the street and saves the self-respect of a million or more men. Psychologically and morally and spiritually, the war has undoubtedly left its scars, but these, from their nature, are not readily observable. The feelings of the people are largely hidden, some — as the nationalists — from patriotic motives, others — probably the great majority — to prevent the tears from flowing afresh. Public reference to the war seems to be in bad taste. The living victim of the war, the cripple, is not seen; somewhere they are probably hidden away, to emerge only on grand occasions.

Whatever effects the war may have had on the German people is therefore so well concealed from superficial view that one might well wonder if this land has really known the most cruel strife in all history, which took away two million or so of her finest men and women, made her inhabitants go through six to eight years of soul-agony and physical hardship, and which brought her, beaten and helpless, before the bar of her enemies and proclaimed the moral perpetrator of this great crime against civilization. But of course it *has known*; of course it *remembers*. You cannot readily discern the signs of the terrible tragedy on the streets, but contact with the people in their homes, sympathetic questioning, delicate allusions may bring forth the tragic story which each family has to tell and which in its heart it keeps fresh, vivid, and searing. No, the German people haven't forgotten; they have simply disciplined themselves to say nothing. My landlady is a good example. She was showing me some pictures the other day: "This," she said, pointing to the picture of a fine-looking young man in the uniform of a German student corporation or fraternity, "this is my nephew. And here he is in an officer's uniform. He is dead now, killed in the war. I lost another nephew, too." That was all. Seemingly a simple statement of fact. But I looked at her, and the eyes and the face showed me everything — a world of woe, too agonizing for utterance. Memories too painful over which to linger.

Dr. X is another example. X is as poor as a church mouse. Lives in a room costing $7.50 a month and eats for 30¢ to 40¢ a day. By scraping and struggling, he attained a doctorate of philosophy in sociology and is now looking for a job. But jobs are hard to get in Deutschland. About two million men are out of work. By waiting

10 or 15 years he might get a professorship at a university, but how is he to live in the meanwhile? "Ah," he said, "if I were only well-to-do, I could become attached to a university as *Privatdozent* [a qualified assistantship], then by drinking beer with the other professors, I would get recommendations, and in a few years I would become a professor. But now . . ." This man was well-to-do once. He was 15 when the war broke out, with quite a tidy fortune to his name. His guardian was compelled to invest practically every penny of it (25,000 gold marks) into Imperial War Loans. The rest is known: came the war to an end and the inflation period set in. The government generally paid off this debt as it did thousands of others, but it wasn't enough to buy a pound of butter.

In the meantime, X, though just a boy, had joined the army and with him a brother and seven cousins. The brother and six of the cousins were killed, and for four years he was a prisoner in France. Today X is a sad-eyed, serious-visaged man, a fervent apostle of peace among mankind, and an embittered critic of his people. "My people," he said, "have in many respects a *Sklaven-Nature*, a slave-nature. They are a *gehorsames Volk*, an obedient people. It is in their blood to obey, to fear the whip. They love a master, one who rules with an iron hand. They liked the Hohenzollerns because they were firm and showed power. For a thousand years and longer during their entire history, the German people have known constant war. Fighting has become second nature with them. Each German gloried in the achievements of his *Vaterland*. In each burned a zeal to repeat the victories of his forebears and to make even more glorious ones. The German loves a uniform and a sword. The German has a mission to perform, to bring the double eagle to all the world and let the universe ring with the might and greatness of the German name.

"Today, things are somewhat different, but the old spirit lives on undimmed in a section of my people. There are the so-called German Nationalists. Defeat has not humiliated them. Quite the opposite. 'Germany is victorious in her defeat,' say they. 'See how she stood out for four years against a whole world. We would have beaten Europe to her knees if it hadn't been for America.' And in this way these people talk, having learned nothing from the war, devoting all their energies to bringing back the Kaiser, the aristocracy, and the days of the Hohenzollerns. The rest of the people are living peacefully enough, satisfied with what they are pleased to believe is at last a government by the people, but still fearing authority, still *gehorsames* — sober and group-minded." These words coming from an unusually intelligent, educated German must be listened to with respect. To what extent my own experiences with the German people will bear out his characterization remains to be seen.

Is there any perceptible loosening of moral standards in the Germany of today? Not having known the Germany of the past, I cannot make comparisons, but if one is to credit the general talk on the subject by thoughtful Germans and observe certain phenomena which meet him at various turns, it must be allowed that a good many undesirable things are being done today in Berlin. From what I can gather, the German stage is today on an extremely low plane. Nightlife is characterized by an open exhibition of vulgarity and downright obscenity. The spread of erotic eccentricities or perversions — call them what you will — is the subject of comment of those whose profession it is to know these things. The extent to which art is perverted under the guise of such titles as *Die Nackten Menschen* (The Naked People), *Ideale Ehe* (Ideal Marriage), and *Der Schöne Körper* (The Body Beautiful) would be laughable, did it not have its serious phase. America, in the last three or four years, has also been flooded with the same sort of travesty on art, but in no way does it compare to the openness, boldness, and lewdness with which the traffic is carried on in Berlin. Corner newspaper stands, bookstores, picture shops, dance halls, cabarets, theaters — all are devotees of the "cult of the naked" and reveal their devotion by exhibiting representatives of the nude body in every conceivable mode and setting. And who should gainsay them? Are not we Germans hailed for our rationalism? Haven't we always been in the world's vanguard in the matter of breaking the chains of superstition and leading mankind into the full white light of reason? Does not science, reason, tell us that the human is Nature's finest handwork? How long, therefore, are we to remain under the spell of Christian asceticism and medieval prudishness? Away with darkness and superstition! On to the body beautiful!

At the present moment in Berlin a murder trial is taking place which has aroused all Germany. It is on everyone's lips. The papers have been featuring it for weeks. All one hears is "shocking," "horrible," "unbelievable." Briefly, the facts are these: Hildegard Scheller, a girl of only 15, and her brother, Gunther Scheller, age 18, were left at home by their well-to-do parents while the latter were visiting in Denmark. The children took advantage of the occasion to stage parties in the house — *orgies*, as they have been described. Hildegard was quite a wild little girl and had a young lover, Paul Krantz, also 18, a good friend of her brother. But she was considered a coquette and played him false. One night, Paul and the brother, Gunther, chanced to discover that Hildegard was in her bedroom with one Hans Stephen, a boy of 17 or 18 and a friend to all of them. The two boys, therefore, decided to end the matter in a manner worthy of true philosophers and heroes. Both penned notes to the common friend, Hans. Paul Krantz wrote: "I believe that love has brought me to the end of everything. There exist girls who have aroused in me such an all-pervading sweet feeling (*Durchdringende*), such a blessed delirium and excitement (*Rauch und Tummel*) which you, to your good fortune have never known and which I can never forget . . ."

Then Paul lent his revolver to Gunther. Both knocked at Hildegard's door and found Hans, whom Hildegard had hidden behind a trunk. Gunther shot Hans to death and then killed himself. Paul picked up the weapon to shoot himself in accordance with the death pact, but was prevented (as it was brought out in the trial) by Hildegard, who rushed up and seized the weapon. Now Paul Krantz is standing on trial, accused of having invited Gunther, through jealousy of his rival, to kill Hans. Whether he really intended to carry out his part of the agreement is still slightly doubtful, but most people believe that he was sincere, and in the last day or two the state prosecutor has so acknowledged.

Now such a case, bad though it is, is yet nothing overly startling to us Americans. We have had our Loeb-Leopold affair and our Edward Hickman barbarism. This picture of people actuated by vulgar curiosity crowding the courtroom, the presence of imposing and high-titled alienists, psychologists, and whatnot, is all very familiar to us. But in Germany it is apparently a new thing and has aroused therefore a serious interrogation of whither Germany is going. Intelligent, loyal Germans seem unable to believe that such an affair actually took place in sober, orderly, industrious Germany. And their hurt is all the greater when they look around and observe how lightly the tragedy is being taken in many quarters. Their indignation has been aroused to a white heat by the report that the Scheller parents, apparently unmoved by the terrible tragedy in their own family and despite the fact that the trial is now going on (the trial actually took place last June), are staging a ball in their home within the next few days! Another example of the moral callousness and lack of delicacy of feeling which has taken possession of many Germans is found in the play *Madame Pompadour*, now running at one of the larger theaters. In one of the scenes, Louis XV becomes angered at the fickleness of his mistress and asks his minister whom else he has on his list that might serve the King's pleasure besides Madame Pompadour; the minister is made to reply "Hildegard." This provokes mingled applause and hisses by the audience. Just think of the brutality, the moral perversity! The terrible tragedy entirely lost sight of, and the 15-year-old girl publicly branded as a prostitute.

But from the foregoing one must not get the impression that moral turpitude holds sway in every German home and that German sobriety, respectableness, and solid virtue is a thing of the past.

First of all, the examples I have given are taken from Berlin, and Berlin is not Germany any more than Chicago is the United States. All I have attempted to do is to show that there exists a noticeable loosening of moral reins among a considerable number of Berlin people, that old values are in danger of being discarded, and that, few for the most part, unwholesome tendencies have come to a head. Whether these are typical of other bits of Germany as well, I have yet to find out.

One of the evening newspapers in large front-page type asks, referring to this trial now in progress, "Have we already American conditions in Berlin?" — a good sidelight on how Europe looks at our crime conditions, and with what dread.

February 17, 1928. Berlin

German Eating Places and Eating

One characteristic stands out predominately in the German cafes and restaurants which distinguishes them from similar places in America, and that is that practically every one of them has a beer or liquor counter in connection with its food service. It is sometimes hard to make out whether the food is served incidentally to the beer or liquor, or vice versa. Water at mealtimes is literally all but unknown. I know of no place but one, and that is a sort of boarding house, where water has not to be asked for specially, and then it is served to you in a glass about the size of a small wine container, just about 10 to 15 thimblefuls. Usually you have to put in your request twice or three times before the waiter is sure you said "water." The great national drink of the Germans is unashamedly *beer*. It is a rare sight to see a table in a Berlin eating place, from the highest to the lowest, without its beer thereon. Men and women, young and old drink it equally. No cafe is complete without its beer fountain, its sparkling glasses of every shape and size, and its gold-lettered or placard advertisements of its brands of beer. The varieties of beer are endless and must be asked for by a specific brand.

If beer is the German national drink, then *wurst* (or "hot dogs," as we call them in America) is the national food. And for every type of beer there is at least one kind of *wurst*. They are short and long, thick and thin, hog or cow, boiled or broiled. There is none of that slight shamed-facedness which prevails in America when one is caught eating a wiener at a Coney Island wiener stand. There are scores of restaurants here where sausage is the greatest staple item on the entire menu. The Aschinger chain of restaurants is a good example. Aschinger's is to Berlin what Thompson's is to America. They are exceedingly popular, though the self-serve department (they usually have table service also) does not have anything like the great variety of eatables that the Thompson places have. By far and wide the most popular section of the counter is where the wurst is kept. Here, men and women of every class flock to get their two wieners, potato salad, and one bun, pay 50 pfennig (12¢), and then purchasing a glass of beer, go to the closest table where they can squeeze in alongside of the other people and, standing, eat their hot dogs and sip their beer. Yes, they stand, for unlike Thompson's, there is only standing place in Aschinger's self-service departments. However, this is the exception in Berlin, for the Berliners usually sit down to their meals and eat them with much greater slowness than we in America.

There are other curious features, from the American standpoint, of the majority of Berlin eating places. One is the entire absence of butter with the meals, and another is that bread or buns are usually figured separately. Thus, a customer has to tell the waiter how many pieces of bread and buns he has eaten and the price is thus added to the bill. A natural question arises for an American at this point: "But doesn't the waiter know beforehand how much bread the diner has eaten?" The answer is yes or no, depending upon whether the bread is already on the table or not. But in any case, the customer has to tell exactly what quantity he ate, just as he must itemize everything else, for in the average Berlin restaurant or other eating place the waiter does not give checks but depends upon the diner telling him what he has eaten. If the latter should prove dishonest, then the waiter is in hard luck, for he is charged with everything he takes out of the kitchen. Personally, I don't like the system, for I am a heavy bread-eater and must, therefore, pay considerably extra.

A characteristic of Berlin restaurants is the prevalence of music at the meals, usually two or three musicians and often regular orchestras. This is true of even very small places. A very large number also have dancing in connection with their food service, but these are really more of the specific night-type of places.

The Germans drink very little tea, and when it is asked for in restaurants, it tastes horrible. I don't drink coffee myself, but I am told that the usual coffee served in Berlin is a very poor affair, and the cost is relatively quite high: 25 to 35 pfennigs (6¢-9¢) a cup.

Prices in German restaurants are, and yet are not, cheaper than in America. In the ordinary small place, the prices are about the same as its counterpart in America; in the larger places, considering the quality of the surroundings, appointments, and music, they are cheaper. At places in Berlin where the meal is, say, one dollar, a similar place in New York or Chicago would charge at least two dollars.

Monday, February 20, 1928. Berlin

I am beginning to think the Berliners are a very polite people, so much evidence have I witnessed of this trait. The place where I usually eat my dinners is a sort of private restaurant or small boarding house. Here come students, people of the neighborhood, and others. One goes through a courtyard, climbs two flights of stairs, and rings a bell in order to enter. At the door, he is greeted by *"Mahlzeit"* ("mealtime" – really the last word of the expression *Ich wünsche ihnen keine gesegnete Mahlzeit*: "May your meal be blessed"), to which he answers in a similar fashion or with "Good day." When he enters the dining room, he says *"Mahlzeit"* to the people in the room, whether he knows them or not, and they return the salutation by the same expression. When one leaves the room, the same formality is also observed. This greeting of the morning or day or night is observed to an almost universal extent. At almost any neighborhood store, and even in the larger stores, there always takes place an exchange of polite expressions, topped off by the famous *auf Wiedersehen* (goodbye). In cafes, hotels, and such public places, the greeting is always given. To an even greater extent, however, sometimes to the point of tediousness, is heard the words *bitte* (please) and *bitte schön* ("please" or "don't mention it," corresponding to our "you're welcome"). Everyone uses them on the slightest occasion. If you are buying a number of things from the grocer, he will say *bitte schön* after each item that he has filled. The motorbus conductor will always say *bitte* in asking for fares. The hard-boiled-looking policeman will always say *bitte schön* in answer to your thanks. And so on down the line. Often these words have become a sort of habit, something like our "yes, yes," and a man wanting to be very polite or helpful will say *bitte bitte* (please, please) any number of times. Needless to say, the words "thank you" (*danke ihnen*), "many thanks" (*schönen dank*), and other expressions of gratefulness are heard at every turn.

How much respect for age, weakness, or similar forms of helplessness prevails, I am not living here long enough to say. The coin has, however, a reverse side. Women are seldom accorded a seat in a bus or car, except very elderly ladies. There is a good deal of shoving and jostling in getting onto the transportation vehicles, and one has to move fast if he expects to get on at all. But on the whole, the people conduct themselves very orderly in such vehicles and maintain the very noticeable and marked characteristics of the German: orderliness, quietness, and sobriety.

The health cult seems widely spread here. In general, it manifests itself by a more or less open display of the nude body. Thus, it may take the form of a complete exhibition of the naked body under the name of art — or "ideal marriage," or "the body beautiful" — which is confined to art studios, the theaters, illustrated magazines, painted pictures, or postcards. Or it may take a less extreme form in a sort of youth movement that seems very general in Berlin. Everywhere one goes, one sees children and youths going bareheaded and displaying naked chests and knees to the chilly blasts of the winter winds. Such a movement can easily go to fanatical lengths, but I must say that I have seen some wonderful specimens of youth here: straight-bodied, solid, flushed-cheeked, clear-eyed youngsters, very pictures of health. Most of them, I imagine, belong to a sort of boy-scout organization and probably represent the best of German youth. How much the cannon-fodder idea is behind all this, I have yet to find out. At this point, it is perhaps appropriate to remark that the physical appearance of the average Berliner is very good indeed, and I have seen some really splendid specimens. Somehow, I don't remember seeing in any one place so many clean-cut, straight, fine-looking men as I have here in Berlin. As to the women — well, I shall leave that for another occasion.

The policemen here are a fine-looking lot also. They are very military in their bearing. Their uniforms help accentuate this impression. The famous German helmet, with its striking metal emblem and its peculiar shape, is worn by every copper. Each is a walking arsenal. Not content with a billy club and a gun, the German cop must carry a bayonet in addition. Really, I don't quite see the necessity of it all; the Germans are such a quiet, orderly people.

No wonder, in the face of such an armament, such efficiency, and such military bearing, the words *"Polizei verboten"* (forbidden by police) have such a magical effect. Everywhere it is seen: public vehicles, parks, restaurants — everywhere. Sometimes I wonder if the words aren't used just to intimidate or frighten people, without the sanction of the police department. For example, in a cafe and dance hall where I happened to be, I saw the sign "Standing in this aisle *Polizei verboten.*" Foreigners have for years been snickering about the universality of this sign *Polizei verboten*, or *Verboten*, and during the war it was used in ridicule of the Germans, to show the ubiquity of military rule in their land and their subservience to the ruling caste. Judging from its prevalence at the present time, the situation must have actually prevailed in prewar days. However, this must be admitted: such a regime has certainly made for order, cleanliness, and similar virtues in the public action of the people — at least, I don't know what else to ascribe it to. I can't believe that by nature the German is any less destructive or disorderly than any other people. Some force, or fear of force and punishment, must therefore have operated on him for years and generations, until his present-day characteristics have become ingrained.

Nevertheless, one must be cautious about describing the German as having a shudder of fear every time he sees the 'law.' This was good war propaganda and may have had some truth in 1914, but today it is different, as I can bear witness. The arsenal which the cop carried about him made me think that no citizen would even dare affront or even talk back to 'his majesty,' but I learned differently when I saw a taxicab driver sass back the cop — in fact, two of them — in the most vigorous fashion, and Mr. Policeman just answered in the same key: no bayonet was drawn, no bullet was fired, no strike-him-dead-on-the-spot tactics, as the war propaganda would have it, were indulged in. All of which proves we mustn't judge too hastily and be guided too much by external appearances.

Friday, February 25, 1928. Berlin

On Tuesday, the 22nd, Berlin had the appearance of a national holiday. Unter den Linden and several other of the important central streets were decorated mightily. For a moment, I had the thought that it was all in honor of our first president, but I soon learned differently. No less a person than the King of Afghanistan was coming to Berlin. It was really laughable, the way republican Germany put itself out for royalty. Even the former Crown Prince put in his appearance. Every royalist heart must have beat faster as he observed these elaborate preparations. Hindenburg and all the officialdom was there at the station to greet His Royal Majesty. A jewelry store in the downtown section exhibited in its windows a whole array of decorations which the Mohammedan monarch intended to confer on worthy Germans — this despite the fact that the present constitution forbids the acceptance of foreign decorations by German nationalists, just as our own constitution does in the case of American citizens. The socialist papers got a good deal of fun out of the whole affair and waxed very sarcastic about the strong democratic leanings which the administration was showing. It really is puzzling why the government made such elaborate arrangements to welcome this prince from such a comparatively unimportant country, particularly for Germany. If it had a political motive, it is difficult to discover what it might be. But of course, in reading this, the usual caution must be observed to distinguish between official acts and popular endorsement. I'm sure the great majority of Berliners were as bewildered about the affair as I was. And yet, Washington's birthday did not go entirely unnoticed. I don't know how it was at the American Legation, but above the door of the American Express Company there hung two large banners. I confess to a real thrill as I observed them. Remarkable how one's patriotism and affection comes to the front when one is away from one's country. This holds true for one's family and community also. You might think that one would soft-pedal his Americanism abroad, particularly in Germany, where they have little cause to relish us, but such is not the case. Whether it is imaginary or not, the American expresses by his entire attitude and conduct the conviction that his nationality is a passport to any door. He holds his head a little higher than the others and readily and proudly proclaims his origin. And the quite noticeable thing is that he is really received with great respect wherever he goes. If there is any truth in the reports current in the States that the American is now everywhere in Europe disliked and ill-treated, I haven't been able to observe it.

Perhaps, at this point, it would be interesting to bring in my German barber and state his views on Americans, particularly in respect to their connection with the recent war. Like practically every German above 26 or 27, he has his story of misfortune or tragedy to tell. The war lost him his nice barbershop and all his savings, by the usual route of the postwar inflation. He served on three fronts and witnessed all the horrors. The memories still survive, and he was anxious to unburden himself on me. Without particular pride, as a simple statement of fact, he brought out how marvelously Germany held out against the overwhelming enemy. America alone turned the scales. America and Germany had always been friends; there always existed reciprocal admiration and good feeling, until the French came along and 'be-dirtied' Germany to the Americans, just as she traduced her to every other country. America fell for French and English propaganda, and to this same contributed the *verrückt* (crazy) Kaiser and his ministers. The 'jackass' had notions of ruling the whole world, grandiose conceptions of world glory and world reign, and in this he was supported by his stupid officialdom. If Bismarck had lived, it would never have come to such a pass. The Kaiser should have been shot exactly as any other soldier who in time of war deserts the colors. The Kaiser was afraid for his precious hide and fled to Holland. No, America should never have been permitted to come into this war; it was a sheer piece of *Dummheit* on the part of the cocky leaders of Germany.

No talks of further war by this man. The French may be a malignant and ungrateful people, but he wants no war of revenge: "If a Frenchman comes to my shop, I treat him with exactly the same courtesy that I treat others."

Several things can be generalized from this man's talk, to include the great majority of the Berliners and probably the German folk: that the Kaiser is certainly not wanted back; that the military regime under which every German lives is a fine thing; and that the average man now feels himself more free, less shackled to any oppressive system. Withal, there is a rather regretful looking back upon former days when, despite the cocky warlords and officialdom, the despotic policemen, and the overbearing office class, each man had a steady job and was even able to put aside something; when things seemed more permanent, more certain; when old institutions and old conventions were stable and respected, not as today, with the poverty and the God-knows-where drifting. If only these good things could come back and the bad stay away, that would be ideal.

The Kaiser is damned by practically everyone, and the memory of Bismark is taking on an ever-increasing luster. The one represents failure, the other success. The one, Germany at her nadir, the other, at her zenith. The Germany that the iron chancellor brought to its peak of glory, and the Germany that Wilhelm II reduced to shreds and patches. It is interesting to speculate how differently German history would be written if in 1918 success had come to its arms instead of defeat. Bismarck, to be sure, would have retained his great place, but some sense of balance in weighing his merits would have been maintained, while the Kaiser, instead of the unenviable position he now has, would have been lifted to a place on an equality with Bismarck in the Valhalla of Germany's great ones.

It must be acknowledged that, outwardly, the Germans whom I have so far seen appear by no means the ragged derelicts that are often imagined in the States. It is really remarkable the respectability of their dress and their homes. The movies, theaters, and cabarets are packed. I haven't seen a dozen beggars (open mendicants) since I am in Berlin. The shops are bursting with fine things and there seems no lack of buyers. The school-kids are as fine-looking and healthy a lot as can be found anywhere. If abject poverty exists in Berlin, it is certainly hidden on the street. The French may well wonder then who really won the war. Certainly not they, for the general impression that one gets there is far more unhealthy.

The people and surroundings look poor and probably are poor. In France, wages are terribly low; in Germany, low as they are, they are yet higher than in France. In both lands the taxes are high, but whereas in Germany the government has practically no internal debt, having resorted to the simple trick of inflation, in France the administration is staggering under a load of inconceivable size. Yes, the French may well wonder if they really won the war. Norman Angell may have been right after all in his *Great Illusion* when wars were pictured as financial successes for the losers and failures for the victors. He pointed out the effect upon France of the defeat of 1870 and showed that she waxed prosperous soon after, whereas Germany suffered from depression. Certainly the parallel seems to hold here.

There is another phenomenon surely affecting my disposition, and that is the institution of dog keeping. Really, it has spread to insane lengths. Wherever one turns he meets the animals pulling or being pulled by their masters. No day is exempt from dog exercising, but Sunday is the *occasion par excellence*. Yesterday, too, was an unusually sunny day, just ideal for walking, so that the array of hounds and masters was larger than usual. It was a most extraordinary sight. Only the rather dull sense of humor of the German can explain why he does not burst out laughing at himself and his neighbor being jerked and pulled by a canine, struggling at their leashes.

Unter den Linden is probably the most important street, on the whole, in Berlin. On this street, thronged by visitors, out for their Sunday's pleasure walk hundreds of dog owners with their animals. Apparently when it comes to dogs, the Berliners lose all their ordinary standards by which to measure good taste or beauty. Actually, some of the dogs are the size of lions, and the ugliest and most awkward beasts that one can imagine. Or else they are these small, rat-like affairs, fly-legged curs, and everything else that is odd and tasteless.

The animals are as carefully kept as babies. The little ones have their nice-colored blankets. All are sleeked and washed and combed. Some have fancy haircuts. All wear collars. Sometimes, husband and wife each has his favorite, so that they will walk down the street and before them, carefully wrapped and tidied, will walk their two dogs. The Berliners may be poor according to reports, but apparently their poverty does not prevent them from paying about 70 marks a year in taxes for each beast.

It is noted that dogs are more often kept by people having no children, or at any rate, no young children. This explains why the institution enjoys such great favor in the large cities. Chicago has more than its share of dogs, but it in no way compares to Berlin either in number or tastelessness in the dogs owned. Many stores here have 'parking places' for the animals — the reason is obvious. How many dog hospitals are found in Berlin I do not know, but I'm sure almost as many as lying-in [maternity] hospitals. The Germans have a word, *verrückt* [insane], which is very expressive. They would do well to get a little sense of humor and apply it to about one out of every ten of the Berlin population.

Tuesday, February 28, 1928. Berlin

In one of today's papers, a reference is made to an article appearing in the *Los Angeles Times* in which the writer, an American, praises Berlin as the cleanest city in the world. On the basis of my own limited experience, I am ready to endorse this statement. The cleanliness and neatness of the city is truly remarkable. By contrast to American cities of anything like its size, its preeminence in these characteristics is only the more unchallengeable. There are none of those begrimed and smoky buildings as in Chicago, for example. I have yet to see a cluttered-up backyard or alley, yet to see empty lots with the grass uncut and piled high with rusty iron, old lumber, and other junk. And if the backyards and empty lots and street railroads and elevated-railroad rights-of-way are all so clean and orderly, one can imagine what models of neatness and sanitation are the streets and boulevards and parks. Everything, whether the house doorsteps or the brass knockers, the gutter or the pavement, bears the unmistakable evidence of a people who are tireless in their wars against dirt and all forms of untidiness. Everywhere this condition holds true — in the factory-workers' district no less than in the richest neighborhoods. And it is all the more wonderful when it is recalled that Berlin is an old, old city, going far back into medieval times. There are none of those tortuous, narrow streets overhung by the upper stories of ancient tenements that are so characteristic of other old cities of Europe, like Paris, for instance, or the Italian towns. Instead, every dwelling place is a substantial structure of heavy stone, limestone, marble, and compositions, with massive doors and windows, and tile roofs. The streets are wide and paved. There is no bar to the light and warmth of the sun, no standing pools of water, no great holes in the sidewalk or street. Even the pushcarts are entirely without refuse (for Berlin, a big city, has also this antiquated method of doing business).

The business houses, from the largest down to the common grocery store or delicatessen, are no less remarkable for the same general phenomenon of cleanliness and good appearance. Take the small grocery as an example. All the delicatessens are under cover in a sanitary case or container. The tins are packed in symmetrical order. No abutting or jutting out of boxes, and bags are carefully arranged and displayed on the floor. Even the very name-sign over the doorway is artistically made and spotlessly kept. Practically all the sanitation and refrigeration devices known in America are to be found in daily use here. I do not know to what to attribute this unexampled love of cleanliness, other than to a sort of national peculiarity or quality. Certainly, the argument that it is a product of a people who always pinched and scraped in order to exist and hence could allow no wastage through deterioration, decay, or general inefficiency isn't satisfactory. Else how to explain the quite unlike record in the matter of cleanliness of, say, the French or the Italians, peoples historically just as pinched by poverty and want as the Germans.

In the retail and general middleman business, Berlin — and probably all Germany — exhibits no such tendency toward trusts and chain stores that is characteristic of the United States. Aside from one notable exception: the Aschinger chain of restaurants and *Conditoreien* (combination ice cream parlors, cafes, and beer and liquor saloons). All places like bakeries, shoe stores, clothing stores, groceries, and delicatessens are independent establishments. Germany has certainly disproven, if other countries have not, the prediction of its famous son, Karl Marx, as to the quickness with which the small entrepreneur will be swallowed by his large neighbor. Retail business here possesses two characteristics, among others, which are worthy of note: first, it is generously spread in all parts of the city and not concentrated in a few localities to anything like the extent that occurs in the States, and second, most of the establishments do not occupy individual buildings but form part of the ground floor of dwellings (we call them tenements or apartment houses), or the basements, or else are conducted in one of the upper floors.

Thursday, March 1, 1928. Berlin

A good example of the hard-working German person is our servant girl, Luzie. Luzie is quite an interesting personality in herself. Hails from Upper Silesia. Came to Berlin a year ago to satisfy her curiosity as to what the big city is like. This trek toward the towns is clearly not an exclusive American condition. With Luzie came one or two other of her girlfriends. They seem to have readily adapted themselves to the new environment, but Luzie has not. She is too domesticated; the heritage of the hard-working rural life is too strong within her. She likes to dance, but only occasionally. To drink, to pet unrestrainedly — that Luzie cannot do. She was just made for the farm and the house. And what a tireless worker, and so faithful! It is a thing of amazement, the thoroughness with which she daily straightens and cleans my room. Once a week is not enough; daily must the place be dusted and tidied. The girl is up at 7:00 in the morning and works without a stop until 10:00 or 11:00 at night. Her only leisure is a few hours on Sunday. She could have Thursday afternoon off too, but she doesn't care for the rest. Luzie sweeps and cleans the entire apartment of seven large rooms, keeps the stoves going all day (no light task), cooks all the meals, serves the two roomers with their breakfasts (as well as the landlady and her husband), buys all the provisions, does a hundred other things daily, and as a finishing stroke, washes the family clothes — all this for room, board, and 40 marks ($10) a month!

Now, really, such a wage for such incessant hard labor is outrageous. No man would even dream of working for such a ridiculous compensation. It is a mighty poor commentary, incidentally, on the generosity of women to their own sex. The poorest paid labor, in reality, exists where women are the employers and their own sex work for them, for instance, their wages to washerwomen, to maids, to servants. And this is no less true where the woman is extremely wealthy or can afford to pay well as when she cannot. In the case of Luzie, the unfairness is all the more striking when it is recalled that for my one room alone, the landlady exacts more rent per month than she pays Luzie wages.

And so, taking it all in all, our Luzie is not content here and longs for her parents' farm in Silesia with the fine countryside and the neighboring forest, where on a Sunday she would always go and spend the day in delightful pleasure.

The maid or servant girl is a very common creature in Berlin, despite the war. Almost every family of any means whatever possesses one. The low wages paid undoubtedly explains the fact. The girls here seem mainly of German stock, though a large number of them are probably of other origins, perhaps Bohemian or Polish. A negro servant girl would create excitement, so unheard of is she. I haven't seen a single negro, male or female, all the time that I am in Europe. Orientals, too, are much rarer than in the States. The Chinese laundry, or the Japanese restaurant, so familiar in America — all that is unknown.

Sunday March 4, 1928. Berlin

The New Free Synagogue of Berlin

Curious to gather my first impression of German-Jewish divine worship, I paid a visit to the New Free Synagogue on Oranien Strasse last Friday night. Despite its name, 60 or 70 years have passed since its doors first opened, and other synagogues have been erected, newer and larger. But in its day, it was the finest in all Berlin, and it is yet numbered among the best. And as its name indicates, it adheres to the 'free' or 'liberal' category of Jewish worship — halfway between the old orthodoxy and its opposite, German Reformism.

In its architecture alone is to be found the epitome of German and Jewish-German history. The structure abounds in the classical features of European church buildings, with its massive walls and doors, high ceiling, narrow stained-glass windows, division into two side aisles, heavy benches and pews with their rich coating of varnish, and, particularly characteristic, the deep gloom and cheerlessness which enshrouds the entire place. Above each side aisle is a balcony running along the entire length of the interior, where sit the ladies, for though the synagogue calls itself liberal, the traditional seating arrangement is preserved. The upper portion of the apse, which meets the nave at its lower end, is encircled by two superimposed galleries, the lower one of which holds the organ and the choir of ten people and its leader. In the center of the apse is a high altar whose handsome ornamental features, covered by a thick layer of gilt, show forth impressively in the reflected light of the many tallow and electric candles that stand before it, on the railing around the altar, and on the table bearing the sacred books. The electric lights are lit, but they are too few and scattered to chase away the shadows, and the interior bears the same dark and gloomy visage which characterizes it by day.

Architecture is, of course, an expression of people's moods and outlook on life — *Weltanschauung*, the Germans call it — no less than painting or music or poetry, and in the structure and features of the synagogue we are told the story of a people who have not yet outlived their past heritage. *Fear* made the medieval Europeans erect their buildings of the heaviest materials and in the most substantial manner: fear of their fellow-man, of fire, of all the other natural elements or accidents of life. Then, too, life was slower and men's thoughts sluggish. There was no rapid alternation of styles or bewildering succession of new materials and conveniences. There was no wholesale migration. A man would build a house with the certain expectancy that his remote descendants would inhabit it, untouched and unchanged. And this heritage of ponderousness in thought and building came down, and at every hand it is to be seen today in Berlin, as in all Europe, in the way the houses are constructed — for example, in their heavy stone material, the massive iron front doors, the huge brass doorbells and knockers, the weighty keys which recall those of a medieval dungeon — and in the public buildings, the churches, in everything.

And the Jews, though a wandering people, mayhap yet adopt the ways of their hosts. They may have been hounded from pillar to post as seen from the perspective of history, but as measured by the span of years of the individual, their sojourn in each land and place was quite long, and the Jew (the young one), not having the experiences of his father, with none of his fears and forebodings, felt himself secure and permanently attached wherever he was. And so the Jew built him his home and his furniture and his 'church' strong too, and the New Free Synagogue is but the heritage.

The synagogue is peopled by older men — heads of households — with few young people present and two-thirds of the seats vacant. Germany, too, has its problem of the empty synagogues. And, besides, the places of business do not close until late. There are a few women, but they are off to themselves in the two side balconies. Most of the faces are clearly those of imported Jews from the East: from the German provinces, the Baltic states, Poland, and Russia. But quite a few are Germanized, with fair skin and blue eyes and erect gait, and several wear dignified black cutaways and silk toppers. All comport themselves quietly — German orderliness and discipline has had its way here, too. The synagogue is a picture of cleanliness and sobriety. The deacon, cantor, and rabbi are in immaculate black, on which the silk and embroidery of their prayer-shawls stand out in pleasing relief.

German Jews take their services seriously, soberly. That is evident. The silence is profound. The faces are big with seriousness. How deep his emotions are, I do not know, but certainly in silence each sits alone or rises with the congregation. The solemnity and gravity of the occasion is impressed on one still more by the black or dark clothing each wears, and by the gloom of the nave. The cantor and the choir sing beautifully, and the organ is impressive, but the audience does nothing. Even the one or two short prayers are said for them by the rabbi, just as in the Catholic church. Could this be German militarism at work, where one or two lead and the rest obey in silence, just as German orderliness and sobriety and cleanliness are also at work here?

The services start exactly at the minute announced on the blackboard in the lobby (5:34, if I am not mistaken) and end no less punctually. Each person walks out in the same methodical, silent way that he entered. Only in the lobby is there an occasional handshake and word of greeting. In an extraordinarily short time, the synagogue empties itself, and hardly has the last back left the doorway than the lights are turned off and the doors are barred, as the House of God is left to its gloomy solitude.

In silence, I too then turned away, overcome by a strange and heavy depression, wondering if my imagination was not playing tricks on me, that instead of having been in a house of worship frequented by live human beings, I had somehow found my way into an abode of departed shadows, or perhaps into a morgue where the freshly laid-out dead, in their black suits and white waistcoats, had arisen from their slabs and were going through a speechless pantomime of prayer and mock ceremony. And so I still feel.

Thursday, March 8, 1928. Berlin

It has been snowing the whole forenoon and part of the afternoon, not thickly but enough to fill the streets with slush. Must be a sign of spring approaching. Until now, the weather has had snow, yet not as disagreeably cold as I had been led to expect from the northern latitude in which Berlin is located. It is hard to realize somehow that Berlin lies as far north as the cities of northern Canada. Several days of the past two weeks have betokened (at least so it seemed) the arrival of spring. But today's experience disproved the general belief. Last Saturday in particular was a fine day, so clear and sunny that my friend Alex Shilkin and I took a long walk through the Grünewald, a large forest preserve on the outskirts of Berlin. It has been a long while since I was out in the open country and I therefore thoroughly enjoyed this communion again with primitive nature: the army of closely set trees, denuded of all leaves or blossoms, except for the pines, which bore their evergreen needles; the straggling hills covered with their rough growth; the pretty lake, Teufel See – Devil's Lake, they call it here – sat lonesomely among some great hills which all but hide it from view; and lastly, the fine view of the Spree, the river which at this point is joined by several little lakes and is much wider and more unconstrained than in Berlin proper.

Tired from our walk, we drew up at a little place called Schildhorn, and there, sitting by a table in the open-air pavilion which fronted the river, we surveyed the beautiful scenery in complete relaxation. Though the ice had not yet melted from the many little bends and forks of the Spree and summer was far in the offing, the Berliners were already out in considerable number.

Like ourselves, they sat at the tables talking, eating, drinking, and, in their own restrained way, making merry. In one thing we were distinguished from them: whereas we drank hot milk, they were slowly and calmly, as is their custom, emptying tall glasses of beer. Certainly, there weren't many other hastily observable differences, for the Berliner bears a remarkable resemblance to the American of the big city — that is, when taken in the crowd — in the matter of features, clothes, general bearing, etc.

This impression was strengthened in me on this particular occasion by the fact that as we walked into the pavilion, I observed a number of automobiles at the gate bearing such familiar names as Buick, Chrysler, Chandler, etc. And as we sat there looking over the water, held in spell by the peaceful, lovely surroundings, there came to my mind a description of just such a scene from a book I read which at the time made a profound impression on me. The book was written by a German during the early part of the Great War. In one of the chapters he told graphically just how the announcement that Germany had ordered mobilization (or perhaps it was the news of the Sarajevo murder) had come to his ears. How on this beautiful summer day, to escape the blistering heat of the city, he had gone to the edge of Berlin and, with a friend, had sat down at a table, and there, as he was talking and drinking and enjoying the beauty of the Spree — just exactly as I was doing now — and reflecting how completely at peace and harmony the whole world seemed, came the stunning announcement that the dogs of war had been let loose at last. It is indeed difficult to reconcile this peaceful, ordered land, with its abounding, teeming proofs of an industrious, hard-working, plain-living folk, with the military, blood-loving, sword-and-musket people that so large a part of the world believes the Germans to be.

And yet, the facts of history are not to be denied. This is a land that has been baptized in blood from time immemorial. Open the pages of history at any point, and a record of incessant warfare is before you: wars against the invaders and intertribal wars, dynastic conflicts and religious struggles, personal combats and family feuds. None is excluded. No country of Europe has its record. When practically every land of Western Europe had achieved its national unity, Germany was still a congeries of political fragments, each in bitter hostility to the other. And just as her disunity was brought about by the sword, so likewise was her unity. The mighty Germany of 1914 was the handiwork of Brandenberg-Prussia, an achievement largely by the imposition of its power over every phase of life, domestic or interstate, with which that state had contact. Is it any wonder then that the philosophy of Prussia, the unifier, the guiding force in Germany for the last 200 years, should become that of a great portion of the nation — the philosophy that blood and iron alone keep a people vigorous and great.

But, of course, one should be cautious. There is such a thing as a philosophy, a cult, an institution which is that of the ruling group and becomes the official one of the State without it being that of the people at large. It is, indeed, difficult to say how native, how pleasurable, was the cult of militarism to the average German. But this seems true, regardless of the degree of natural like or dislike for the institution in the nation at large: officially it existed, and every man, woman, and child felt its weight and paid its price.

The Case of Sergeant Grischa, which I have just finished reading, deals with just that problem. It is a very well written book, a novel, and has aroused great interest, I am told, owing to its frank revelation of the military system as it worked during the Great War. The individual was nothing, the system everything. This novel, written by a German (one of the most prominent novelists in the State) endorses almost everything that Germany's enemies gave out during the war concerning the grip which the military clique had upon the *bodies* of the people, that it constituted an aristocracy, a castle which enjoyed every type of special privilege and favor and who disposed of men's lives with the same carelessness that it disposed of ciphers in its theoretical calculations. It arrogated to itself the right to identify the *State* with its own ghastly philosophy and thus sanction its crimes and be able to say with impudence, "The individual is a louse; the State, everything," to quote the words of one of the characters of this moving book.

Saturday, March 10, 1928. Berlin

I saw my first movie in Germany last night, a straight comedy scene. Billy Dooley, an American comedian of second-rate importance, in a one-reel comedy, and a six-reel Danish film depicting Pat and Patachon, the two leading movie comedians of Denmark. The latter are highly touted in this part of the world. In America, we would give them third-rate (at best second-rate) importance. A news item and a travelogue completed the program.

Not having been to other German movies, I cannot, of course, compare them to the American, either from the standpoint of buildings and ornamentation or the technical or esthetic excellence of the films. The particular place I went to was quite plain; I went in just to spend a couple of hours. But there are unquestionably some excellent movie places here, with splendid fronts and fine illumination. As to the films themselves, there is no question but what America leads the world in elaborateness, technical excellence, and quantity of production. Berlin features every type of picture — her own, Russian, Italian, French, Danish — but more than any single other, or all others, including perhaps her own, the American. I can't recall all the American films I have seen advertised here, but they include practically all the leading ones. Two playing just now, of those that I happen to have read about, are *The Circus* with Chaplin and *Adventure in Paris* with Bebe Daniels.

American jazz and American automobiles are no less popular — that seems true all over Europe. A large number of the cafes have two orchestras, one to play classical or national airs, the other to pour forth jazz, usually American. However, there are other importations. Argentinian tangos and Hungarian waltzes, for example, are well liked.

As to American automobiles, practically every large make has its agency here. Ford and Chevrolet have several, probably also Buick. The prices are American, with duty added and freight. American brands are certainly liked, but how many are bought I don't know. Probably a good many, else how to explain the many agencies? Perhaps as an investment in groundwork for the future. The prices are so out of reach for the average Berliner. Written in dollars, it doesn't look so bad; in marks, enormous: 4,000, 5,000, 10,000 marks. Certainly the number of private cars is very small compared to an American city of this size, such as Chicago. On the other hand, the number of taxis is prodigious, probably as a direct consequence of the fewness of privately owned automobiles. The rates from an American standpoint are very cheap. I paid about 30¢ once for a distance of between three and four miles. From the point of view of the German purse, that is not cheap, probably. Still, taxis are certainly heavily patronized.

Later on in the evening, after the show, I sat down with Alex Shilkin at a table in the Vaterland Cafe. Cafes and restaurants have an importance in the life of the Berliner — I am told, in all Europe — of which we in America have no conception. A restaurant or cafe (the distinction is a bit difficult to draw) is not merely a place in which more or less hurriedly to eat, as in the States. It is a social institution in a very wide sense of the term. People come to spend not a half hour but the whole evening. To read the paper, meet their friends, carry on an evening's conversation, hold family or social gatherings, observe and mingle with people, dance, listen to music. The Berliners eat — eat heavily — but that is only one function of the restaurants and cafes here. People drop into the most elaborate restaurants or cafes not for a meal, not at all, but for a glass of beer, or a plate of soup, or a cup of chocolate, and it is gladly served them. A complete democracy of menu prevails: beers and wines, soups and vegetables, pastries and confections — all are indiscriminately served in the finest places. Just imagine in Chicago or New York a person walking into a pretentious place with elegant fixtures and elaborate decorations, with two orchestras and a dance floor, and ordering a beer or a soup. It would be unheard of, preposterous. But here it is the usual thing.

The Vaterland Cafe is one of the finest cafes in Berlin. Before the war, I am told, it was the Mecca of all out-of-town, wealthy Germans, particularly the patriots. Today, it has lost its jingoistic flavor (at least, I couldn't readily discover any) but it is no less popular. Everything is elaborate, spotless, expensive. For the two or three hours of pleasure of sitting there, talking, watching the people, listening to the good music, observing the dancers, and eating two scrambled eggs and a cup of chocolate, I paid 35¢, and Shilkin (who also danced) 12¢! There are, of course, more expensive places in the city, but these are few and cater to out-of-towners or foreigners. At the finest places, either with or without a dance floor, you can get excellent dinners in excellent surroundings and hear good music for 75¢ to $1.00.

One thing must be said: from the standpoint of cleanliness, elegance of appointments, general elaborateness, well-attired personnel, and general expensive settings and entertainment, the Berlin restaurants are incomparable with anything in the States. For every one in Chicago on the same order, there are two dozen here. This description, with only some modification, applies to the great majority of eating places here, not just the few. One feature is that all here, without exception, show striking cleanliness. One has only to glimpse, as I did, a few of the cafes in Paris — the ordinary ones, to be sure — to observe the difference and appreciate this splendid trait of the Germans.

I like German cooking, too. Whether it appeals to me better than the French, I cannot say, having eaten so little of the latter, but I certainly like it better than American — and I believe most people would agree with me.

Thursday, March 15, 1928. Berlin, 10:10 p.m.

Yesterday I purchased a briefcase and immediately became, not one of the elite, as would have been the case in America, but one of the great democratic army of briefcase carriers of Berlin. Statistics are wanting to me, but I venture to guess, without too much exaggeration, that there are twice as many briefcase owners here as there are dog owners, which is saying a whole lot. For the first few weeks that I was in the city, I was continuously amazed both at the vast number of these portfolios and at the variety of people who carried them. There was no discrimination in age, sex, or profession. Taxicab drivers, factory workers, department store girls, janitresses, school kids, government clerks, students — all had them. And they weren't empty, either. No indeed. On the contrary, they were all bulging out because of their sizeable contents.

Now I am one who for more than half my life has been nurtured on indirect evidence and hearsay as to the passion for learning which the German possesses, which accounts for his great contributions to the intellectual enlightenment of the human race. So when I arrived in this greatest of all German centers and observed the vast number of briefcases and their amazingly heterogeneous array of carriers, these teachings and this reputation of the Germans was immediately confirmed in my mind. I couldn't help but say to myself, Here is indeed the Messianic Land, the Greek Arcadia, the Platonic Republic — yea, a land even greater than Plato's, for whereas his had only philosophers for rulers, here in this land even the laundrywoman with the clumsy feet and red, swollen hands is a philosopher and a savant, a poet and an artist. What an ideal country, a Utopia truly and actually realized for once, was this modern Germany! That laundrywomen, janitresses, rough-looking taxicab drivers should spend every spare minute of their time in sitting at old Homer's feet or in thrilling to the lyrical cadence of the Lorelei, or in listening to the metaphysical expositions of the great Königsburger [Kant], or mayhap in burning with indignation as the eloquent Jude [Marx] painted the misery of the proletariat — that, that was heaven on earth, indeed! And now, imagine how disconcerted I felt when this entrancing picture that I had visualized was rudely broken by the information that these briefcases for the most part carry not heavy tomes bearing the wisdom of the ages but only sausage and cheese and rye bread and other things to feed the stomachs of their owners! Yes, I am still recovering from the shock. To think . . . to think . . . well, probably, I confess myself entirely discomfited. But it was a good lesson, which is not to jump to conclusions when in a strange land.

Friday, March 16, 1928. Berlin, 8:30 p.m.

My 'country cousin' came to see me today, and I acted about as cold and indifferent — at least for the first minute or two — as the snobbish and wicked big-city cousin in *Tom the Bootblack,* or was it *Ned the Newsboy*? Yesterday my landlady greeted me with the announcement that a relative of mine, also a Joseph Werlin, had called and inquired whether I lived here; that he had a letter for me which by mistake was sent to him; and that since there were so few Joseph Werlins in the world, he felt sure I must be the son of his uncle, Joseph Werlin, who left Alsace-Lorraine for America 40 years ago and had not been heard from since. Too bad I wasn't home, but tomorrow he would come again and make the acquaintanceship of one so dear to him.

Strange how it is, but somehow this sudden discovery of an unknown cousin left me cold. My landlady must have thought it awfully ungrateful and high-toned of me not to go into transports of joy at her announcement. But, of course, she didn't know as I did that my relatives hailed from such an unpronounceable place as Rezhishev instead of beautiful Alsace-Lorraine and had originally borne the perfectly horrid name of Werlinsky. Poor soul, how was she to know all this? And probably Luzie, the faithful little housegirl, must have also felt the same way. Yes, these Americans are peculiar people!

This morning, promptly at the hour set, came 'my cousin.' One look and I was convinced beyond all doubt that he had erred. The sizeable nose, the flapping ears, the big feet — all these unfailing, genealogically fixed characteristics of every Werlinsky — all were absent. One and only one characteristic had he in common with them: unmistakable poverty. Yes, it was indeed unfortunate for me that we weren't cousins, I told him, but wouldn't he sit down and chat a bit anyway? And so we entered into a conversation and I learned all about him and his family, and how hard times were in Germany, and about everything else that can be talked of within a half-hour. A respectable-enough-looking man, but clearly fortune had not smiled on him. His threadbare coat, the condition of his shoes, his whole general appearance — all attested to this fact.

What could one do with 40 marks a week when a good overcoat cost 100 and a suit 120, three times his weekly wages? Poor man, he had hunted me persistently enough. Father had addressed his letter to me "Joseph Werlin, Berlin, Germany," forgetting to add "American Express Company." With only that to guide him, my poor 'cousin' began the search. He had even inquired at the American Embassy, but was told that by some unfortunate mistake his distinguished 'cousin' had failed to report his arrival in Berlin and his address. But a righteous cause is always rewarded, and the next day another letter for me came. It bore the address "13 Cuxhavener Strasse" well enough, but this being a flat and a score of people living therein, the postman was unable to locate the distinguished 'Herr' and had again forwarded the mail to him. Now the trail was much better. Arriving at 13 Cuxhavener Strasse, he was told by some ignorant person that the honorable Herr was unknown, but of course he wasn't to be stopped so easily as all that. Up and down the street he walked, inquiring if anyone knew his distinguished relative *"aus Amerika,"* but by some malignant spite they all pretended ignorance. At last the footsteps took him to a little *"Guten Mittagstisch"* sign and it suggested itself to him that possibly the Herr might eat here. Sure enough, it was so. Herr Hamil did know of an American who ate often at his "good midday table" and that he lived by Frau Kohn on Cuxhavener Strasse. Well, the rest was easy. All he had to do was to come back to 13 Cuxhavener Strasse, ring Frau Kohn's doorbell, and inquire if Herr Joseph Werlin lived there.

Yes, yes, it was almost a pity that we weren't related after all. Poor fellow, I was almost sorry for him, with such hope and persistence had he sought the beloved son of his dear uncle. But what could one do? Pretend relationship? I might have even done that had one single feature except that of poverty been that of a Werlinsky. I looked again to make sure, but no — ears, nose, feet — none was a Werlinsky. But I did recompense him for his car-fare expenditures in trying to locate me, and I did thank him heartily for bringing in my two letters, and I did express regret that I was not the son of his long-lost uncle. What more could I do?

This afternoon a little observation that I made set in motion a whole train of thoughts that had had their inception on the first day that I landed in Berlin. On the bus, across the aisle from me, sat a mother holding on her lap a rather cute baby. The child was prattling and gurgling in German, and the mother was bouncing it up and down and playing with it, as is the wont of mothers to do. I found myself wondering how it comes that a mere infant already spoke the language while I, a grown-up a dozen times its age, was having so much difficulty with it. I even found myself wondering how it is possible that baby talk could be babbled in German at all. And so one absurd thought led to another, until I was back to the first impression that I had gained when I arrived in Berlin: the all-prevalence of 'Jews' and the 'Jewish tongue.' Everybody without exception was speaking 'Jewish.' Did not my own ears hear them, I would not have believed that all these hard-boiled Irish-looking (at least in some cases) policemen were conversing or shouting out commands in 'Yiddish.' That this clearly non-Semitic-looking bus conductor was asking for fares in 'Yiddish' was unbelievable. That all these light-complexioned, blue-eyed, small-mouthed men and women should all be Jews seemed a complete contradiction to all that I had ever seen or heard of Jewish people. But the evidence was indubitable. What these people were saying had an unmistakable

Jewish ring, hence what else could they be but Jews? Well, it might seem strange and rather silly to one, but it took me many days to get rid of this first impression and even now it persisted, as was the case this afternoon. I'll come back to it. One thing this experience in Germany has done and that is to clothe the Jewish tongue in a dignity and a favor that it never before had in my eyes. In actuality, I have tended to despise the language, to consider it as outlandish and somewhat barbarous, to pretend ignorance of it entirely, or when occasionally uttering a word or two, to do so apologetically. This applies undoubtedly to a good many other American-born Jews, and the explanation is probably quite simple. At least, in my own case I believe I can give the answer. One unconsciously absorbs the prejudices of the people about him. The Jewish tongue was identified by me with the Jews of Eastern Europe, whom I looked upon, along with the people surrounding me, as representing all that fine, cultured people should not be. They were cheap, crude, and uncouth; they bargained and talked loud and gesticulated offensively. In short, all was bad about them and nothing was good. The language probably unconsciously appeared to me as a symbol, a living reminder of these hateful characteristics, hence my dislike of it. And now, coming to Germany and hearing a whole nation using it, or what sounds very much like it — such a clean, fine-looking nation, one that I had been taught to revere and admire ever since my first contact with the academic life (though not particularly at home, for Father is a lover of all his people, no matter from where they hail) — is it any wonder that my attitude toward the Jewish tongue should have undergone a complete change? That I am discovering virtues in it that I never observed before? That it is not a meaningless jargon of sounds, that it has the same right to exist as any other language because it serves as a medium of rational intercourse between men and can be made into a flexible instrument for expressing every shade of human emotion, thought, and experience? If it is a wonder to anyone, all I say is, let him see as I have seen. Then, if he doesn't agree, one of two things is true: either he is blinded by super-patriotism, which is only a form of provincialism, or my sense of values is all distorted.

Sunday, March 18, 1928. Berlin, 11:50 a.m.

Saturday afternoon and evening is my usual time for sightseeing and amusement, and yesterday was no exception. In company with Alex Shilkin I visited two cafes, one in the afternoon and one in the evening, after supper. The first was the Rheingold, located near Potsdamer Platz, one of the busiest traffic corners of the city.

In former days, I am told, the Rheingold served as a rendezvous and general pleasure center for the wealthy elements, but since the war, like so many other places, its exclusive character has been broken, and today it is patronized by a more democratic audience, though admittedly still of the more well-to-do classes. The crowd was what would be called in the States an afternoon crowd, interested in dancing a while, sipping chocolate or coffee, talking to one another, and so passing the afternoon. It was much like the afternoon teas in the better hotels of America; in fact, it is called 'five o'clock tea dance' here, too. The admission price, which included refreshments, the cost of checking the coat and hat, and the established fee of 10 percent to the waiter, totaled in all 1 mark 40 pfennig, or about 38¢ in American money. Clearly, from an American standpoint, dirt cheap. And it is. The place, as is so generally typical of Berlin amusement and eating establishments, is a picture of cleanliness and elegance, even more so than ordinarily, for, as I say, the Rheingold is quite an exclusive institution. The walls and pillars are of marble; the fixtures, the tables and chairs, the table service are all of the best; the orchestra, the personnel, the chief waiters are all immaculate.

The second place that we visited was one of the many enterprises of the Aschinger Company. This corporation operates a large number of restaurants on much the same standardized plan as Thompson and Child in America, though with features that are not found in the latter. In addition, it controls a series of *Conditoreien*, and also, apparently, a number of places such as I attended last night, that is, cafes where the chief purpose of the patrons is not to eat but to dance. As I have mentioned before, the word 'cafe' has a significance here that is largely unknown in the States. It may mean what we term a cabaret, or it may mean a restaurant exclusively, or it may mean something that includes parts of both 'restaurant' and 'cabaret'; that is, its chief function might be to serve as an eating place, but in connection with that it offers a musical program and an opportunity to dance. What would more closely correspond to our public dance halls in America is the cafe we attended, a cafe where the dance space is a little larger than in the other types, and where only refreshments — beers and liquors — could be gotten. An exact duplication of our public dance halls is not to be found here at all. There is no such thing as dancing without eating or drinking in Berlin. The Aschinger Cafe or Diele (I believe it was called the latter; *Diele* is the German word for 'floor,' hence *Diele* and our word 'dance hall' have about the same meaning) is clearly below the Rheingold in quality of interior, but it is an excellent place just the same. The crowd was younger and more of the office-clerk class. The admission price was about the same, 1 mark 20 pfennig (about 30¢), and included dancing, refreshments, hat and coat checking, and waiter's tip.

On the basis of what I have seen and heard thus far of German social life, I am tempted to characterize the people, but I realize that this involves great possibilities of error at this stage of my experience with them. After all, my contact with Germans has thus far been very limited. My studies keep me closely confined, and I talk to very few people. All my impressions have been gathered mainly by external observation, not by mingling with these people — in particular the great ordinary masses — and finding out what their greatest interests are: what their ambitions, ideals, fears, hopes; what their prejudices, inclinations; who they love or hate; whether they are silly or serious, pessimistic or joyous; and a thousand other things vital to an understanding of a people. The best procedure probably is to limit myself as much as possible to a narration of easily observed facts and, where indulging in reflections or philosophizing, to reserve the right to alter my opinion as time shows up my mistakes. This is what I shall do — at least, attempt to do, for it is not easy to avoid generalizing.

A very noticeable thing in these amusement places is the relatively greater admixture of young and old than pertains in the States. Alex Shilkin seems to think that this doesn't hold true of nightlife in the big American cities such as New York or San Francisco. He may be right, but this hasn't been my experience. Owing to the relatively low cost, there is also a great variation along the lines of class, profession, wealth, education, and general position in the social order. For example, it is a very common sight to see at these places very plainly dressed, plain-featured, countrified mothers, fathers, old aunts, and even an occasional grandma. They come here mainly to look on and spend the evening — for nothing is more popular here than to spend half of the night just sitting and observing the people about you — or mayhap even to dance. The family or domestic spirit (call it what you will) is clearly still strong here and manifests itself in these and other ways. It must exist far more strongly yet in the smaller towns and the rural regions. In America, in the German rural communities and even in the cities, this same trait of the Germans — to make the dances or singing-unions (*Sängerbund*) or feasts or whatever it may be into family-community affairs where grandma and grandpa, father and mother, uncle and aunt, all go and participate — is also evident. But aside from these, I cannot visualize an elegant cabaret in America corresponding to the Rheingold here, peopled by even the three or four elderly mothers and fathers, in plain housedresses or suits and bearing all the earmarks of good old domestic people, that I observed in the Rheingold. A much more general sight, however, than the preserver of these elderly, family people is the mixture of middle-aged people and those, say, in their thirties and forties with the younger set. These may be fathers and mothers — who usually, however, do not dance in these more fashionable or small, strictly dance, places — or maybe bachelors and elderly girls. As is the case in America, the bachelors range freely among the young girls or else among the women more of their own age, while the spinsters look on or, if the men are gracious, dance with the bachelors or elderly men.

The number of unescorted girls is very noticeable not only in these places but in all phases of Berlin life. Much more so than even in the big cities of the United States. The war, with its effect upon the ratio of men to women, is one ready explanation. Another is the economic one, which is probably of greater force, for the superabundance of women relative to men is not generally observable in the nightlife. It is difficult to pay one's own way, let alone a girl's as well. Besides, most girls work and are in many cases as well off as the men. For that reason, girls in groups or pairs or even singly come and go freely wherever they care to. In Chicago it is quite true that the girls go largely alone to the public dance halls, but I doubt if many examples could be cited of girls without companions of either sex frequenting these places to all hours of the night, and fewer still of their patronizing the cafes, cabarets, and other establishments alone. But here it is *such* a general sight that one never even notices it. One thing must be said, however: the Berliners are a very orderly people and crime is ridiculously low compared to American cities like Chicago or New York.

At this point it is perhaps well to bring in something about the general behavior and character of the people at these places. The outstanding features are decentness, quietness, and general orderliness. My impression of the German thus far is that on the whole he is a very quiet, self-contained person. In a crowd he laughs little, smiles, and occasionally talks low, dances methodically and perhaps stolidly. His features are quite immobile; everything about him is characterized by restraint or discipline, whether in his eating or his dancing, his conversation or his amusement. These I believe are his undeniable characteristics in his public life. Whether one prefers the vivaciousness, color, volatile temperament and other characteristics of, say, the Latin is a matter of personal choice, of course, but that the German traits make for good order and general respectability is probably unquestionable. I now see what the effect of an older, more stable culture is like and can better understand certain facts in American national life. I can see, for example, a certain general crudeness or rawness in the American people as a whole which I had only heard of before and couldn't appreciate. So often had I read or heard without really understanding, though frequently repeating, that the Americans were in a young, rude state of culture, that only after a generation of further history could they expect the refinements, the softer, finer finish of the Europeans. Usually such statements are used in connection with the degree of development in which American art or music or literature finds itself. That it might also manifest itself in the general character of the people – in certain subtle, not easily perceptible ways – I didn't realize so much, for less, apparently, is said on this subject. I had been used to comparing, just as most of us, one group of American people with another and could readily see superiorities and what we call 'greater culture' in one than in the other – for example, farmer folk against country people, Easterner against Westerner or Southerner, Russian Jews against earlier-arrived Americanized Jews, and so forth – an ultra-national comparison, it might be called – but I had never compared the American people as a whole with, say, the English or French or Germans as a whole, probably because I had not had the opportunity to observe the others. I therefore never realized, at least in a serious sense of the term, that the same degrees of difference in the cultural traits between different groups might also prevail between nations. And, as I have said, my present experience with the German folk has revealed many raw, unpolished traits of Americans, considered as a whole, which I had hitherto overlooked or else adopted as characteristic of all people. And if I were to live in China now, more than likely I could discern still finer traits than the Germans possess, at least traits that bear witness to the relatively much greater historical age of the Chinese over the Germans, just as the latter are older than the Americans.

Let me see if I can't be more specific. In my contacts with the American working girl – the stenographer, the office worker, the store or shop clerk – it has often struck me how really coarse, primitive, and what might be termed 'unladylike' so very many of them were. The primitive, rude state was very much in evidence. The separation between them and the still coarse-fibered men of their own class was often very little. They curse, tell smutty stories, are coarse and crude in their ways. When they marry, they have little conception of what a decent, respectable married life is like. More by chance than by calculation, by the pressure of society, conventions, laws, do they somehow manage to lead a passable family life. Now what of the German girl of corresponding classes, which of course means the great majority of all girls, since the rich and educated in both lands are very few? Should I say that instantaneously and overwhelmingly her superiority over her American sister has manifested itself to me? No, for that wouldn't be true. Character differences are very, very subtle things to deal with. Often they can be felt and appreciated without one being able to express just what they are to others or even to oneself in intelligible language. It is difficult, therefore, for me to put in understandable words just wherein lies this superiority of German women in the matter of character, but that it does exist I am prepared to assert after my six weeks of admittedly indirect contact with them, purely on the basis of distant observation, reading, and reports. It is on such occasions as this that words play such an important role and at the same time, unless their contents have exactly the same precise shade of meaning to others as to you, are absolutely useless. Let me hope, therefore, that when I say that German women appear to me to be *on the whole* more genteel, softer, more feminine, more ladylike than American women, the meaning that I wish to convey by these terms will be grasped in full by others. German women as women are probably superior in character to German men as men. The latter is by the same token of historical age and national temperament likewise superior to the average American man. At this point it might be well to interject that I am prepared to admit that what constitutes superiority in character traits is the subject of endless debate, but also that I am not interested in hair-splitting, and that what I mean by superiority is what the average educated man recognizes and appreciates for such. I find him more sober, more serious, more comprehensive of the duties and obligations of family life and community life, better prepared psychologically and temperamentally to take on the responsibilities of fatherhood, just as his women, on their side, are prepared for motherhood. He seems to be older, hence more settled, more dependable, more understanding than the American man in the same general ratio that his country is older than that of America.

But this analysis is subject to certain cautions. It does not say that this picture has not a reverse side, no indeed. It speaks in *comparative*, not absolute, terms. It says the German in these respects is 'better' or 'finer,' not that they are 'the best' or 'the finest.' All along I shall be pointing out German characteristics that I don't like. That there are many such is needless to add. All I am saying here concerns only this *particular* phase of their life and characters, nothing else.

The dress in these places, particularly that of the women, varies of course with their class or wealth and the establishment they frequent, but in general, and with no fear of contradiction, it can be said that it is inferior in quality to the American's on similar occasions. I am a poor judge of women's clothes, but I can readily see that what the women at the Rheingold, a really fine place, wore could by no manner of means be called elegant or expensive: very plain, simple dresses, usually of a single color — blue, purple, and reds predominated — along straight lines, and clearly inexpensive shoes and stockings. The hair is most often bobbed, usually shingled, or with an occasional boyish cut or Ponjola. Many, however, are letting their hair grow out again, as in the States, while quite a few have never cut their hair at all. These last, it should be added, are of the homelier variety, as might be expected. I cannot say with regards to the styles. Owing to the plainness of the attire, the styles do not look so smart or modish, but I imagine that where considerable money is invested in a frock, Paris styles are at once consulted.

The matter of beauty and smartness and general appearance of the German woman relative to the American is again a perplexing topic. Everyone knows how important a part makeup, dress, and a carefree life play in making a woman attractive. On all these points, the American woman has the advantage over the German. If one takes natural beauty — figure, features, hair, etc. — that, too, is not easy to decide. The Germans, as a race, are of course tall. This and their thinness are good assets to feminine beauty. Blue eyes predominate. The hair, while under the general category of blonde, is more often brown than flaxen. The complexion is good, very good, with natural color. Most of these are good points, but on the other hand, too often the faces are unintelligent and lack animation. The seriousness which rests on the German, while usually good for a man, is too frequently unfavorable for the women. The teeth are more often bad than good, but this is less a natural fault than an artificial one, owing to the lack of money to go to the dentist. One thing both German men and women possess is a small mouth with thin lips. But from a classical standpoint, the latter are not a special asset. The lips are inclined to be overly thin and to lack the cupid's-bow. The complexion, too, is often inclined to have a pasty color rather than pink or red. On the whole, the legs — at least those that chance observation has brought into my ken — are not classically desirable: the ankles and calves are more often heavy than not, and the general appearance somewhat unaesthetic. Too, too often the German girl bears the earmarks of centuries of enserfment and domesticity, lacking the proud carriage, the poise, the pride of so many American girls. In the provinces, these last characteristics must prevail even more, I should imagine, than in Berlin or the other large cities.

On the whole, this matter of relative beauty is one of quantity. Each one of these characteristics, good or bad, that I have pointed out have their duplication in the States. Hence, all we can do, as in the case of most other features of the two civilizations, is to compare on the matter of relative quantity. From this standpoint, and on the basis of my own experience, I should certainly say that there are more pretty American girls per 100, or per 1,000, than the same ratio would reveal in Germany. This is measuring them by the standard of natural beauty no less than artificial beauty, but is talking only of the present and does not maintain a theory that the *inborn, inherited* physical characteristics of the average American woman are superior, according to the accepted orthodox criteria of feminine pulchritude, to those of the German woman.

Concerning the Berlin men, I'd say that as men they are physically more attractive than their women, considered as such. They are more often tall than short, with erect carriage, usually thin, with fine-cut features, excellent complexions, and a general neatness that is remarkable. However, like the woman, his face is too often immobile, with a tendency toward stolidity, and the blue eyes are often without quick intelligence. Indeed, their looks are often as their books: ponderous, heavy, serious, lacking humor and delicacy. Very often too, when middle age sets in, their heads, due to the growing heaviness of their necks, appear unusually round and heavy, like a solid sphere. This characteristic is heightened by the very popular type of haircut, especially among the older men, of clipping the hair as close as possible and as far up on the head as to look exactly like the forelock of the American Indian – just a short, thin ridge of hair immediately above the forehead – or else by the complete lack of hair, for baldness is very common here.

In this description of German men and women, this further caution must be borne in mind: what I have been describing here is what I have observed in Berlin, and Berlin is not Germany in many respects. The land is made up, like America, of many diversified localities, differing in type, conventions, and general mentality. What these are like I have yet to find out, but for the present, consider this as only applying to the largest city of Germany.

Tuesday, March 20, 1928. Berlin 10:20 p.m.

For the last few days, one side of my mouth felt uncomfortable as I chewed my food. Not knowing exactly what was wrong but believing it to be the loosening of the one gold filling in my mouth, I decided to visit a dentist. Now, the matter of visiting a doctor or dentist is a delicate one, even in one's own city where one knows personally or by reputation a good many medical men. In a foreign land, where the skill, methods, and equipment are altogether unknown and perhaps altogether different from one's own land, the problem is far more difficult still. My landlady recommended a man personally known to her, but as his office was too distant, I decided to take her second recommendation, a Dr. Silberstein, who lives in the neighborhood. Once in the chair, my troubles began. Yes, the filling is loose – here, it has come out! – and three cavities in the neighbor tooth need filling. No, he strongly advises me against putting back the filling. It is sure to fall out again, the gold would have to be added to, and for the price I would have to pay I could almost have a gold crown. A crown is much better, will last me 25 or 30 years and will give me the greatest satisfaction. The cost? Oh, not nearly so much as in America. There they figure by the dollar, while here we reckon by the mark. For the crown and the three amalgam fillings, 64 marks.

True, cheap enough, thought I to myself, cheap enough for all this work – $16 – but how in the devil does it happen that I need all this work? The dentist I went to five months ago never told me anything about all these cavities. Wonder if this fellow is trying to ensnare me? After all, big jobs don't come every day, not in these hard times in Germany, where the average weekly wage is hardly more than half 64 marks. But no, he's so positive about my condition, and besides, he has just shown me in the mirror the cavities. At least, they look like cavities. But what about the crown? I've had this same gold filling put back half a dozen times, why not again? But he says it has become too small. Damn, what shall I do? I don't like his touch exactly, but maybe it's my imagination, and perhaps when he gets down to serious work he'll be better. Anyhow, I've got to have that filling back in my mouth, so might as well let him begin now.

Well, the first contact of the drill against my teeth caused a sinking of my heart. At the end of the first ten seconds I was convinced I had made a mistake. God, how brutal that man was! And with the speed of the very devil did he do his unholy work. My *"Gehen Sie Leichter, bitte"* (Take it easier, please), repeated several times, only brought forth the answer that soon, soon he would be through. And he was. In an amazingly short time he had cleaned two of the holes and had filled one.

Now I did something that never before had I done. In the chair, under the torture, I had formulated the plan to pay him for the work done, take back the filling, and find me another dentist who perchance might be more merciful than this fiend. But, alas and alack, how much easier said than done was this! In halting tones I told him that I wanted to enquire at another dentist as to the advisability of the crown before having him do further work, and that if he concurred, I would come back. And now what was my bill?

Oh, merciful heavens, shall I ever lose from my memory that wounded look, that stab of pain and surprise that came to his countenance? Shall I ever cease to hear that torrent of moving words that fell from his lips with the force and speed of a raging mountain stream? For ten minutes I listened to a speech of self-righteousness and outraged professional pride in words so eloquent, so heated, so passionate that the very stones would have wept had they heard him. Every word weakened my resolution, every phrase convinced me that I had done a great injustice. "For twenty-five years I have plied my profession. Take my work to any dentist in the city and he will praise it. Why should I dawdle and fake about your mouth and make a whole theater scene in order to fool you into paying me more? I didn't take advantage of you because you were an American, as many others would have done; I charged you exactly what I charge the German people. You are a Jude, no? Then we are brother believers. Surely, I wouldn't deceive my fellow religionist; nay, not only him, not even a Christian, either, etc., etc."

I ask you, what could I do? Long before he was through, I was convinced that I had made a terrible mistake. His every word pierced me to the heart. His "then we are brother believers" was the finishing stroke. I could contain myself no longer. Out came the filling from my pocket and dropped on the table before him. Involuntarily, automatically, my mouth poured forth words of apology and regret. "I didn't know . . . you see . . . foreigners . . . ignorant of dentistry . . . thought, maybe . . . Will come again . . . tomorrow, next day, any time you say."

Thus closes the first episode of my contact with a German dentist for the first time. Other chapters will follow in the order of their chronological succession.

Wednesday, March 21, 1928. Berlin, 10:25 p.m.

How little did I know yesterday at this time what the morrow would bring! Who would have thought that my affair with the dentist would have ended so painfully for me — yes, and possibly has another chapter yet to go! As I write, I am acutely aware that something is wrong with my mouth. A spittoon stands on the table beside me, and every few moments I add to its contents. The tooth that figured so prominently in my 'memories' of yesterday is no longer in its customary place but in my vest pocket! Heavens, what a shame, what tragedy! The faithful companion that has served me so loyally all these years exists no longer. Cruelly broken in two, forcefully drawn from his time-hallowed abode, bleeding, mutilated, stone dead he lies, wrapped in a paper shroud, in the vest pocket of the friend and master whom he had so faithfully served. And I, his lifelong beneficiary, cannot forget him. With pain and regret am I constantly, momentarily, continually reminded of this old friend and of the home, now entirely empty, a mere yawning cavern, that once housed him.

This afternoon, promptly at 12:30, I presented myself at Herr Doktor Silberstein's office. All in smiles, apparently entirely forgetful of my great injustice of yesterday, he escorted me to the chair and began his rapid but brutal work on my inoffensive teeth. He finished filling the remaining cavities and then turned to the tooth that had caused the visit in the first place. To my horror, he came out with the statement that he had just that minute discovered that one of the roots was broken. He was, if possible, more excited than I. Yesterday the tooth was whole, he could swear to that. Something had happened in between yesterday evening and today noon. Could I recollect a cracking noise in my mouth within that time? I turned pale — at least, I must have. I did remember such a noise. This morning, just before I came to see him, I had bitten a hard piece of rye bread and had felt a cracking noise. Well, from that moment until the moment he had pulled out the last piece of the faithful molar, I was a sick man, not from physical pain, for the operation did not hurt, but from mental-spiritual chastisement of the cruelest sort. "Why," I kept mercilessly and ceaselessly saying to myself, "why are you always such an ass, such a fool? All your life you have learned only in the school of hard knocks. Most people learn by experience, but there comes a time in their lives when they profit by these lessons, not only not to repeat their former mistakes but to avoid others in the future, at least those closely akin to the former ones. But you, you damn fool, never profit by anything. Your history has been one round of payment — payment in money, in pain, in mental and spiritual anguish — not once lighted up by a glimmer of forethought. For the last dozen years you've been hanging around laboratories, doctors, dentists, clinics, and you have learned nothing, absolutely nothing. Couldn't you have foreseen that any pressure placed upon the mere shell of a tooth (which is all that it was when the filling was absent) would be sure to do damage? No, you had to yield to your glutton appetite and eat a piece of hard rye bread that you really didn't want, and had to eat it not on the other side but just the side where it would produce a catastrophe. Served you right. Hope the dentist half kills you."

I shall spare myself a detailed account of the extraction. Suffice to say it was, if not a painful thing, yet very unpleasant. All the more so because of my relentless self-chastisement. Finally, the last piece was yanked out and then, merciful heavens, will I ever forget the happiness which overwhelmed me and filled every crevice of my being at that moment! There, on the last root just ejected, was the *beginning of an abscess*. In four or five weeks it would have developed to such a point that I would have suffered great pain, necessitating the immediate removal of the tooth. At the same time, the cost for the crown would have been wasted, and the discomfort in fitting it would have been in vain. It is indeed an ill wind that blows no good. The lack of foresight which gave me present pain saved me pain in the future. I certainly felt better after this announcement. Not that I had reason to congratulate myself on any amount of prudence or common sense whatever, yet matters were certainly not as bad as I had painted to myself. As to the Herr Doktor, I'm his bosom friend now. I feel better toward him and he feels kindly toward me, partly because I paid him in full, partly because he feels a bit guilty about not having warned me of the delicate state of my tooth. So warm does he feel toward me that he insisted upon showing me his little daughter of five or six years and inviting me to spend a few hours with him, since a fellow Jude from *Ausland* is not encountered every day.

Thus ends Chapter II of my dentist story. How many more will follow is in the hands of fate alone: I am only the helpless agent.

Friday, March 23, 1928. Berlin, 9:30 p.m.

Yesterday afternoon, feeling somewhat indisposed to study because of my tooth extraction of the day before and attracted by the warmth and pleasantness of the weather, I decided to pay my first visit to the Berlin Zoological Garden, which lies in the general neighborhood of my rooming house. I have been to only one other large zoo besides this one — that of Philadelphia — and am therefore not in a position to make comparisons. But I am almost willing to wager that there is not another in the world that is any more ideal. It is simply magnificent! Everything gives evidence to the most careful planning and greatest disregard of expense in order to bring about the desired end. The welfare of humans was no less considered than that of the animals. Playgrounds, a 'reading hill' with an arbor where adults could read in comfort, stone benches artfully placed, a fine restaurant, a refreshment stand, a huge bronze statue on a marble base of Jason and the two buffaloes, trees, patches of meadow — everything to make a day at the zoo memorable. Some of the animal houses are really architectural gems, while all without exception are built for enjoyment and permanence. The monkey house, for example, is built on the order of an Indian pagoda, with all the characteristic terraces, domes, ornamental features, and resplendent coloring. Before the stalls of the American buffalo stood several genuine totem poles and other little touches reminiscent of the days when the Indian rested in solitary human majesty on the wide and open plains of the North American continent, and buffalo by the millions roamed the land and served as food and clothing for the Red Man.

Most interesting of all, perhaps, was the Aquarium, where is displayed various forms of fish life, set off by exhibits of amphibians, reptiles, insects, etc. It is astounding the amazing completeness with which was carried out the plan of showing creatures in their natural surroundings. Each type of fish or fish group, for example, is surrounded by a section of the rock or cliff or coral or other formation that enveloped it in its natural habitat, by the sand or soil that formed the ocean or riverbed, by the attendant water-life, and by all the other physical and biological phenomena natural to it. All through the exhibition the same motif held true. Everything was uncannily complete and perfect.

To me, not having seen such an exhibition before, it was all amazing. The curiosity that drew me here and to the zoo in general might have been that of a kid, but the reflections were those of an adult. Involuntarily the phrase recalled itself: "How great is Thy handiwork, O Lord." As I looked I thought to myself, How marvelous is nature and overwhelmingly inexplicable. The incalculable diversity in plant and animal life; the infinite assortment of sizes, shapes, colors; the astonishing variation in protective and attacking apparatus — now a shell, now a color, now a claw, now a fang — in method of obtaining food, in procreating, in ways of existing; the intelligence that each showed in getting its food, in avoiding danger, in protecting its young — all were testimonies to the great mystery. And everywhere, everywhere, I was impressed by the overwhelming, heart-sickening evidence of the cruel arrangement or situation under which all of us, from the most microscopic to the greatest of us, are forced to exist. Everywhere the survival of the fittest; everywhere slaughter and murder, violence and brutality. The big eat the little, the strong attack the weak; no pity, no love; all kill and hate, all doomed from birth to kill or be killed, to eat or be eaten. No, the universe gives the lie to a just and peaceful God. He may exist, but he loves neither peace nor justice nor mercy — not if we trust our human senses or understanding.

My conclusions may not be admitted, but that I received a real lesson in religion from my visit to the Berlin Zoological Gardens cannot be denied.

Sunday, March 25, 1928. Berlin, 10:30 p.m.

This afternoon I witnessed the Russian film *The End of St. Petersburg* and was greatly impressed, as must have been many others. It has been running for quite a while in Berlin. How extensively it is being shown in other lands I do not know, but I doubt if very much. I believe it has appeared at a few theaters in America also, but the great mass of the people probably never are able to see it, owing to its specialized appeal.

I am entirely unqualified to speak of its technical side, but purely as a layman I would say it is exceptionally good, approaching the American films and probably superior to the great run of European pictures. This includes the photography, the scenic settings, balance and proportion in the treatment of the theme, handling of mob or crowd scenes, and general directing. The acting is up to the well-known Russian standard, which means very high. An interesting aspect is that most of the characters are played by genuine representatives: laymen, not professional actors.

The theme itself consists of separate scenes and phases of Russian social life before and during the World War, connected and turned into a drama by the interweaving of a simple story. The class character of Russian society — at least from the viewpoint of the communist — is shown throughout. Alternate scenes of peasants' and workers' lives are followed by the depiction of the capitalist and his environment. These are followed in more or less chronological order by scenes showing the growing disaffection of the workers, the threatened strikes of 1914, the outbreak of the World War and Russia's decision to enter, the carnage of battle, the hunger of the population, the riots of March, the declaring of the provincial government of March 1917, the events of November, and the triumph of the proletarian revolution. As propaganda, the picture is excellent. The present-day Russians are masters of the art of producing the desired effect. They tugged at every heartstring. Every emotion was skillfully called out — anger, hate, pity, sympathy, enthusiasm. You left the theater exclaiming, "What a glorious revolution, how utterly unselfish and courageous the Bolsheviks were, what a noble work they have done, how deserving of sympathy and approbation of all decent, righteous men they and their achievements are!" Like a skillful master of the violin, they sound every note and half note of your heart and soul. Frequently, this end was achieved by a minimum of artificial supplementation. The sight of typical

Russian peasants and workers in their usual surroundings, which means the absence of all but the barest necessities of life, was enough to arouse your pity. This was transformed into anger and indignation as the next scenes showed you heavy-pounded, sleek-looking capitalists and their corps of servile assistants. Here was disgusting materialism and selfishness. Money, money, money — that alone mattered. Fat brokers were shown at the stock exchange fighting like maniacs in order to sell or buy the congealed sweat and blood and misery of the worker and his family.

War breaks out and the paunch-bellied capitalist and his coarse, be-diamoned wife become hysterical with love for the dear fatherland. They shed big crocodile tears and call upon their dear and beloved brothers, the workmen and peasants, to join the glorious struggle for God and country. War scenes then follow, and genuine hot tears almost pour from your overfull heart as you witness the horror and slaughter of the most terrible war of all times, or as you look into the tortured, uncomprehending eyes and face of a typical Russian peasant soldier who, in the agony of his suffering, is saying haltingly, "Why, for what are we dying?"

The scene changes, and you are back among the sleek and selfish capitalists, whose whole time is being occupied by stock reports and speculations on the market, and your indignation waxes hotter and hotter. Then comes 1917, and proletarian mothers are shown storming the food shop for bread, for they can bear the cries of their starving children no longer. Strikes break out, the workers are in a ferment, and only one thing remains: expel the Tsar, and as a sop to the masses, declare a republic. This is done, and again the fat capitalists and their jewel-decked wives are now shedding crocodile tears of joy and love for the worker. But the worker has had enough. He knows who are his true friends — the Bolshevik labor leader and the peasant — and, together with the army, brings about the glorious revolution.

The last scene is especially impressive. The great halls of the Winter Palace stand silent and empty. Through them walks hurriedly a proletarian woman, the wife of one of the labor leaders. She is looking for her husband. She finds him, wounded and bleeding but alive, and on all sides of him lie other workers. Her husband and one of the peasant characters are revived. From the pot that she carries, the woman takes out boiled potatoes and hands each of the wounded and the workers one or two, which they put into their mouths. Brotherly love, comradeship, equality, communism, is thus symbolized, and the picture comes to an end.

Now what are some of the thoughts which sober reflection over this truly masterful picture brings about? That first of all, this is focalized propaganda, that is, deliberate, conscious propaganda, calling attention to the Russian achievement of 1917 and to the ideals that prompted, and inferentially are still prompting, the Russian leaders. That such pictures are powerful agencies for enlisting friendship for the socialistic proletarian cause among the great majority of workmen everywhere, if only they get to see them. That among intellectuals and just-minded people, a kindlier feeling is kindled for the Bolsheviks, at least for their efforts in helping rid the people of the chains of the old system. That a new force has come into the world, the force of proletarian will, viewpoint, and general philosophy, heretofore entirely inarticulate, spoken through the mouths of others, or expressed in disjointed uprisings or revolutions. That all conventional interpretations of history in the broadest sense of the term are seriously challenged. That all present-day institutions and viewpoints are called into question. In short, that we are at a landmark in human social evolution, the significance of which promises to be enormous.

Sunday, April 1, 1928. Berlin 9:30 p.m.

And so the old story repeats itself: a Jew is a Jew the world over. For instance, Mr. Glusman. Thursday at the Russian embassy, where we were both waiting for Moscow's decision, he introduced himself to me.* One word led to another, and soon the usual exchange of autobiographical high points took place, with Mr. Glusman, as the elder, doing most of the talking. He had come from Canada, from Winnipeg, Manitoba. Had a general store there. Was on his way to Moscow to see the mother and brothers and sisters whom he had not seen in 23 years. The passage of time was bearing heavily on the mother. Seventy years she was now, and the Lord alone knew how much longer her soul would hold out. He longed to see and be with her for Pesach — perhaps the last Pesach for her — but Moscow was delaying permission. Eight days already was he in Berlin, and lonesomeness in the strange city and anxiety to see his mother and relatives were driving him almost wild. He had arrived on the 21st; now it was the 28th and still no word from Moscow. Eloquently he had put his case to the Berlin official, pointing out the anxiety and suspense with which the old mother awaited the son separated from her for so many weary years. The man appeared to be moved and had promised his best efforts. Day after day passed and still no word. Finally, a wire came from the Moscow relatives asking where are his papers, that the Foreign Office had received nothing. This morning he had rushed to the embassy and demanded an explanation and was

---

* For a more extensive account of Mr. Glusman and other acquaintances Werlin meets, see "Correspondence," beginning April 1.

told that the papers were sent from Berlin on the 26th. True, they had promised to help, but mail was sent to Moscow once a week only, and this ruling could not be broken.

All this Mr. Glusman told me, not in a crying tone, to be sure, but in one that left no doubt that he was in great agitation. I sympathized with him but couldn't tell him that I was surprised at his predicament. From my own experience, I knew that Moscow acts slowly. It was six weeks since I had applied for a visa and I was still waiting. What could he expect with only eight days of cooling his heels?

The mutuality of our plight, our reciprocal commiseration, our common English tongue, the kinship of race and religion, all exerted influence, and before we knew it, we were on the streets seeing Berlin together. Mr. Glusman knew Jewish — in other words, not German — and hence had been compelled to stick close to the hotel. I, on the other hand, possessed the advantage of eight weeks in Berlin, and had come to Germany with the extra advantage of not knowing Jewish well, and so was able to play the mentor to some degree. Where we walked, there we looked. Mr. Glusman, being in the dry goods and grocery business, found every shop window and every price tag of interest. The department stores called for many comments from him: "Fine! . . . Big . . . bargain . . . have to hand it to the Germans," and the like.

By this time it was getting on in the afternoon and our stomachs began to complain. I asked my friend where he would like to eat, a Jewish restaurant? Oh, with him it was all equal, he replied. "One place is as good as another. But maybe . . . yes, let's eat in a Jewish restaurant!" And so we went to Bernstein's, on Dorotheen Strasse. The bill of fare read "Kosher," and the people looked Jewish, acted Jewish, were Jewish, but somehow, somehow, he couldn't feel at home among them. The reason was clear: they spoke German and he spoke Jewish. What good is it to know that your neighbors are sons of Israel if they speak a language unintelligible to you?

At his room in the hotel the next day, I learned more of Mr. Glusman's life. Astonishing how alike Jewish biographies can be. Twenty-three years ago saw him leave Odessa and arrive in New York. Three months later and he was in Canada, in Winnipeg, Manitoba — the endless story, almost monotonous by duplication, of the wandering Jew repeated. One shoestring led to another, the pushcart gave way to the store, the store to a larger one, real estate entered, and so today Mr. Glusman is comfortably fixed, with property, a car, an established business giving him a "nice income," and best of all, a "fine family." The two boys have finished high school but they don't want to go to college. The youngest is a "what you call it? Hookey

. . . hockey player, dot's it." Good boys, both. Honest; won't take a penny from the cash register without asking Father; won't cheat anybody; got good business heads. But only one thing is not good: they don't take an interest in intellectual things, read only the football and hockey papers and detective magazines. "Not good, but what can I do? Fine boys. Treat me like a brother. Come up and hit me on the back and say, 'Pop, how goes it?' " He had spent money — plenty of it — for Hebrew lessons and wanted to send them to college, but they refused all. What could he tell his old mother? She would ask him what kind of grandchildren she had in America, and he could only tell her that they were fine hockey players. No, not good, but what could he do?

Knowing my man, I proposed a visit on the next day, which was to be Friday, to one of the Berlin synagogues. Of course, he would be glad to go. A father of children away from home, lonesome, never before in a German synagogue: "Sure, let's go!" So, the next evening I took him to the New Free Synagogue on Oranienburger Strasse. Now, if there is one thing every Jew of orthodox persuasion feels himself privileged and capable of doing it is to pass on the merits of the cantor. Like an experienced wine drinker samples a new wine by taking a small sip and then pausing for a few moments in critical examination of the taste, so my friend went about judging the cantor. With head cocked to one side and ears extended, he took in the first few sounds and in weighty silence proceeded to analyze their quality. The result I couldn't tell exactly, but all through the service I could see that my friend was not comfortable. He kept squirming and twisting about, now adjusting his hat, now leaning forward. The services, the cantor, the rabbi, the organ — all were strange to him, and he couldn't feel at ease.

The services over, we walked out and were joined by a fellow worshipper whose acquaintance we had made earlier in the evening. The man was from Vienna and had been in Berlin only three weeks. He had lost his mother ten months ago and had since then said three times *Yahrzeit* [a ritual for the bereaved that includes reciting the Mourner's Kaddish]. He didn't act quite right, as though a bit tipsy, and spoke loudly and passionately of his religiosity. The New Free Synagogue was a fine place and all that, but it's a shame that they held Yahrzeit services only once a day.

At this point, one of the regular members of the congregation, who happened to hear the slur on his synagogue, joined in without invitation and said that he was sorry to contradict the statement but Yahrzeit was said [i.e., a Minyan was gathered for Kaddish prayers] twice a day in the synagogue, and he proceeded to prove it. The Viennese admitted that he was wrong but emphasized that in

Vienna the services were repeated thrice daily and that all true synagogues should do likewise. Whereas the regular rejoined that for his part the Viennese could say it a dozen times a day, but so far as the New Free Synagogue was concerned, twice was enough.

Well, one word led to another until finally a warm, though polite, polemic was in full swing, with the principals and listeners standing in the street, in considerable danger of an automobile arriving and relegating the dispute and disputed to Paradise for settlement. The discussion finally got around to Reform Jews, the Viennese mentioning the astounding fact that he heard there are Jews in Berlin who pray without their hats and on Sunday, and that such Jews are apostates, traitors, not Jews at all. Meanwhile, the regular maintained that neither hat nor Sunday service makes a difference, that a Jew shows his worth by his deeds, not by the length of his beard or by the degree of force and number of times he punches himself.

We finally got the two separated and proceeded with our walk. The Viennese, however, couldn't forget the argument. He repeated his great dislike of Reform Jews and pointed out to us that the old rabbis ordained the wearing of the hat in order to distinguish the Jew from the Christian, who took off his hat in church, and hence Reform Jews were no better than Christians.

At this point, my friend Mr. Glusman could hold back no longer and spoke his mind. While the other two men were talking, he had been of necessity compelled to keep silence, for they spoke in German. Now that they had parted, and the Viennese with great difficulty had given him the drift of the argument, he could contain himself no longer. Both disputants were partly right, partly wrong, but as to the origin of the hat-wearing, the Viennese was dead wrong. He would tell him how it came about: In reality it goes back to the time when the Jews were in the desert, fleeing from Egypt. The sun was so hot that Moses, seeing what a torture it would be for the Jews to stand bareheaded in the broiling sun and pray, ordered them to cover their heads, and thus the custom had its beginning.

At the hotel that night, I bid Mr. Glusman goodbye, and as I walked, there involuntarily came to my mind the expression "And so the old story repeats itself. The Jew is a Jew the world over."

Wednesday, April 4, 1928. En route, Berlin–Warsaw *

The train left Berlin at 6:18 p.m. It is now 7:30 p.m. I am in a third-class car packed with people, mostly Polish peasants. Everyone carries enormous packs, and many have sacks filled to

---

* See "Correspondence" for a further account of the travel experience to Moscow.

the top, probably with vegetables. Many men are unshaven, with matted hair, rough skin, filthy clothes. In my compartment are two Poles, a young husband with his wife and small daughter, and a German in a sports outfit of golf knickers, sport socks, and all the other trappings. The German is spick and span, with a clean red face and nice blue eyes, well-cut brown hair; looks like an American scoutmaster. He is silent; looks on casually. Probably a bit contemptuous, conscious of being better than the less well groomed Polish couple. But they are friendly and talkative. The young husband speaks German. Gives me advice about stowing my grips [suitcases]; makes room, and cordially invites a couple of men who have just come in to sit down.

A new world all about me. The Teuton is giving way to the Slav. Rapidly.

<u>8:13 p.m.</u> Arrival at Frankfurt an der Oder

The Slav Belt is upon us. People are talking loudly, incessantly, as good an indication as any that I am leaving Germany behind.

Have been thinking of my experiences at the Polish Consulate in Berlin. Openly deferent to Americans. I wonder if it's part of a plan — to flatter the showerer of favors? I wonder if the doorman pulls the same trick on all Americans that he played on me. He took my passport, looked me understandingly in the eye, and asked if I didn't want the formalities hurried. Naturally, I did, though I knew it was going to cost me a little bribe. The fellow went through some flourishes, as though trying to show me special attention, but when the pass came back, I found that the others got theirs just as quickly, if not more so. But, of course, a condition is a condition. I had to slip the knave a mark, anyway. He had absolutely no power; he had cooked up this scheme as a way of increasing his income — probably poor enough. Thus is an American compelled to pay for his nationality in Europe!

The Poles about me are doing considerable drinking; lots of whiskey in evidence.

<u>10:00 p.m.</u> Stentsch [Szczaniec], German-Polish border

Sitting in a little restaurant at the railroad station in Stentsch, the last town in Germany on this line. Drinking tea, with people all about me doing the same, or else drinking beer. Line of men in front of the money-changing booth. Money-changing is a big business in Europe; a new border is crossed every few hundred miles. Many men become rich merely by being canny in money speculation.

I'm not so backward myself. Bought 70 rubles in Berlin at 37½¢ a ruble. In Moscow would have had to pay 50¢. Rather dirty trick on the Russian government, but I'm a poor man and can't afford to lose 25 percent on my money, or rather to be more exact, neglect the opportunity to make 25 percent. It's all but impossible to sell Russian money abroad. That is why it is offered at a discount in foreign markets.

World is becoming the same. Advertising signs on all the German stations, just as in America: "Baccarat Cigaretten," "Enver Bay" and "Muratt" cigarettes, "Halpaus Mocca," "Kant Schokolade," "Der Rhein Schokolade," "Deutschlar," etc.

Dress of people about me entirely modern and remarkably good, considering — stiff white collars, immaculate ties and shirts, good suits and shoes . . .

Jews are becoming numerous. Six in the station just opposite me. Quite Chicagoese or New Yorkish in appearance. Have seen their brothers by the thousands in the States. The day of the yeshiva type (the greenhorn) is apparently gone. Yes, the world is becoming one.

Can't help but think that I am so far, far from home, and getting farther. Drizzling and cold. Must wait an hour here. People about me talking Polish, sounds a good deal like Russian. A few are speaking Jewish. The tea tastes good. Shows conclusively we are getting out of Germany, where only beer is known and the tea is abominable. Every one of these types about me has his duplication in America; these are the proto-types of the Poles, Russians, Jews, and Germans in the States!

<u>11:50 p.m.</u> Bentschen [Zbąszyń], Polish customs point

They have just taken up our passports. A passport in Europe is as important as one's soul, more important, in fact, for without it you certainly can't live in modern Europe, whereas without a soul there is still a probability.

And now come the baggage inspectors. Toll borders are a reproach to civilization, a crime against mankind. A tremendous hardship on the poor devils about me. Their enormous packs are wrapped in paper or blankets, or enclosed in paper cartons or wickerwork baskets, and are tied with ropes and strings and straps. Every inch of space in the car is taken with their baggage. Even the aisles are packed halfway to the ceiling. It is impossible to pass without squeezing oneself or climbing over something. Imagine, then, the confusion, excitement, and real hardship which results from having to open every piece of baggage, box, and sack in order that the customs officer may have a peep — in reality it is only a peep, unless a 'hard-boiled' inspector is met. I've never seen anything yet that was found subject to duty among these poor people. I suppose the preventive idea operates, but just the same, it would seem that some way could be found to exempt people from this unnecessary trouble. Lucky for me I took along only two small grips.

A whole clan of Chinese have just gotten on the train, a rare sight in this part of the world. Their luggage beats even that of the Poles. A breath of China: one of the men is bent 45 degrees by the weight of two tremendous baskets hanging from the ends of a long pole which he carries on the back of his neck and shoulders. The baskets are filled with every type of household article and must be very heavy. About three or four families: wives, children, babies and all. Seem out of place here. Must be on their way to China via Russia and Siberia. Everyone eyes them curiously, makes them the subject of lively comment. Probably saying, "What outlandish, queer, inferior people these are," not for a moment reflecting that they themselves strike me just the same way. So is the ego of people! In actuality, between the Chinese and a good many of them there is little to choose.

The great variety of people so readily observable in this part of the world — where every three or four hundred miles reveals a different people, varying in language, dress, appearance, and grades of culture — is at times very depressing in its effect upon me. I am filled with a sort of sadness. If all were pictures of health and well-being, intelligent and educated, it wouldn't be bad, but the actual tragic fact is that they are not, that everywhere I see the opposite, everywhere poverty and destitution, great suffering, breeding, grubbing for food, living and acting like the animals of the field. If only there were fewer of us! It is sad to think that these unfortunate beings are numbered in the millions and hundreds of millions — like ants, swarming and fighting, toiling and moiling in a desperate effort to fulfill the miserable end that they didn't ask for but which they nevertheless must carry out. Helpless, pathetic puppets, victims of a blind, voracious, cruel nature. The Chinese more than all give me this feeling. There are so many of them, so many.

And yet, cruel as it is, life has another side. These poor beings do not realize their misery — not in full, anyway. They do not reflect and hence do not realize that they have a terrible grudge against nature. It must be allowed that for the most part they are not sad. On the contrary, if they are not suffering too much and their stomachs are full, they laugh and love and breed and live out their lives quite uncomplainingly.

<u>2:40 a.m.</u> Posen [Poznań], second city in Poland

<u>4:40 a.m.</u> Somewhere in formerly German Poland
Hurrah! The dawn is breaking — my first moment of daylight since leaving Berlin.

<u>4:50 a.m.</u> Ostrów

That travel makes strange bedfellows is axiomatic. My own experience is telling me so right along. For instance, at this moment in the next compartment is one of the Chinese families. I wish I were an artist. The spectacle that it presents just now deserves to be perpetuated on canvas or in marble; there is something so charming about it. On one of the two benches lies the mother and the three children, all sound asleep. One of the kids lies lengthwise, the other athwart the bench, half lying, half sitting, but dead in slumber, while the third, a tiny infant, lies with eyes tightly shut, suckling at the mother's open breast. The upturned faces are a perfect study of charm and unforgettable quaintness. The skin is marvelously smooth, and the faint dab of red in the middle of each cheek, set against the light yellow background, somehow recalls to me hard-preserve pears, which I have often seen in just that combination of colors. The slant eyes, small but well-chiseled features, the close-shaven heads, their purely Chinese dress, together with a sort of cherubic innocence and beauty which their features reflect as they lie fast asleep, enhance the charm of the picture. Haven't any idea whence they are coming. Heard one of them say something about Hankow. Perhaps they are going there.

<u>5:25 a.m.</u> Kalisch [Kalisz]

First town in former Russian, or Congress, Poland. Countryside hilly and pretty. Few trees to be seen at the moment. Everything under cultivation; the fields carefully laid out. The first village I glimpse is in the form of a cluster. The houses vary in size and in type of building material. Mostly small and poor-looking. Majority made of poor red bricks with either shingle or tin roofs.

The landscape now changed. More trees and more hilly. I now glimpse my second village. There's an old-fashioned Dutch windmill just a-turning, and there are the two spires of the village church. The Poles have a reputation for great religiosity. Quite remarkable how far the banner of Roman Catholicism spread itself. In the light of modern means of transportation and communication, distances in Europe are not great, but even today it is a healthy distance when it takes a fast train 20 or 30 hours to cross a country. In the days when Roman Catholicism reached this land, it was a really tremendous distance. It meant going by foot or boat or oxen; it meant going through untracked forests of wild and impossible growth, among a widely dispersed people who, where not outright savage, were totally ignorant and barbaric. Yet, despite these great difficulties, these standard bearers of Catholicism accomplished their mission and, in the case of the Poles, did an excellent job, as everyone knows.

__7:10 a.m.__ Passing through some wonderful countryside. The fields are beautifully worked and the houses and villages clean and picturesque-looking. How the insides of the houses look is another story.

Smooth, rolling terrain. Country has certainly the appearance of prosperity. Where is all the poverty that one hears about?

Haven't seen a sign of an automobile.

Many ramshackle dwellings have come into view near a railroad siding. Unpainted frame affairs, falling to pieces. In Germany such houses would be all but impossible to find.

__7:30 a.m.__ Arrived Lodz

One of the larger towns of Poland — which doesn't mean much from an American standpoint. Getting close to Warsaw. The East and the Slav are becoming more and more apparent. Can be seen in a score of ways: the poor assortment of food of the station vendor, his arm basket instead of a little wagon, the ragged look of the station.

The houses now are very shabby. Not a sign of a paved street. Patched, crude fences. Crudeness, rawness everywhere. Reminds me of certain villages in America.

A factory village just hove in sight. How entirely different from a German! The ugly brick buildings and homes, all a dirty brick-red in color. Lack of paint everywhere noticeable. Many of the houses covered by straw roofs.

The roads very primitive, only for lumbering carts and horses. Just saw a cobblestone road — unusual. Good enough for horses, I suppose. No need to build them for automobiles, as there are none in these regions.

A few ugly white cottages came into view. Along the track runs an entirely unimproved dirt road.

Can see it's getting toward spring, but air still chilly. The fields quite nice.

__8:30 a.m.__ Houses are getting poorer. Brick is rare. Every one is an unpainted one-room structure with matted straw roof. But fields continue nice. Just passed a pretty good dirt road, also one or two houses with tin roofs. An old wooden windmill! Way out in one of the fields is an upright wooden cross. Flat country. Patches of trees now and then, but scrawny affairs. Wonder if Germans during the war had anything to do with lack of big trees in this region? Another village, hence another church! Usually the finest structure in the village. God must be served.

Where are the toilets to the cottages? Manure probably too valuable.

Wow-wow-wow! My Chinese certainly are at it now. I don't know what it's all about, but the man and woman are at it hammer and tongs. Her face is red with weeping, but her tongue is going like a trip-hammer. They have been keeping it up for at least a half hour, with absolutely not a moment's rest. The woman is talking at the top of her voice and the man in a lower but just as insistent tone. The whole car is watching them, but many are turning away, weary of the apparently endless battle of words. I never knew Chinese could be so loud and so indifferent to white people around them. These Chinese seem to speak a little Polish; perhaps they have learned that the Poles are tolerant, not like the Americans? About five of the little kids are playing by themselves, entirely unmindful of the painful discussion of the elders. Certainly look quaint. Two are little girls, wearing earrings of tin or some other metal, in the form of flat squares in one case and hearts in the other. One wears a pigtail, an unusual sight to me. In Philadelphia, as a kid, I used to see many pigtails, but the Chinese have since ceased to wear them for the most part. I am told that pigtails were originally an enforced sign of submission to the Manchu conquerors but that the practice is now all but given up, owing to the overthrow of the dynasty and proclamation of the republic in 1911 under the leadership of Sun Yat-Sen.

9:50 a.m. On outskirts of Warsaw.

Thursday, April 5, 1928. Warsaw, Poland

The city presents quite a contrast to Berlin. The latter is the acme of cleanliness, using the word in its broadest sense: in the condition of the streets, courtyards, factory surroundings, and empty lots; in the generous administering of paint and varnish, and the readiness with which buildings are repaired; in the appearance of the people, who, often poorly dressed, are pictures of neatness. The German word *Sauberkeit* [cleanliness] is very fitting for this state of things. Warsaw, at the very first glimpse, already showed itself different. The railroad station is an abomination: no sanitary devices, no system, no order. The ghastliest waiting room. Sort of country-fair type of structure, unpainted, cheerless; no conveniences, no aids in the way of bilingual signs.

I walked or rode through a considerable part of the city, including representative parts of almost every district: the financial area, big business, and hotel sections; the secondary business districts; quite a few of the residential streets; the Ghetto, or Jewish quarter; the riverfront; and others. All revealed a vast difference from Berlin, and no euphemistic language which kept anywhere near the truth could make it aught but inferior to Berlin. One is the world of the Teuton, the other of the Slav — at best, the Westernized Slav — and the Slav's is undeniably the poorer in every sense. The best business district is second- or third-rate by an American or German standard: small stores for the most part, with no elegance inside or outside, with stocks that are very limited in quantity and assortment, and displayed in the show window with about the same artistic effect as our small, second-rate stores.

Aside from a few public buildings and one or two churches, there does not appear to be a building that deserves second notice, unless it be from an historical, architectural, or other specialized point of view. The entire city has the general appearance of being scattered and is probably in actuality so. There are but few what we term solid blocks of business houses. This phenomenon, as found in New York, Chicago, or other of our large cities, is not very noticeable even in Berlin, and in Warsaw still less. There will be two or three stores together, then a house or hotel or empty lot, then perhaps a few more stores, then again this mix, and so on. The buildings are usually two, three, or four stories high, but with little uniformity in appearance, again interfering with the block or solid effect. Most of them are old — 30, 40, or even 100 years — and show it. The Slavs do not believe much in repairing, apparently, or when they do, it is palpably patchwork: a board here, a strip of canvas there, a rope elsewhere. The Germans possess far more skill in making the repair an organic part of the old.

The town in its layout is clearly medieval. In other words, excepting a few main thoroughfares, the general phenomena of the old European town are noticeable in the tortuously winding, very narrow streets, the blind extensions, the many lanes, the narrow sidewalks, the cobblestone pavements, the old-fashioned gas or electric streetlamps, the dirt-bank waterfront coursing in zigzag fashion, and in many other features.

In some shops, as I was able to observe, modern appliances for efficiency, sanitation, refrigeration, and the like are lacking, with but few exceptions. Germany in this respect is also somewhat behind America — I am speaking now of Berlin; the smaller places must be worse — but it represents the zenith of a mechanical age compared to Warsaw. Not even a close photograph could adequately picture the terrible conditions in some of the butcher shops, delicatessens, and groceries that I have seen here. How horrible must it be in the very poor districts and in the smaller towns!

Warsaw is not only largely medieval, it exhibits also many Slavic or Eastern features (which are almost the same thing). This can be seen, for example, in the architecture of many of the structures, particularly the churches. It shows in dress and appearance of the women or the men. Contributing to this effect is the enormous number of Jews, with the distinctive dress and features characteristic of most of them, but of these I shall speak separately.*

Europe in general seems to reveal more than not of the characteristics which we ordinarily think of as belonging to the pre-modern, pre-mechanical age, but Warsaw is behind all the others that I have thus far seen. But that is to be expected. I now know on the basis of my present experience that what the world accepts as a postulate is really true: that the farther east one goes, the more the older, more general world of bygone days comes to view. I have read and listened to many arguments in favor of this older world, but for the life of me I cannot see it as anything but gross inferiority in every way, that is, dirtier, uglier, more barren, more cheerless, more coarse, more cruel.

The prevalence of the military here is really tremendous. Everywhere one sees soldiers and officers. The number of officers is truly astounding, though I suppose the fact that Warsaw is a military center has something to do with it. They are handsome, fine-looking men for the most part, but that doesn't take away from the observation that they are a curse to the country, a privileged, pampered lot, an absolute aristocracy. They are nothing but an idle breed, nothing but parasites, literally living in this impoverished land on the sweat and suffering of the masses. Nothing but plumed cocks with their pomp and show, their ribbons and medals, their boots and spurs and swords. By their glitter and glamor, they make war possible. It makes war appear merely a parade, a beautiful pageant, deceiving them along with the unhappy others. The light of sanity, of peace, of understanding, will not come from the East, certainly not from Poland. The people are too bowed down, too chained to the wheel of their military, their arrogant and bureaucratic aristocracy. Mayhap, this light will come from the Soviet. More likely still it will come from the West, for poor as its record has been, omnipresent as the old elements and features still are, the signs of a new and saner dawn are nevertheless on its horizon.

It is the second day of Pesach, and in order to get a notion of the Warsaw synagogue and how the people conduct themselves, I visited one synagogue this afternoon and one this evening. The latter was the Grosse Synagogue, the largest in Warsaw. It was very fine indeed, built on the order of the New Free Synagogue of Berlin but considerably larger and, unlike it, painted solid white

---

* See correspondence with Rose, April 5, 1928.

on the inside, which, reflecting the light of the fine electric illumination, made the place hospitable and cheery by contrast. The choir, and particularly the cantor, were really fine. (One of my neighbors volunteered all sorts of information, including that the cantor is only 28 years old, comes from Vilna, was selected from among ten candidates, and receives the enormous sum of 2,000 zlote — about $250 — a month.) The people kept unusually good order. This is the wealthiest congregation of the city and is considered very "modern." The old, more orthodox Jews do not go here, consider it too *vergoyeshed* [Gentile]. It is a strictly orthodox schul — there are no other kind in Warsaw — but there is less bowing, more restrained emotions, and fewer of the signs and characteristics so dear to the heart of the older Jew; hence, he doesn't like it. I almost didn't get in. Tickets were necessary, and two officials, backed up by three or four Polish policemen, stood at the door to let no one pass without a card. I didn't, of course, have one, and was at first refused entrance. Some of the people standing about told me to go back and show them my passport and tell a moving story about coming all the way from America. I was anxious to get an impression of the place, so I took their advice and it worked nicely.

Here too, in the Ghetto, the light of the West, for better or for worse, is penetrating. It hasn't reached every nook and cranny yet, but it's coming. The signs are many: in the services and general behavior of the people of the Grosse Schul, in the fact that scores of businesses kept open Pesach, in that the majority already work on Saturday, in the lipstick and silk stockings of the girls. There is, at every hand, sign of a quickening and a stirring of the sluggish stream of Ghetto life. The Ghetto is dying, slowly but surely. How much better the newer thing will be is another story, but that it is on the wing and around the corner is undeniable.

Living conditions, always unenviable here, have been made still more oppressive by the war. If one were to go by the general dress of the people in the synagogue and on the street on the second day of Pesach, he would say that they are well off; but if he judged less hastily and remembered that the Jew, as in fact all other people, always manages to find somehow, somewhere, means to look his best before the Lord — *Welcher Yid hat nicht ein neue Hut oder Rock für yom tov?* [Which Jew has not a new hat or skirt for holy days?] — he would come to other conclusions. The poor bodies and wan faces tell the story. Since the war things have become much worse, though at the moment they are a bit better. The Jew here suffers not only economically, though in this he is no worse off than his neighbor, but also politically and socially. Under the guise of defense of

Fatherland and true patriotism, the Poles have excluded the Jew from every post of responsibility or have limited his university numbers (in other words, his strength in the professions) to about 5 or 6 percent ratio, grant him no allowance for sectarian purposes as they do the Catholics, and in countless other ways treat or endeavor to treat him unfairly. The Poles, the greatest prewar yellers, crying about their condition, the greatest tear-shedders and most successful sympathy-getters of all the oppressed peoples, turn around and do exactly the same thing to others. So goes history. The Italians today in the Tyrol against the Germans, the Serbs against the Bulgarians in Macedonia, the Romanians against the Jews in Bessarabia and against the Hungarians in Transylvania — all are alike. In doing away with open pogroms, the Morgenthau Commission did a lot for the Jews in Poland, but they are still oppressed and subordinated.

Friday, April 6, 1928. En route Warsaw–Moscow, 11:00 a.m.

Train passing through outskirts of Warsaw. City is much bigger than I had first imagined, extensively spread. Had made the error of not remembering that Warsaw was a former city of the Russian empire and was developed toward the East, not toward Germany or the West. That is why in approaching it from the German side, the station, as it were, met the plain without the usual suburbs and outlying districts in between (at least I believe this is the explanation). At the moment, we are passing through a residential suburb, a new one. Some nice brick and stucco homes are an anomaly, the new in juxtaposition with the old.

I don't see any improved roads, only primitive dirt ones. Must be terrible in rainy weather. Good roads are largely a creation of the automobile age, and these lands are still in the horse era. Warsaw has quite a number of taxicabs, a large part of which are Ford touring cars, converted into taxis by the simple application of a sign — "Taxi, 50 Groschen/Kilometre" — but for the most part it still relies on the traditional *droshky*, the open plush-seated carriage with the driver high up in front. Berlin still has a few of these, but they are considered more in the light of a curiosity.

Just crossed the historic Vistula, which flows through Warsaw and at whose lower end is the famous Danzig.

<u>1:15 p.m.</u> Just got through with lunch in the dining car. Tricky scoundrels. Advertise their meals for 6 zlote, or 75¢. From an American standpoint this isn't much for dining-car prices, and I took a chance. Some things can only be learned by experience. How

was I to know that the entrée and the soup that they served without asking me was not part of the dinner? Or that the tea was not a logical climax? Or that 15 percent would be added for service (this is not so excusable, since 10 percent is customary in these parts, but one does forget)? Actually, therefore, the bill, instead of the announced 6 zlote, amounted to 10½ zlote, or about $1.30. Clever!

The meal, however, was well cooked and served with all the finesse and flourishes customary in such places. The service, cleanliness, and general attention was much the same as one gets in an American dining car, no better and no worse. All the waiters are, of course, white. The menu may be interesting: salad of sliced eggs, strip of ham, strip of herring, greens; bread and butter; pureed soup; entrée choices of cooked fish and potatoes or roast beef (medium done), peas, and mashed potatoes; dessert of sliced pears and sweet rice pudding; plus tea. A good meal, but too much for one occasion.

A traveler in these parts with only one language is lost. German or French will get one by; English, rarely. My poor Russian came in handy in Warsaw. Enabled me to read quite a few things and understand a few spoken words, and also in asking the policemen how to get to the station, though on one occasion I was misdirected. Could it have been my Russian? Polish, of course, is not Russian, but the latter helps through having accustomed one's ear to the general sound of Slavic. This is already a great advantage: you are not listening to mere gibberish. Remarkable how many people here speak two or three languages and in some cases even more. If they don't speak German, they know French, or else they know Russian. The Jews for the most part are even better off. By speaking Polish, they have an introduction to the various Slavic tongues; by speaking Jewish, they are on the road toward the Germanic tongues. Their Hebrew would also be an advantage if they should travel in Semitic lands.

The countryside through which we are riding is very pretty: rolling landscape and artistically patterned fields. The peasants, however, appear to be much poorer than on the west side of Warsaw. Practically all the huts are unpainted, with only one room, and covered with straw. Occasionally, I sight a painted house or a tin or shingle roof.

2:00 p.m. Getting close to Bialystok. The aspect of the landscape has changed. More hilly and rolling and continues this way uninterruptedly for miles. Everywhere the fields are beginning to exhibit a short growth of green. Patches of unmelted snow and ice are still in evidence, for we are traveling steadily toward the northwest. Now, again, the countryside has altered: patches of forest and undergrowth.

<u>2:25 p.m.</u> Bialystok

Apparently quite a town. The approach to the station, and the station itself, presents the usual non-Western aspect. The same ubiquitous phenomenon of army officers — booted, spurred, and bearing swords — and soldiers. Nothing particularly noteworthy about the people. So far, I haven't seen the picturesque peasant that one hears so much about. The people about the station are wearing entirely Western clothes. A group of Jewish people have just met one of the train passengers. The girls are outfitted in fashionable fur coats, the latest pumps, silk hose, etc. The etiquette around here is interesting. The Jewish people, men and all, kissed each other, but the Poles do it differently. An elderly lady just got off the train and a young man and woman met her; both kissed her on the mouth and then on the hand. Hand-kissing is a usual thing here. Seems natural when the woman is well dressed, a 'lady,' but not where she is dressed like a workwoman, as in one case I observed.

Nothing pretty about this city from the station. Some scattered effect of the houses and general arrangement of the city. Scores of ramshackle houses, mud and dirt lanes for streets, etc. From this point of view, a good deal like some of our small towns of Louisiana or Texas. One thing is very noticeable as well as curious about all these places, large or small. They all lie only on one side of the railroad, so that from the train the whole town lies in full view, while on the other side are the open fields. This is probably due to the fact that the railroads came to these regions after the towns were already in existence, for most of them appear to be very old. The railroad was constructed on the edge of the town and continued in this relative position owing to the slow increase in growth of the latter, or its entire dormancy — which must often be the case, for Eastern Europe is not America.

The car I am in is divided into three sections: two sections for non-smokers and one for smokers. I am in the latter, not because I smoke but because the others were occupied when I took the train at Warsaw. The number of passengers has been progressively decreasing since we left the latter city, until at this moment there are only five of us in my section: a young girl, an old Russian, a young Jewish man and woman, and myself. The Jewish pair are speaking in Russian. Possibly later on I'll enter into a conversation with them, if they speak German or Jewish, and learn a few things. The time is passing quickly between writing and looking out the window, so I am not very anxious for company.

<u>4:00 p.m.</u> Getting closer to the Russian border. Still have five hours. The villages are becoming fewer and fewer. One vast sweep of

plain and rolling terrain with an occasional lonely hut. Just passed a village: very, very primitive. Log huts with the bark still on the walls and crowned with straw. Say, there's a cute little hut! A red tile roof, too! Now comes the straw roofs again. For all the world like the Zulu kraal are these villages, with their huts set closely together and their straw roofs built in a pyramid shape. Hurrah! Civilization! A soldier stands on the side of the track.

<u>4:15 p.m.</u> Wolkowysk [Vawkavysk]
Quite a fair-sized town, as the towns here go. Nice depot, white stucco with red tile roof, most unusual. There's the graveyard; people die here, too.
My use of the term 'village' in this region is misleading. 'Hamlet' is the more fitting word for most of the places. Just two, three, or four dozen huts, perhaps 100 to 200 people on average. Most of them are too small to have a depot and lie away from the tracks. God, it must be a lonely, soul-killing life. Prison would be far, far preferable to the average person raised in the city; the lonesomeness and isolation would kill him. Look at that village on the right! The Zulu kraal entirely! Imagine 100 to 200 unpainted, rudest sort of huts, covered with a heavy layer of compressed dirt-mixed straw! There's the church. A considerable village, therefore. The church is made of brick, the only one I see this way, with two exceptions. The latter must be the town hall and some other public structure.

<u>5:15 p.m.</u> A lonely ride. Nothing but solitary, naked plain and hill, hill and plain, interrupted by an occasional hut or hamlet. Just the monotonous *zh-sh-sh* of the wheels on the tracks and the occasional sound of the steam whistle of the engine. There are two peasant women for a change. One of them — but I'd better not say what she's doing. No shame, anyway.

<u>5:30 p.m.</u> Slonim
Very nice station: white stucco, tile roof. Seems to be a military post. These officers are getting on my nerves. Caricatures of ordinary men with their shining uniforms and ever-present dangling swords. These fellows never had the opportunity before to play the soldier; the Russian farmer-lords were the officers. But Versailles made a change, and so the Poles are now on top. It's the same old thing — the breed and the uniform-color have merely been changed.

<u>8:00 p.m.</u> Stolpce [Stowbtsy]
Last town in Poland on this line. Again, the horrible routine of giving up passports and standing by for inspection of baggage.

Everywhere the military and police, all with swords, bayonets, rifles, pistols. All Poland is an armed camp. One class of bureaucrats and parasites changed for another, that is all.

I have been speaking to the Jewish pair. Both are working for the Russian Trade Representation in Berlin and are going back to Russia on vacation. The man is on pins and needles to catch the first glimpse of the land he hasn't seen for six years. An ardent socialist he is, too! Thus, before the winds of reality fall the straws of internationalism.

<u>9:30 p.m.</u> Rah! Just crossed the border. Russia at last! The Russian passport man just came in! My first glimpse of the Russian official and uniform! I don't know whether it is imagination or not, but I feel as though a load has been taken off my chest in leaving Poland. I don't like the spirit there. Something is bad, very bad, when a country is so completely ridden by the military caste. Already a difference here. My Jewish friend in his excitement and happiness has just shaken hands with the two passport officials and said "*Tovarish*" (comrade). But let's not be too hasty; let's see what the future brings. Certainly entering Russia under favorable auspices. The full moon is out, though covered with a heavy film; it looks out palely in the frosty air — a typical Russian moon, I do believe. Last night in Warsaw, by the way, it was out in all its glory, and my thoughts turned involuntarily toward home and a certain person there.

<u>11:00 p.m.</u> Minsk

Capital of White Russia. A great home of Jews. Shown by the fact that one of the four languages in which the name of the station is written is Hebrew, or rather, Jewish with Hebrew characters.

Saturday, April 7, 1928. Still en route Warsaw–Moscow

6:15 a.m. Had a good night's sleep. These Russian third-class accommodations are the best in all Europe. Getting deeper into the interior of Russia. Can tell we're going north: the ground is frozen hard, with banks of snow and ice everywhere. The great Russian plains already visible in eastern Poland are now in full evidence. The peasant huts stand out bleak and gaunt in the cold morning air. They dot the plain in self-contained silence, not as in Poland, where they are gathered into more-or-less compact villages.

No land-hunger here. Miles and miles of empty plain awaiting the touch of a human hand, but clearly not giving it a warm invitation at this moment.

How stamped with the seal of poverty are these huts! Poor as they were in east Poland, they are even poorer here, if it is possible. There, a painted cabin showed up occasionally; here, at least at the present writing, I fail to see even a single one. Practically all are built of logs and covered with shaggy straw, so typical of east Poland. The logs, ordinarily, are stripped of the bark but now, owing to the effects of time and weather, are as black as though the bark were still present.

The fields have now undergone a change. Scrub trees and stunted growth of all sorts are visible, a truly arctic scene. The Old Russian landlord-noble was truly a dog-in-the-manger: despite these thousands and thousands of empty acres, the peasants still had to pay exorbitant rent and taxes for the little that they used (exorbitant, of course, in relation to their niggardly return from the land).

<u>8:15 a.m.</u> The scenery has now changed. The flat or rolling terrain has given way to hills and forests. But still the same primitive habitations and rude nature.

A young Englishman and his wife are on the train with us and we are getting very chummy. He is an engineer for a British mining concession in the Urals. He had been in Russia for a whole year before and is now returning from a vacation in England, bringing his wife with him this time. Brave woman! Imagine living in this utterly primitive region, a thousand miles from Moscow. I don't know how far he will be from a railroad, but he tells me that the chief concession of his company — gold mining — is on the Lena, 1,200 miles from a railroad! In summer, the trip to the nearest railroad town is made by boat; in winter, with rude sleighs, of which every peasant has one. He has learned to speak a little Russian. It is all new to his young wife, and I imagine her feelings must be a compound of fear and thrill. Really a game girl, must be admired. How many other modern wives would follow their husbands into this primitive wilderness? How many would be willing to forego their city comforts and baubles for such adventure and isolation? That's loyalty. That's love. That's true womanhood!

<u>2:30 a.m.</u> Smolensk
Halfway to Moscow. My first view of Russian peasants in real life.

<u>9:55 a.m.</u> Certainly, on the dining-car prices and tip system, Russia has the world beat. For two glasses of tea and all the bread and butter I wanted, I paid 70 kopecks — about 35¢. In Poland, Germany, or elsewhere, it would have been at least twice as much.

Tipping is forbidden and would be refused if offered. None but a traveler in European lands can appreciate in full what this means.

2:20 p.m. Got to talking with the English couple and the other passengers and failed to write down my impressions. But the talks were valuable, particularly with a Viennese who is making his 19th trip across Russia to China and who lived seven years in America. About 15 minutes from Moscow — on the outskirts now — the great radio station — a church comes to view. Moscow!

April 8–24, 1928. Moscow

First Impressions of Moscow

It will not be easy for me to forget my first impressions of Moscow. The station itself was not at all bad. On the basis of my experience in Warsaw I had prepared myself for much worse and was quite agreeably surprised to find a rather neat, well-kept station upon my arrival in the capital of the U.S.S.R. This was particularly surprising in view of the appearance of every other station through which the train passed since leaving the Polish border. 'Abominable' does not really express the true condition of things. Great holes in the cement floors of many, discolored walls, not the slightest element to cheer or to comfort. A wooden bench or two would stand against the bare, damp walls, and on these would sit, or else would lie on the cold cement floor, some of the most ragged and miserable specimens of humanity that I have ever encountered. This Russian muzhik is certainly not the type of peasant we know, or Western Europe knows. Perhaps certain parts of the Balkans have his match, but that is to be doubted. It does not seem possible that anywhere, short of perhaps India or China, such uncouth specimens of human beings are to be met.

It must be allowed that the time of the year had something to do with this impression. Unpainted, dilapidated huts, or such stations as I have described, look even more wretched and disagreeable in the barren, cheerless environment of winter as they know it in Russia than when surrounded by the blossoming trees or green fields of summer. The same is true, undoubtedly, of the peasant when he leaves off his shaggy sheepskin coat, which he wears with the hide on the outside — about as unsanitary and ugly a thing as one can imagine — and the strips of rag which he winds around his legs and boots to keep them warm, and the horrible-looking cap which he usually wears. I imagine his unshaven face and ragged beard look better, too.

In coming to the station at Moscow, initially I was pleasantly surprised, and I prepared myself for a revision of my opinion of Russia, formed on the basis of my experiences thus far. But this revision never took place. The first glance outside of the station prepared me for the worst. I cannot touch in detail all that I encountered on my first ride through the streets of Moscow, but perhaps I can convey the ensemble. Imagine, then, streets covered with thawing snow and standing pools of water; imagine great holes in the streets and sidewalks; imagine the most cheerless, decaying buildings and shops; imagine, above all, hordes, not crowds, of people, absolutely Asiatic for the most part, walking in the streets or on the broken, narrow sidewalks, dressed miserably in general, unshaven, haggard, dirty, looking far worse than our worst workers. Imagine that and you have a picture of what I encountered. Whatever it was, it was certainly not the West as we know it. People, dress, surroundings — all are strange to me.

Housing

It is difficult to imagine how cultured people are today forced to live in Moscow. Comforts are all but unknown. Rugs, carpets, painted or papered walls, ornamental woodwork, new furniture — not two out of a hundred have them. But cheer-less as the interiors are, they are not to be compared to the exteriors. The latter include sagging uncarpeted stairs, broken bannisters, unpainted doors, dingy one-lamp hall lights, horrible smells, piled-up dirt and debris in the courtyards, and unpainted wooden courtyard gates.

Crowded as conditions are, it is yet not so bad as the West sometimes imagines — that two or three families live in a single room and the like. By one of the new housing acts, each person or family is assigned a certain amount of room-space in accordance with a standard which the law established. The amount of room-space which a family may occupy depends on the number of members, their ages, and certain special circumstances. If only a mother and a child, then one room and perhaps a small cubicle to serve as a kitchen or pantry; if a family of parents and two or more children, then perhaps two rooms and a small kitchen or pantry. In very few cases are more than two rooms per family allowed, except under those circumstances where the children are grown up and are workers. But while the law figures out a theoretical amount of cubic space per person or family, it cannot be applied literally at all times. Allowances must be made for peculiar architectural or structural conditions of each tenement separately. Walls usually cannot be taken out in order to allow each person the exact amount of cubic feet allowed him by law. However, many a former pantry or corridor has been converted into a living room for one or more persons.

The rent is fixed by law and varies in accordance with the profession and earnings of the individual, not (at least usually) in consideration of the conditions of the dwelling or neighborhood. All who come under the 'workers' classification are the best treated; those in other categories are treated in accordance with their social utility, as measured by the conception of utility predominant in present-day Russia. The worst off — that is, those paying the highest rent and being considered last in all applications for living space in new or old buildings — are persons classed as 'bourgeoisie.'

By citing the case of a family I know, perhaps a better understanding will be had. This family consists of three sisters and two children. By good fortune, they managed to obtain an apartment all to themselves, the rarest of rare occurrences. One of the sisters has a small child of about three years and possesses on that account a larger room than her eldest sister, who lives with her boy of 13, for as the law sees it, a little child needs more room than an older child and (at least the theory so has it) is entitled to as much room as an adult. But the elder sister, despite the fact that she shares a room with her teenage son, is adjudged to have more space than she is entitled to and must pay for the excess. This excess is proportionately always much greater than the normal amount, and this fact, together with the fact that this particular lady does not happen to be a member of the trade union, compels her to pay 16 rubles for rent each month, while her earnings are 80 rubles — in other words, 20 percent of her wages. On the other hand, the youngest sister, who has no child, who has a smaller room, is a trade union member. She pays only 8 rubles a month, despite the fact that she makes 100 rubles monthly — in other words, only 8 percent of her earnings. In addition to the three rooms, the apartment consists of a corridor and a tiny toilet. They do not pay extra for these amenities. The latter room contains a little cooking lamp and serves as a minor kitchen.

A feature true of almost all buildings is the community kitchen. This is made necessary by the fact that most former kitchens have been turned into living rooms, and therefore people had to be given some place where to cook their meals. In these community kitchens all the housewives or servants cook meals and bring them to their respective apartments or rooms. On Sunday the kitchen is closed, and therefore unless the family eats a cold meal or has an auxiliary small kitchen (which is very rare), they must prepare enough food on Saturday to last for two days.

A novelty introduced in the housing situation in Soviet Russia is the cooperative. All the tenants constitute the cooperative, from whom a chairman and an executive committee or board is appointed, with all power to act during intervals between meetings of the full cooperative. This board has charge of all problems connected with the administration of the dwelling: repairing and cleaning of common property, such as walls, corridors, and stairs; arbitration between tenants; safety concerns, etc. When some project is considered that involves any considerable outlay of money, such as remodeling or repair, the entire cooperative is convened and the plan approved or disapproved. For all small things, the board controls the treasury of the cooperative (whether there are ever any funds and ever any repairing is another story).

In addition to the common kitchen, the cooperative members, or tenantry, are entitled without further charge beyond their rent to all general services, such as heating, maintenance of common areas, and cleaning and heating of a common bathroom (if such exists), kitchen, etc. This is a service paid for by the management or board of the cooperative, the balance being turned over to the government (?) or used to pay the interest and principal, if it is a new dwelling.

How efficiently this cooperative system works is another story. In general, the interior of each private room or section of the building is in extraordinarily better condition and appearance than those parts of the dwelling considered as common property. The latter is too often an utter abomination, lacking the most elementary care or attention. Dilapidated steps and stairways, unpainted doors and corridors, broken lights, hanging wires, bad odors, and general cheerlessness and disorder are evident in the portion considered common property. The interior of each private domain, poor as it is, is a Christmas carol by contrast. Here, each housewife does her utmost with her terribly limited means to keep up the atmosphere of a home. Here may be a frayed tablecloth, but it's clean; here may be a meager patch of carpet, but it serves to hide an ugly spot or counteract the impression of bareness. Here is light and warmth and cleanliness by comparison. It is so because people feel that their allotted space is their own, while the rest is held in common, and yet by no one. At a time when everyone is pinched for every kopeck, it is as natural as it is understandable. First comes one's own self and family, only later come others. A bannister stick is broken, a step fallen in, a doorknob missing, the front doorbell out of order — the most elementary things to repair — but no one thinks of fixing them. Each says, "It's not mine; it's everybody's. I've got too much of my own troubles to think about. Let the blamed thing be as it is. Maybe someone else will fix it." And so it goes. The result is that no one fixes anything and the dilapidation and disorder multiplies.

A cooperative member has certain other privileges or rights. Once a member, his room space is his permanently. No one can take it from him, except under extraordinary circumstances, such as intolerable habits (an almost unheard-of cause for eviction), outright refusal to pay rent, etc. As long as he meets his rent obligations, it is his for all time. He has the full privilege of living elsewhere and re-renting his space to someone else if the cooperative votes to accept the new member. This is quite common, I am told. It may occur as a result of a temporary exchange of rooms. For instance, a tenant finds it more convenient to live elsewhere for a time — perhaps it is closer to his work — but does not want to give up his space for good. He may enter into an arrangement with a member of the other household, both agreeing to go back to their original quarters at the end of a certain period. More common still is the renting of space and going to live with a friend or relative and so obtaining an extra income. This, however, is not an open transaction. By law, no worker may be ejected because of lack of means to pay his rent. On the contrary, if he is out of work, he pays no rent whatsoever.

Cooperatives are often formed by members of the same union or the same factory or trust. They agree among themselves to put up a new building or repair an old one and to permit only fellow workers to be the co-tenants. This is the prevailing tendency now. The financing and ownership of a number of buildings now being erected, or already erected, is on the same general plan of cooperative ownership that prevails in Chicago and other parts of America. Workers get together, decide to form a cooperative among themselves, and take in as many members as necessary to finance the corporation. Each subscribes a certain sum, and the balance, usually the much larger part, is obtained as a loan from the government banks.

I am told that there is really a large amount of building going on. One thing that keeps the pace slow is the fact that owing to the terrible Russian weather, construction can only take place four or five months in the year. There is no doubt that the housing situation is gradually improving over what it was. Two or three years ago it was absolutely unbearable. Six to a dozen people in a room was common. Families were divided in order that the men should be in one room and the wives and children in another.

I visited one of the newly erected dwellings. It was one of ten or twelve built at the same time in this neighborhood and was exactly like its neighbors. In fact, they together formed a sort of independent community numbering 5,000 people. Of the tenants, 77 percent were factory workers and the others were office workers, specialists, professors, etc. The buildings were divided into apartments of two living rooms, kitchen, and a small toilet. Central heating and electricity existed, but no gas or running hot water. In all ten buildings there was not a single bath. I was told that this was because of the lack of funds, and that in the very newest buildings (these were one year old), each apartment has a bath.

Rent is in proportion to wages. My hostess paid the average rent — 24 rubles a month, or $12. The only other expense was for light. To join the cooperative she had to pay 100 rubles — $50. Despite the fact that the buildings are all made in the plainest and most inexpensive fashion (just box-shaped, rough brick dwellings with the minimum of ornamentation), the workers consider themselves in Paradise, and in comparison with the way they lived under the Tsar, it is almost true. They cannot imagine living better than they live now. This has a deplorable result, in that the corridors, staircases, inner and outside walls, doors and doorsteps, and all other commonly owned portions of the buildings already show, despite the fact that they are only one year old, the effects of misuse and neglect. For instance, the staircase walls of the building I was in were all scratched up and marked with writing and figures by the children, yet no one thought of doing anything about it. For one thing, it was common property; for another, the residents really didn't care. Most had been used to far worse things. Why be concerned now with a few scratches or markings?

Transportation

Conditions in this respect are very bad. Since the Revolution, the population of Moscow has swollen two or three times over what it was before. Imagine a population of two million having to rely only on streetcars and a handful of motor buses. New York at six o'clock in the evening doesn't compare with Moscow at almost any time of the day. The heavy coats and wraps that people wear only increase the difficulty. They want to get home or elsewhere, and since every car is crowded, all rules of politeness, gentility, or patience are broken. It is certainly a case of every man for himself and the devil take the hindmost. Women, being weaker, suffer most under such a regime. It's remarkable, however, the way they have learned to fight. When the streetcar pulls up at the waiting platform, the free-for-all begins, and if it isn't a pretty spectacle, it is certainly an edifying one. One learns then more about human nature, the beast that is in man, than at perhaps any other time. For the first few times your more gentle training keeps you back, but after thoroughly tiring of standing by and giving your turn to unappreciative folk, and wanting to get somewhere, you join the melee and struggle with the rest of them. Thus is environment a teacher.

Costs of transportation are not so bad, yet not so good. They vary in accordance with distance, ranging from about 4¢ to about 7¢, but with no transfer privileges.

What Is Being Done for the Workers?

Without touching the question of how thoroughgoing or satisfactory the efforts on behalf of the workers are, the following benefits can be cited as included in the official program of the State:
1. Social insurance laws of all kinds: health, accident, old age, unemployment.
2. Abolition of fines and punishments in connection with labor.
3. All pregnant women-workers allowed about four months' unemployment on full pay prior to delivery and one or two months thereafter. For abortions, two or three weeks.
4. Free hospitals, clinics, etc.
5. Sanitoria or rest homes where workers can go and recuperate health or strength. Many of these are in Crimea and also on Strelitea [Sestroretsk?] Island in Leningrad. All service, food, etc., is free.
6. Vacations with pay.
7. First preference in all applications for rooms.
8. First preference in merchandise and food at time of scarcity.
9. Free education from grade school through university. Support by government of indigent students of worker category.
10. Workers' clubs, reading rooms, restaurants, etc.
11. Half prices to theaters, *kinos* (movies), etc.

Disease and Health Measures (from Talk with Doctor Brodski)

Large work in this direction is being done. Vast spread of literature, lectures, institutions, etc. Infant mortality in Russia before the war was about 500 per 1,000 births — now about 150. The general mortality rate is reduced in all respects. Sexual diseases and others are reduced or entirely stamped out. The large number of health institutions helps in solving the disease and health problems and are mostly free of charge. The cost of drugs for is low for everyone, and for the poorest, entirely free. Dental work is not covered but is quite low. The result of disease-prevention measures is already being shown. The population is steadily increasing. Only economic pressure can keep down the birthrate, or else voluntary restriction by the more intelligent people.

Considerable study is being given to ensuring the health and safety of the worker while at his labor, addressing such matters as appropriate work clothing, safety devices, ventilation, heating, etc. There is great interest in the most desirable sort of working uniform, from the standpoint of hygiene, durability, warmth or coolness, etc.

Wages

The highest paid workers are the so-called specialists — that is, professional men, such as engineers, technicians of various sorts, and managers of large enterprises of a technical nature. Many of these earn as much as 500-600 rubles a month (particularly the engineers) and seldom less than 200 rubles ($100). Workers in factories average about 110 rubles, while wages of clerks, office people, etc. range from about 60 to 150 rubles. Communist officials, by law, are forbidden to receive more than 250. This includes all the leaders of the State, from Kalinin, President of Council of Commissars, and Stalin, Secretary of the Russian Communist Party, on down. However, the more important ones obtain certain privileges and favors which greatly increase their income, such as living free of charge in the Kremlin, permanent seats in theaters, State automobiles, servants, etc.

Prices

Wages, of course, are important only in relation to prices, and here we get another story. Without touching the problem of the availability of food and clothing, the following is very interesting. In general, it may be said that staple articles of food in Russia, such as butter, eggs, and bread, are about on the American level. Other things, such as canned goods, preserves, specialties, or dainties, are always above, sometimes 50 to 100 percent. But it is in clothing and furniture that we can get the most interesting figures. Some examples:

	Russia	America
Cheapest ladies' cotton hose (in America could hardly be found, so cheap are they)	$0.85	$0.25
Good ladies' lisle hose	$3.00	$1.25
Silk hose	$4.00-$7.00	$1.50
Cheap man's hat	$7.50-$10.00	$3.50
Cloth for suits	$45.00/meter	$5.00
Cheapest quality shoes (good shoes almost impossible to obtain)	$7.50	$2.50
Ordinary wooden bed	$40.00	$15.00
Ordinary iron bed	$50.00-$75.00	$20.00
Bedroom suite	$500.00-$750.00	$250.00

When it is recalled that good wages are 125 rubles ($63.50) a month, and this sum is compared with cost for clothing and food, then one can understand why the Russians today are living so miserably. The wages are just enough for food and for nothing else. Only by the greatest pinching, usually by depriving oneself in some other sphere, is one able to buy the pair of shoes, the stockings, or the other article of clothing that he absolutely needs. Usually these extras for clothing come from not spending a penny on the living quarters, cutting down on amusements, and renouncing everything except the absolute necessities for the time being. Measured in dollars, the German worker gets only about half the wages of the Russian worker — that is, about $30 (120 marks) a month — but his marks will buy about 50 percent more than the Russian ruble, so in actuality he is earning more. As to the way the two live and dress, there is no comparison. Poor as the German may be, his clothes show the evidence of constant repairing, brushing, and painful efforts to keep clean and neat-looking. The Russian worker is an altogether different-looking person, allowing for many exceptions, of course. He dresses ragged and looks ragged, not to mention dirty. The Russian has not that tradition of personal cleanliness and love of neatness that is characteristic of the German and which marks the latter as an upstanding man, a self-respecting person. Besides, the Russian worker is a terrible drinker and spends far more for this purpose than the German, himself no small drinker.

The Vodka Industry

An enormous sale of liquor prevails now. The excuse of the government is that it seeks to stamp out homebrew (at least, this was the original excuse), but it doesn't hold. The peasants cannot afford vodka, at about 1 ruble 80 kopecks a bottle, whereas homebrew costs about 25 kopecks. In former days, I am told, there were only about a dozen or two government stores in Leningrad where whiskey was sold. It was also retailed in restaurants, but this source was too expensive for the worker. Now, however, liquor is sold in practically every cooperative and in scores of special liquor stores. Thus, the sources for purchasing liquor are about 20 times as great as before the war. Formerly, also, government shops for the sale of whiskey opened from 11:00 a.m. to 6:00 p.m., whereas now they remain open until midnight. The opportunity to buy the stuff is so easy, so at hand, that drinking has greatly increased. The Russian worker, always a terrible drinker, is even worse today. All the liquor shops have attractive window displays, which is more than can be said for 95 percent of the other stores.

This matter of encouraging the drinking of liquor by increasing the opportunity for its purchase is a very serious charge against the Soviet government and cannot be lightly answered. The usual reply is that it brings in about 25 percent of the budgetary income, but that only arouses a stronger sense of repugnancy.

Old Merchandise

The story of old merchandise, particularly old clothes, is a very interesting one in Russia today. One of my acquaintances, for example, a man who employed four servants in his home before the war, now wears an overcoat 16 years old, a felt hat 15 years old, and a pair of trousers that his father wore 20 years before. In prosperous days he would have thrown them in the attic or in a trunk; now he has resurrected them and congratulates himself on his foresight. The same holds true for all people, and on a larger scale in the shops. As in America during the war, where merchants got rid of almost every type of junk they possessed, especially such stuff as had come from Germany and the other enemy countries, so with Russian shops today. It is hard to picture, unless one has been to Russia, the meager and miserable display of goods the shops offer, except the very largest. In particular this holds true of the few score private shops in Moscow and Leningrad. A few have nice merchandise, but for the most part, owing to their harrowed existence and the necessity to survive, stores accumulate any sort of junk — a few remnants, second-rate or third-rate pieces of clothing, and the like — and display them in the window.

Who Are Bourgeoisie in Soviet Russia?

The term 'bourgeoisie' is used so very often in Russia today, and yet so wildly, that it is extremely difficult to know who comes under that category and who does not. There are about 2 or 3 percent — relatively very few — who are deprived of voting rights and many privileges, who apparently come under this head. These include certain categories of owners of private enterprises, certain members of old families powerful in former days, certain important members of the old bureaucracy, and certain people in a vocation or profession that does not come under the worker classification. In the case of private enterprises, it is hard for an outsider to appreciate the distinction between one who is a bourgeois, and is accordingly deprived of nearly all rights granted to others, and one who is not a bourgeois. For example, owners of private barbershops and restaurants, street hawkers, keepers of sidewalk stalls, etc. are not considered officially as bourgeoisie, whereas practically all owners of established businesses that deal in goods rather than services, or private manufacturing establishments, are so considered and suffer the consequences. The distinction is partly governed by the qualification that the latter employ labor. But this is not satisfactory, since the lone merchant behind the counter is a bourgeois while the hawker on the outside is not, although the former does not employ labor and might have a stock of merchandise even smaller than the hawker's.

The Kulak

The kulak also comes under the bourgeoisie classification: he is the "bourgeois of the country." In reality, the term describes the peasant or farmer who is in somewhat better circumstances than his neighbors. The government considers him a danger from various points of view. The following are the charges against him:

1. He lends the simple peasants small sums of money at enormous rates of interest and keeps them permanently indebted to him.
2. This enables the kulak to have a sort of mortgage on the crops of his neighbors.

3. Through this fact, he influences the smaller peasants to hold back their grain and speculate for higher prices. This is particularly bad at a time like this, when the government relies upon the raw products of the peasantry as the chief source for the capital that it so badly needs.
4. The kulak is an employer of labor and so endangers the present socialistic system.

How true this is, or how mistaken the entire viewpoint, is another story. Nevertheless, this is how the kulak is regarded.

Present Reaction Against Bourgeoisie

I am told that hundreds of private enterprises have been forced to shut down in the past six or eight months as a result of one of the latest fluctuations in policy. This did not take the earlier forms of simply chasing the owner out and declaring the enterprise government property, but through an unbearable increase in taxes. The Trotsky-Zinoviev opposition of the last two years seems to have had an effect after all, though formally repudiated and their members driven out of the party.* As a result of the closing down of many of the private shops, several thousand people throughout Russia were thrown out of work (at least, so I am told) and the already great unemployment increased.

Economic Situation at Present

There is unquestionably great unemployment. In part, this is due to the drastic economic policy that the government has instituted in all its enterprises. This policy has its origin in the New Economic Policy, or NEP, of 1921, the historic Retreat. After the Revolution of 1917 everyone was given a job. Since the State and the people are one and the same thing, since all are members of one big family and all are equal, all must work and all must eat. But, as is well known, this could not be maintained. Since the introduction of the NEP, government establishments are run more like private businesses. They must show profit, if necessary by laying off workers or cutting salaries. For example, each government or trust, factory or enterprise, at the beginning of the fiscal year

---

* The meaning of the "effect" of the Trotsky-Zinoviev "opposition" in this context is not clear. Grigory Zinoviev was a leading Bolshevik who, along with Leon Trotsky, was expelled from the ruling Communist Party in 1927.

makes out a budget, or a statement of plans and needs, for the current year. The government as the banker will consider the budget and grant appropriate funds on loan. But if during the year, due to inefficiency, or excessive costs for labor, or unforeseen problems, the enterprise needs more money, the government may refuse to lend more, and hence the factory will be compelled to economize. This is the occasion for strikes that every once in a while were heard of in Russia over the past few years. Each enterprise must stand on its own feet. Its deficit cannot be made up by others. Such is the law.*

Morality

Things in this respect were apparently very bad after the Revolution. There were a great number of divorces, free sex relations, gross immorality, and any amount of unregistered marriages. Now there is considerable improvement. A considerable minority of sexual unions are still unregistered, but by one of the later laws, should children ensue, the parents' relationship must be registered. The very latest enactment seems to require that all unions must be registered. Separation does not require court action at all, while divorce is freely granted and can be obtained by either party without requiring consent of the other. However, in the event of children, the father must pay one-third of his income for support, unless the mother is working, in which case the amount of alimony varies with her earning capacity.

The Intelligent Russian Woman's Viewpoint Today

The extent to which woman has become equal to man in Russia today is not approached by any other country. The Russian woman participates to an unbelievable degree in professions and work which heretofore have been considered man's domain. She is to be found in high executive positions in all the professions and trades, in all work, whether of brain or manual in nature. The intelligent, thinking Russian woman has accepted the most extreme doctrines as to what constitutes woman's emancipation. Woman is not to be an ornament or a drudge, but to have exactly the same freedom — in the most rigorous sense of the word — as man. To be a personality, not a plaything. To have a responsible position in society. She wants no

---

* The NEP was rescinded and centralized planning reintroduced under Stalin in late 1928. (This note is a vast oversimplification, but Joseph Werlin is not attempting to show a larger picture, as he will in his academic endeavors.)

special privileges or empty chivalry; she wants equal obligations but also equal rights. True, the ready separation and easy divorce — this freedom in morals — goes harder on the woman. She cannot change her affections so readily as a man; she will remain loyal longer than he, more willing to put up with incompatibility for the sake of the children or in memory of earlier happiness. But just the same, she prefers this hardship — and it is a very real one in Russia now — to the older system; the independence, with its possible drawbacks, to the ornament/drudge existence.

The Present Conditions of the Jews

As in most other things, the story you will hear in this respect depends upon the person who is doing the relating. One of the first persons to whom I talked at length on this subject was a quite intelligent, educated woman whose husband is manager of one of the Moscow papers. She was very bitter. Formerly, she had been told the troublemakers for the Jews were the Tsar and the old government. She had labored hard for the Revolution. For three years she had gone into the villages as a nurse and medical adviser to the peasants. Now her reward is the same old cursings and hate of the Jew, the same old *Zhidski Mord* (literally, "Jew snout"). She cited instances of anti-Jewish hate. One case was that of a Jewish schoolboy in the south who was taken by two or three non-Jewish schoolfellows to the woods, tied to a tree, and left in the bitter cold. After leaving him alone for several hours, the boys became frightened and brought him back to the town half-dead from cold. A trial was held, but the only punishment that the boys received was a reprimand not to repeat the act again. She couldn't be hopeful of any near solution of the Jewish problem. There are no people so cruel and ungrateful as the Russian people, she said. It is the same old murderous hate of the Jew as before. On the streets, the boys sing anti-Jewish songs. She stands in the bread or butter line and hears all around her the word "Jew." Her neighbor next door, a Communist too, hates Russians with "all his soul."

"We are getting old," she said. "We are tired of making sacrifices and giving up all our strength and endeavors and thoughts for the sake of the Russian people. Now that we have made the Revolution at such a bitter cost, we want relief and serenity in our old age. We don't want to wait a hundred years. We are tired of promises. Seeing how everything is in reality, we just can't be enthusiastic; we can't join the chorus in singing that the glorious day has come. The Revolution itself was a wonderful thing; it must be praised. It delivered Jews and all from the cruel hand of the old system. Now we have rights; now we can lift our heads as human beings. But the people themselves have changed little toward the Jew. God only knows what will happen to us if the Communists lose power. There will be a terrible massacre of the Jews the very first thing. That is why we continue to work so hard for the Communist cause. Our views are not shared by many Jews, perhaps by a minority. They are enthusiastic for the Revolution; they speak about the Golden Day having arrived, that now all is brotherhood and oneness. But we, my husband and I, can't see it that way. I hate the Russians, hate them with all my soul. I tell my daughters, 'Marry a Chinese, an Indian, anyone, but not a Russian.' Much as I love my daughters, I shall separate from them and send them to England, America, anywhere, but not Russia."

I spoke to another Jewish woman, also educated and intelligent, on the subject and repeated what the first had said. Her view was that such talk was hysterical, such views unfounded, the result of a very sensitive imagination, of a case of 'nerves.' That such people shut their eyes to reality and see only the petty few incidents. No one pretends that the Russian people have been purged through and through of all prejudices. That is silly. Ten years cannot do such a thing. But tremendous progress has been made. The instances the first woman cited were isolated ones, exceptional, not reflecting the true conditions. Wherever anti-Semitism raises its head, it is crushed like a viper the moment it is discovered. Any number of contrary examples can be mentioned. Take the case in Kharkov [a city in Ukraine]. A Russian Communist had a servant who wanted to join a trade union. His wife told the servant girl that if she did, she would be discharged. However, a Jewish Communist living next door gave the girl advice on how she should go about being admitted to the union. She followed his advice, entered one of the unions, and was soon afterwards discharged by the Russian. The Jewish Communist, for his part in the affair, received a letter from the Russian reminding him that the days of pogroms were not yet over. The incident came to the attention of the papers and was reported to Communist leaders. A trial was held and the Russian was immediately excluded from the Party. Another instance which my informant related to me happened in the same factory where her sister worked. A Communist there was heard to say that he himself was witness to a ritual murder. The case came to a hearing and the man was deprived of his Communist membership. No, said my informant, the first woman I talked to was wrong. In reality she was still a bourgeois, couldn't forget her prosperous condition of the past, could only see the contrast between her present and her past life.

A third person with whom I talked was a Jewish physician. Before the war he had had a private practice; now, like most doctors, he was working for the government in one of the many newly erected institutions, this one being called Workers' Psychological and Health Institute, or something on that order. He represented a middle point of view on the Jewish question. He admitted that the feeling was stronger now than at any time after the Revolution but refused to be alarmed by every report or to take on a case of 'nerves.' As he saw it, the outlook was quite optimistic, and he pointed out the many things that the government has done and is continuing to do for the Jews.

Another person I conversed with was a Communist, one of the government legal prosecutors and an undeniably intelligent, reflective man — a Jew, too. As he weighed the pros and cons of the matter, he felt the results showed a change for the worse, but not in any degree to cause alarm. He also pointed out the many things the government is doing for the Jews, and to the fact of the great role which they were playing in the State today. According to his viewpoint, the frowning and resentment of the non-Jews was understandable: "No nation of 150 million would be willing to be ruled by a minority group."

A fifth individual with whom I discussed the question was a former well-to-do pharmacist, deprived of everything as a result of the Revolution, now working for the government as an instructor at one of the universities. Before his misfortune, he had concerned himself very little with Jewish matters and even today remains distant from them. He was, therefore, in a position to give an impartial opinion, at least more than the others. His viewpoint was that anti-Semitism is today very evident, as bad as in the Tsarist days. The Jews are cursed everywhere as the authors of all the troubles. Communists officially can say nothing; privately, they join the chorus.

Here, then, we have a variety of opinions. On the basis of what I heard from still others, and as a result of my impressions generally, I should say that the moderate viewpoint is the more correct one: while isolated incidents of outright anti-Jewish episodes are heard of and mutterings have appeared in certain sections, there is no specific instigator pictured. The government itself seems to be above suspicion. Within it, there still rules the philosophy of workers' internationalism — that is, race and religious hatreds are at bottom caused by the system of private property, and the disappearance of the latter is automatic. True, man being as he is, he is unable to shake himself of his old antipathies and prejudices immediately, but it is only a question of 5, 10, 20 years, at best a generation, until the elders have died out and the young ones, trained in the newer system, have taken their places. To be sure, there is the question of why the Jews no longer occupy the prime posts, why such outstanding leaders as Trotsky, Zinoviev, and Kamenev are no longer in the saddle, but the answer which most Jews in Russia seem to give is that their dismissal was purely an intra-Party matter, that not only they but also a large number of Russians were officially decapitated for their opposition tactics.* But if no Jew can be found in the Council of Commissars or in the Political Bureau of the Party — the two highest bodies in the State — he can be found occupying any number of positions in the secondary order, and in general he plays a role in the official life of the State far in excess of what his numbers entitle him to if the numerical ratio standard is adopted.

On the economic side, all one can say is that the Jews are in the common boat: their future is inextricably bound with the future of the economic conditions in Russia generally. When the World War came to an end and the several peace treaties finally were signed, Soviet Russia was left with about two and a half million Jews. Since most of them had been engaged in middleman occupations — "petty-bourgeoisie," in Communist terminology — they were the hardest hit by the nationalization measures and by the Revolution generally: firstly because their goods were confiscated, and secondly because most of them lacked a trade and therefore could not join the trade unions. What this latter means, only one living in Russia can fully appreciate. The Soviet Union is openly and belligerently a worker's State. To be a worker, and in particular a trade-union worker, means to have first choice on jobs, rooms, butter, eggs, bread, and anything else that is scarce; to have access to clubs, cooperatives, universities, hospitals, and rest houses. Not to be a worker is the equivalent of being without access to these benefits. But in the course of time, by one means or another, about half of the Jews were absorbed into various State enterprises — as administrators, managers, clerks, or simple workmen — or else entered into such businesses as meet government approval — through cooperatives of all sorts, or as hawkers,† etc. — and another 75 to 100 thousand settled on the land.

The balance are very badly off and live for the most part in the same regions they inhabited formerly, that is, the Ukraine and White Russia. I was told that the government is really attempting to do what it can for them, that it is a fact that between five and ten thousand families are settled yearly on the land. The government

---

* "Officially decapitated" is meant figuratively. Zinoviev and Kamenev were executed under Stalin's watch in August 1936. Leon Trotsky was assassinated in Mexico City in August 1940.

† "Hawkers," it appears, referred to licensed peddlers or street vendors of goods obtained through government-sanctioned operations. "Cooperatives" at this time were sanctioned associations of craftspeople or service providers (such as barbers) whose profits were shared and distributed according to communist principles.

is held back in its ameliorative work only by the lack of capital, by nothing else. The Jews, on the whole, appear eager to engage in farming enterprises. A good example of this is in connection with the district along the Amur River in Siberia, which the government has recently opened to Jewish colonization. Over 12,000 people immediately applied for land as soon as the project was announced. When it is considered what hardships the colonists would have to put up with, what an entirely new and distant environment they would be thrown into, their eagerness is really remarkable. It causes one to wonder just how much truth there is in the statement that the Jew hates the soil.

The religious situation of the Jews in Russia is one that will bring very little comfort to many people. For this, the Jews alone are accountable, no one else. True, the official policy is to frown on religion, but this is only an attitude. In practice, the people are left alone, and whether they maintain their sect or not is a voluntary matter. Money, of course, is a factor in supporting the more external forms of religion, such as a church or a priest, and the lack of it in present-day Russia might account for the neglect of the synagogues or inability to keep a rabbi. But of course, that can't be the real explanation. The truth of the matter is that the Jews, more than any other sect in Russia, have endorsed and literally carry out the views of Communist philosophy on religion, which are that it is a fraud, an "opiate," at best only a superstition that has no excuse for existing among intelligent, rational people. It would appear that the great majority of the younger Jews openly profess atheism and that a large number of the elders, while not going so far, have dropped the outward forms of religion, such as attendance at synagogues and observance of the holidays. In Moscow and Leningrad the Jews have gone the furthest in this respect. In the Pale regions, where the Jews still live in greatest number, the percentage of believers is higher.

Considered in totality, the Jewish situation is no better and no worse than that of the people about them. Russia is an extraordinarily poor country today and people are living there in desperate poverty. However little there is, it at any rate is being shared equally (if we exclude a relatively small percent that comes under the bourgeois classification) by all. Whatever the present lot is, whatever opportunity it offers for satisfaction or improvement either for the time being or for the future, the Jew is on an equal footing with the others. And this is really something. Only Jews who have lived in Russia under the Tsar can appreciate in full what this means. From being a pariah, the Jew has become a citizen in full and in honorable standing with all other members of the State.

He now lives where he wants to, participates in political life, enjoys some of the most responsible positions in the government, lifts his head as high as the next man, and feels — the grandest feeling of all — on a parity in every respect with every other man in the land. It is safe to say that 95 out of every 100 Jews in Russia today would be positively unwilling to give up their present troubled existence in exchange for their former life under the Tsar. At the price of material well-being (and this price has been very high in many cases), they have received a certain type of spiritual satisfaction which is beyond the power of money to measure. Now, at least the future is before them; if not they, then their children will profit by their sacrifices. Such is the hope. But under the Tsar, there was lacking even this sustaining hope. It is not mere whim or adventurousness that drove the Jews of Russia in waves to America; it was hopelessness.

There is another reason, a very potent one, why the Jews of Russia support the present government: the fear that a new government might mark the initiation of a series of terrible massacres against them. This is a real fear. The deposed elements, bitter members of the old ruling and aristocratic orders, lay the chief responsibility for the Revolution on the Jews. Should they return to power, it takes little imagination to picture the dark days that would befall Israel. So willy-nilly, the Jews are closely bound to the new order and are compelled to support it.

Atheism in Soviet Russia

Atheism is very widespread among the people today. As might be expected, the more educated among the people have gone the furthest in this direction. To what extent this is a thought-out condition, to what extent it is fashion, to what extent it is only a dropping of religious observances and not a denial of a Creator, is difficult to say. It is safe to state, however, that on this matter, as in most other respects in present-day Russia, the people have accepted the official philosophy or point of view without subjecting it to criticism. For that reason, their professed atheism cannot be taken too seriously; it is lip service, just as it is lip service in the other respects. But for the moment atheism is certainly in the ascendancy, if we are to assume this by the fact that the synagogues and churches are all but deserted, except by the old peasant men and women, the old among the city population, and by the very young children. The holidays, however, find them more well attended. For instance, the first two days and evenings of Easter in

Moscow, the churches were quite full with almost all classes of the worker population, though it was difficult to find among them persons of the educated strata.

The young generation now growing up is taught to laugh at the notion of a God. There is strong, conscious propaganda in this direction. In schools, clubs, meetings, and books, the young are taught that the belief in a God is idiotic.

The Grand [Bolshoi] Theater in Moscow

The theater was built to contain the Tsar, the nobility, and the wealthy. As one sits in the pit today, it is easy to imagine the spectacle which the past must have presented: the ladies in evening gowns with their glittering diamonds and other brilliants, the gentlemen in severe black suits and shining white waistcoats, the general air of festivity and ceremony. One could imagine the great ladies leaning down from the boxes, talking to some of their friends in the pit, or eyeing their neighbors in the other boxes through their lorgnettes, or filling the air with their chatter during the entr'actes; it involuntarily recalls one of the scenes from Tolstoy's *Anna Karenina*.

Now all is gone. Times have rolled on, covering the old and uncovering the new. The day of the worker and the clerk has arrived. The Tsar's box and those of the former mighty are now reserved for the new 'princes' and powers of the realm. The other boxes, the pit, all the choice seats are now filled by humble people, just 'you and I.'

Did this mass of new people seem out of place in these rich surroundings? No, indeed. Poorer dressed, undoubtedly, but as intelligent and as appreciative as any audience we know. Nor was the dress uniformly plain. One could see quite a few sleeveless gowns, quite a few lorgnettes, a large number of opera glasses.

The ballet that I witnessed that night was called *The Red Poppy* (*Krasnil Mak*). Created only in 1927, it could be described as propaganda in the form of exquisite art. The Grand Theater deserves its great fame. The astounding richness and variety of the scenery, the extraordinary fertility in conceiving and the unbelievable skill in executing the ideas, the lavishness of the display, the gorgeous costumes of the players, the excellence of the group and individual dancing and pantomime, the fairy grace of the central figure, named Taï Choa — all went to make a superb and unforgettable spectacle.*

---

* This vivid description of the story is somewhat at variance with the plot as described on Wikipedia.

The motif was a very interesting one, particularly as it reflects the aims and philosophy guiding Russia today. A Soviet ship, symbolic of the U.S.S.R., arrived in a Chinese port. The coolie longshoremen, cruelly treated and working for next to nothing, learn from this ship's sailors of a newer and better world. They are taught the value of cooperation and division of labor by the sailors, who show them by example how a ship by such means could be more quickly unloaded. The force of this example and general instruction encourages the coolies to consider a rebellion in order to rid themselves of their cruel employers (contractor) and adopt the newer system. The employers and their henchmen, fearing for their lives and wanting to maintain the old system which brings so much profit to them, form a plot to kill the captain of the Soviet ship, whom they hold responsible for inciting the coolies to rebellion. (In other words, to overthrow the present leaders and government of Soviet Russia.) Taï Choa, a beautiful and exquisite Chinese dancer, is chosen as the instrument to execute the foul deed. She does not want to, resists, but all in vain. By blows and cruel tortures, the employers force her on. But just as the captain is about to drink the prepared cup of poison, she loses her fear and dashes the cup from his hand. A great uproar takes place. The Chinese coolies rise in rebellion and pursue their oppressors.

Taï Choa does not live to enjoy this new and finer world, for one of the henchmen shoots her. Her last moments are very touching. She is carried in profound silence and reverence to a dais, and as she lies there dying, mothers and children group themselves about her, reaching the sky with their lamentations. Taï Choa half rises several times and entreats the people not to weep for her, for she is dying happy in the knowledge that her sacrifice was not in vain. A brilliant red streamer, the flag of the Revolution, is suspended above her, and another is draped by her side. One of the great red poppies that she loved so well in life is brought to her; she crushes it to her breast and, with a few gestures of agony, expires. Throughout the entire absorbing spectacle of three acts, not a sound is uttered. Everything is done by pantomime, dancing, and symbol.

All theaters in Russia today are instruments for 'conscious' propaganda. I witnessed two other plays in Moscow, one called *The Man with a Portfolio* at the Theater of Revolution, the other at the studio of the Little Theater, and both carried out in striking fashion this same objective.

The Museum of Revolution

This contains a collection of documents, portraits, pictures, and articles of events and persons relating to the revolutionary movement in Russia, beginning with the Pugachev Uprising* in the eighteenth century and ending about 1917. Every radical movement and every protesting group in the history of Russia, so far as visual evidence has come down, has a place of honor. Even such a purely 'bourgeois-liberal' affair as the Decembrist Conspiracy† of December 1825 occupies a niche. History is being fast rewritten in Russia; in fact, the rapidity and extent to which the old has given way to a new interpretation already is astonishing. The righteousness of the protesting or rebellious cause, or the true motives that inspired the leaders, are not considered. It is entirely sufficient that they struck a blow against Tsarism and the wealthy in order for them to be idealized, or at any rate occupy a place of some rank in the Hall of Fame which, low as it might be, is yet higher than that occupied by the best of bourgeois or Tsarist heroes. Not that the Soviet rewriters of history (which in every case means Party men or Party protagonists) hesitate in the slightest to voice their feelings against all movements and groups in the Russian past which did not have a point of view identical to that prevailing today. There are few literatures which contain such violent and persistent denunciation of opponents, oftentimes differing on points so slight in the polemical sphere that an outsider fails to detect any differences. But apparently there is respect for the dead. The dead cannot rise to repudiate them or to harm them (as yet is the case with certain of the groups still surviving and in exile) and hence can be accorded a place of respect, not because their ideas or methods were in line with those prevailing today, but because they represent another nail in the coffin of the Tsarist-bourgeois order, another link in the chain of revolution (from the Soviet standpoint, a solid chain) connecting the remote past of Russia with the last and greatest revolution, that of 1917. That is why in such an important Soviet institution as the Museum of the Revolution, where schoolchildren and peasant workers from every point of Russia are brought for instruction and inspiration, are to be found lumped together so many groups and individuals differing from every standpoint except

---

* The Pugachev Rebellion was an ill-fated uprising of the Russian peasantry against their virtual enslavement by the nobles who owned the land on which they lived and worked.

† The Decembrist Uprising was started in St. Petersburg by Russian army officers leading their soldiers, protesting the succession of Tsar Nicholas I to the throne. In time, it seems, the term came to symbolize wider opposition to the oppression of the Tsars.

one: troublemakers for the old order. For instance, side by side in the museum are to be found such a crack-brained, illiterate person as Pugachev; such aristocratic, mild constitutionalists as the Decembrists; such liberals as Alexander Herzen; such nineteenth-century dreamers as the Populists of the seventies; and, from the Bolshevik standpoint, wishy-washy 'milk and water' socialists such as Georgi Plekhanov and the Menesheviks.

But this is only one example of the new history in Russia. Everywhere, the process of changing history to conform to 'truth' is taking place, in the changing of names of cities, of streets, of buildings, of bridges, of institutions; in the rewriting of textbooks and in teaching; and in countless other ways.

The Sun Yat-Sen University

This is a university in Moscow for Oriental students, the great part of whom in attendance now are Chinese. Here the students are taught economics, sociology, and history from the standpoint of Marxian revolutionary socialism. Located a short distance from the Kremlin, the building is not new but contains several good classrooms, reading rooms, and restrooms, and a good library. Lectures are in English and Chinese (in the elementary classes), in Russian alone, or in Russian interpreted immediately into Chinese. Slides and projection machines are used quite extensively, and the diagram method is extremely popular.

The good-fellowship which prevailed among the students was very marked. This is a training school for revolutionaries. A large number of the students already have a revolutionary background. Many were forced to flee from China to save their lives.* Everything — books, tuition, etc. — is free, and in many cases allowances for living are supplied.

The Students of the Moscow Institute of Oriental Studies

I visited the dormitory of the students of this institution. They were not only Orientals but Russians, sons of peasants and workers for the greatest part. My hosts were sons of miners in the Don basin, and another was the son of a Ukrainian peasant. They themselves had worked side by side with their fathers formerly but now were

---

* Reference is to the Chinese Revolution of 1911, which overthrew China's last imperial dynasty. Sun Yat-Sen was the revered first president of the republic and honored by the Soviets for his compatible ideals and cooperative initiatives. Sun Yat-Sen University closed in the mid-1930s.

studying at the Institute, preparing themselves for diplomatic or political posts in the Orient, the chief purpose of the Institute. These simple workers' sons were studying Japanese and English and showed unexpected intelligence. Their faces betrayed clearly their worker origin but were animated by zeal for knowledge. Much of the latter comes from excessive concentration and drill, but is gained nevertheless.

The government allows these students 80 rubles a month. Charges are only 6½ rubles a month for the average room in the dormitory. Rooms are small, less ornamented than our dormitory rooms and more inexpensively constructed, but comfortable just the same. Corridors, lavatories, bathrooms are all quite poor, however, built on the cheapest order. But this is characteristic of all Moscow dwellings. Private rooms are always the best, the common portions of the dwelling always poor.

What can be the attitude of such students and workers? In actuality, it is only gratefulness and loyalty to the government. For them, it is Paradise itself. When before in Russia have workers been so excellently treated? They lived in the old days in basements with outhouses, in garrets, in the most ramshackle, antiquated buildings, in cold, wet, dirt, and misery, very often one and two families and more in a single room. If one only knew the severity and horror of Russian winters (and summers, too), he would appreciate how the poor man in Russia was forced to live and why strikes and conflicts and killings were so frequent in this land. Not only was the worker materially oppressed, he was deprived in addition of all hope for improvement and betterment. There was practically no schooling, no opportunity to move out of his worker class and enjoy some of the nice things of life. It was unheard of before that simple workers' and peasants' sons should not only aspire to places in the diplomatic corps — always jealously kept for the better families in the Tsarist regime — but should actually be taken from their homes, permitted gratis attendance at the university, be paid enough to live in modest comfort, and secure a position upon completion of their studies. It is therefore no wonder that the most satisfied elements in the Soviet Union today are the workers of the cities. It is they who parade so enthusiastically on the national holidays, who are the mainstay of the government.

Is Everyone in Russia Satisfied?

It is natural that the answer should be in the negative. There are those who remember their better life of the past, those who are weary of the constant privation, those who are pessimistic as to any improvement, those who stand outside the trade unions and therefore cannot get the many extra privileges which come to the latter, those who cannot enter the Communist Party and hence are excluded from most positions of trust and responsibility, those who want extra material (monetary) reward for unusual service — such as an invention or discovery — or improvement in the rate of compensation generally (specialists of all kinds), those who are deprived of practically all privileges and benefits in the State (private merchants or entrepreneurs), certain members of the old officialdom or aristocracy, and those who are unemployed (very many, now).

Extra Privileges to Communists

In actuality, many privileges or favors are accorded to members of the Communist Party, though in theory this is supposed to be impossible. It is natural, where almost every other post of responsibility is filled by a Communist. Gladly will he give a fellow Party member a little extra bit of attention or favor, serve him first, waive aside many formalities, often charge him nothing — or at any rate, less — for a service, etc. I had a personal experience to this effect. At the administrative division of the Moscow soviet where I applied for permission to leave the country, I was asked if I were a Communist, and upon answering in the negative, I was charged the usual rate of 22 rubles for the outgoing visa. Had I been a Communist, I would have had to pay nothing, or at least only a nominal sum, and would have been saved many inconveniences, such as waiting in line, for example — one of the worst evils in present-day Russia.

The Barbershop and Dining Room of Hotel Europe

How does socialism work in practice? Let us take my experience with the Hotel Europe. At the barbershop I was given a haircut. A good one, but with none of the frills and flourishes, none of the gentle tapping, massaging, smoothing so dear to the heart of the average American man. The barber took a fair amount of precaution against hair falling down my collar, etc., but was unconcerned with any close examination to observe that all loose hair had been removed from my face, ears, etc. There were none of those shining mirrors, bottles, and marble shelves and few of those dozens of little examples of cleanliness or items palpably designed to please or humor every customer, even the most fastidious or exacting. The same with the restaurant in this hotel, the second largest in Moscow. Clean, but with the cleanliness of a poor home. Linen white, but not too white. None of that anxiety to immediately remove a tablecloth that was soiled here or there. The general impression was that two or three or even a half dozen spots don't really matter. If the food is not served in such elegant or spotless crockery, or the knives and forks and glasses are not so shiny or clean-looking, what of it?

Now, such examples seem almost bound to be the case where no additional income can come to a man or an enterprise. If the barber knows that no tip can come to him (tips are theoretically impossible in Russia but are accepted by many quite readily when offered) and that his salary will be just the same whether he is attentive or inattentive to a customer — within bounds, of course — why should he exert himself? Why should he, when he is somewhat tired or has just had a full meal and feels somewhat indisposed, go to the trouble of preparing suds in order to avoid any possible smart connected with shaving off the loose hairs about the earlocks or back of the neck, or be overparticular whether any hair clippings remain on the nose or in the ears of the customer? Or in the case of the waiter, who also can get no tips and whose salary is assured, when there is no headwaiter to call him down and no irate customer to complain, for this is a worker's State, why should this waiter increase the speed of his footsteps to serve a customer who might happen to be in a hurry, or care if the tablecloth is heavily spotted from the carelessness of the preceding diner, or see that water or salt is on the table without being asked for it?

And these instances can be multiplied indefinitely, shown in the way the grocery clerk will help you, the way the official at the administrative bureau will serve you, the way the employee of the State store will fit your clothing or sell you shoes.

But the sympathizer will reply, "What do all these frills, flourishes, and extras matter? The important thing is that you are getting a haircut and are eating. If this is done with a reasonable degree of speed, efficiency, and cleanliness, what more should one want?" Yet, really, what does it matter? A very complicated question, in truth. It involves so many things: That your selection of ties should be limited to a dozen instead of a hundred different patterns, and the same for your suit and shoes and hat. That in buying a pair of shoes you should fit them on yourself by balancing on one foot with one hand on the counter, or go over to a vacant chair and try them on, instead of having a polite (if sometimes over-polite and unctuous) clerk show you to an upholstered chair, delicately remove your shoe, give your foot a smoothing pat, and carefully and patiently try on one shoe after another, offering an endless succession of styles, qualities, and sizes. That in buying a suit, one should be handed to you over the counter along with a half dozen others passed to as many different customers and that you go over yourself to the mirror and see whether the thing hangs halfway decently, instead of a smooth-tongued, well-dressed salesman, along with the tailor, giving the thing a little heave here, a little pinch there, making the fit smooth and exact and 'latest.' Yes, a complicated question, truly.

The sympathizer will reply that socialism does not exclude variety or style or comfort or luxuries but does everything in reason: it distinguishes between sheer extravagance or waste, and necessity, between useless frills and fancies, and service. It is based on the principle of the Greatest Good to the Greatest Number, not on the eccentricities or caprices of the individual.

The opponent will answer to the contrary, that socialism does and must by its very nature and ideal exclude style and variety and luxuries, for it gives no incentive to initiative or inventiveness. By controlling all capital, socialism does not allow the individual to put into practice his ideas or to market them. It accepts only those few ideas or improvements which are suitable for application on the widest scale, on a national scale, not where they are in demand by a limited few of the population. Its standards are the standards of the great mass instead of the cultured, intellectual few, and hence it labels as luxuries that which cannot be given to the great mass, but which to others are really necessities. It therefore makes life dull, prosaic, and standardized, instead of allowing it to be rich, varied, and interesting. It operates to drag the progressive, intellectual, delicate-natured few down to the level of the conservative, un-resourceful, coarse-fibered *many*, instead of lifting the latter to the level of the best.

Russia and the World's Underman

On one of the walls in the Hotel Europe, I observed at some length a poster that is typical of countless others to be found in Russia today. It showed workers of the leading races — white, black, yellow — standing together, shoulder to shoulder, in good fellowship and fraternal love, while at the bottom was a slogan which expressed the solidarity and mutual affection of all workers of the world. Russia today, in word and in deed, is representing the 'underman,' acting as the greatest force in history to propagate the cause of the 'oppressed,' or poor, man. Other lands have or have not benefited the working man, but nowhere has his cause been so persistently, tenaciously, openly supported as is found in Russia today. The present leaders have been brought to power on these slogans, and they must make good. It is practically impossible to retreat now, even if they wanted to; they have talked and promised too much to go back. So Russia has become the headquarters or the asylum of safety of all the revolutionary, radical, dissatisfied elements the world over. Under her banner has collected everyone with a grievance. She, in her turn, makes use of every dissatisfaction, every protest — social, political, economic, or otherwise — to further her ends. Everything which hurts capitalist countries — rebellion, crises, strikes, etc. — is hailed with glee. A good example is the present unemployment situation in America. This is viewed not sympathetically but with happiness. I heard it from many people: "America has over four million men out of work. Strikes are taking place in every city. Great crisis is sweeping over America. The beginning of the end is at hand."

The Opposition in the Communist Party

History is capable of being interpreted as a resultant of forces or as a resultant of the action of personalities. The Marxist viewpoint, the one that is prevalent in Soviet Russia, is to emphasize the former and to overlook the latter, except in so far as personalities assist the action of the former. According to the Marxist viewpoint, forces are at work in history which are the logical, inevitable, inescapable product of past and contemporary conditions. These forces (social movements, in particular) are inhuman, in so far as they are entirely independent of the will of a single individual to call them into existence or arrest them permanently. At best, the single individual can only halt or divert them temporarily, and then not the entire movement (or tendency) but only its epitomized or what might be called its 'sensational' expressions, such as a political party. Because of this, leaders and adherents may alternately drop out and rejoin, but the movement will continue regardless. From this viewpoint also follows the corollary: original motives of individual leaders do not count, only results. That is why, for example, Lenin has been elevated to godlike holiness, a man without a blemish, always pure and exalted in his motives, always unimpeachably correct, always possessed of uncanny vision to detect the most imperceptible current that augured either good or bad for the proletariat.

Now, here is where the contradiction lies. To examine the personality of Lenin and to emphasize *motives* when this examination will prove that each phase or period of his life or motives led directly to Revolutionary success is, from their standpoint, legitimate historical procedure. To come to a negative or opposite conclusion, however, is unhistorical procedure, and now they fall back on the principle that *results* count, not motives.

This contradiction or inconsistency is shown in the case of Trotsky, Zinoviev, and the other opposition leaders now in disgrace. To justify their severe punishment, their traits, characteristics, conduct, etc. inconsistent with Revolutionary success are emphasized; in other words, results are here considered less important than motives.

Friday, May 25, 1928. Berlin

Any American suffering from dyspepsia, gout, or any other form of ill humor should have been here in Berlin on May 20th — or the days just before — when the Reichstag and Prussian Landtag* elections were held, and a sure cure could have been guaranteed him. Nothing could have provoked a heartier laugh than these German elections and the whole political campaign. If the Germans were not such a sober, serious folk, they would have laughed, too, and probably a good many did anyway. Ask the average American what is exactly the difference between a Republican and a Democrat, and he scratches his head; imagine then trying to keep clear the respective programs of 30 different parties! It is a task that would stagger the Olympic Jove, let alone one of us frail humans. The Germans are world-renowned for their ability to handle statistics, but here they, too, must throw up their hands in helplessness. The average citizen certainly does not know what it's all about, and my attendance at electioneering gatherings has convinced me that most of the leaders themselves are not clear as to more than a half dozen programs, if that many. In fact, they don't deny it. It's too bad human language is not more elastic; then, perhaps each of these parties would have such a distinctive name that there could be no possibility of confusing one with the other. As it is, some quite bitter enemies have almost the same name, for example, the German National People's Party and the German People's Party; the Social Democratic Party and the German Democratic Party; and the Communist Party and the Left Communists. Others that are just as muddling are the National Socialist German Workers' Party† and the German Social

---

* The parliament of the Free State of Prussia.

† Also called the Nazi Party.

Party; and the Christian Social Reich Party, the Christian National Middle Class Party, and the German Christian People's Party.

The campaign fuel is about as hot, if not hotter, than ours. All the staple 'mud bricks' of graft, corruption, intimidation, violence, personalities, and the like are hurled about freely. Nor are the Germans slouches when it comes to emphasizing words with fists, or real bricks, or even bullets. Just the other day in Hamburg, for instance, Communists and Nationalists fell afoul of each other, and in the result about three were killed and several heavily wounded. The police are always out in large numbers at election times, and the merchants take extra precautions with their shop windows. It must be added, however, that these last elections took place on the whole very quietly compared to preceding years.

There is no end of petty tactics. Every little incident, no matter how manifestly unfair, is used. The German trans-Atlantic fliers* came in for considerable attention. *The Vorwärts* newspaper of the Social Democrats was extremely bitter when it heard that the *Bremen* intended flying the black-white-red flag, the standard of the former Empire, and wrote that it can only hurt the cause of Germany in America "by this laughable exhibition of a symbol which in the entire world has made itself impossible." The papers of the German People's Party, of which Gustav Stresemann, the present well-known foreign minister, is the head, railed at the Socialists for this point of view but on the other hand attacked the German National People's Party, which is even more Right than it, for singling out one of the fliers because his ancestry on one side is Jewish.

Perhaps even more than in America do the various newspapers serve as agencies for the venting of spite and venom against the opposition. The political character of the newspapers is much more strictly defined and recognized here than it is with us. Almost without exception, every newspaper is definitely the organ of one or another political party or group, and each party or group has usually at least one paper of its own. As far as I know, there isn't a paper in Berlin that is strictly independent, that does not adhere to one or another party, though there are papers which are classifiable in accordance with 'tendency' and not with a particular faction. This is true, for example, of such a paper as the *Berliner Lokal-Anzeiger*. Before the war it was a semi-official organ of the Imperial Government, but today it defends Nationalist or Right policies without definitely committing itself to one or another right-wing faction.

---

* The German plane *Bremen* made the first successful transatlantic airplane flight from east to west on April 12–13, 1928.

While we reserve our inalienable right to draw a little humor out of the present political situation in Germany, sober reflection tells us that it is not a comedy that is being played before our eyes but a serious drama, almost a tragedy, in which the comical elements enter only to make the play endurable. Germany is only just now going through the birth pangs of a thoroughgoing democracy and republican form of government. Before the war she had a parliamentary system, but it was only such in name. An entrenched aristocracy, bureaucracy, and military, acting through a semi-absolute monarch, dictated the legislation and policies under which the German lived. Now, for the first time, the German people are really experimenting with representative government and genuine democracy, and because of this must go through the initial throes of unsteadiness and disorder that come with the installing of a brand-new system. A new type of government is difficult enough to establish in times of relative prosperity, but is incomparably harder at a period like this, when poverty is so rampant in the land. The French were almost 100 years in establishing their republican system on a relatively secure and workable basis; in Germany, it will probably go much quicker, owing to the political experience of the people, but it, too, cannot escape this experimental period, as we can see today.

But more than a struggle over outward political forms divides the German people today. It goes much deeper. There is certainly a question of wages, jobs, taxes, and prices, but there is something else besides: intangible things like philosophies and spirits* are in conflict with one another. Old Germany had its own zeitgeist. Through and through it penetrated every pore of German life, affected the school, the church, the home, business life, social relationships, the mind, the soul; molded and shaped and stamped the German individual in a certain peculiar and definite way. So complete and so thorough was its action that the very 'atmosphere' became distinctive from atmospheres elsewhere, and was recognized and labeled as such by the Germans themselves as well as by others. Long before the war, this atmosphere was resented, this zeitgeist attached to Old Germany. Other and newer philosophies were opposed to it, particularly the one called democracy. But the champions of the new were helpless. They had the organized, powerful strength of their opponents to battle, the traditions of 'success' and 'greatness' of the older philosophies to meet. Above all, they had to overcome the inertia of the average man, who feared to experiment and risk exchanging bad for worse. But despite these difficulties, in

---

* It is likely that Werlin originally used the richly freighted German term *zeitgeist* instead of *spirit* throughout this section but that well-meaning transcriptionists substituted the simple translation "spirit."

the days before 1914 a newer spirit, that of democracy, was gradually making its way to more and more people. Then came the World War, the great sacrifices, the tremendous suffering, and finally, the breaking point. The old rulers were thrown out; new leaders took their place, and governmental forms underwent alteration. But the more intangible struggle, the conflict of the older and newer spirits, continued and today has reached such proportions that it is tearing Germany to pieces.

If it were a question only of a struggle between the forces of democracy and the forces of the old regime, the problems of adjustment and compromise might not be so difficult, but it is not. Other philosophies, other viewpoints, have also crossed the threshold of history and are demanding a hearing. In the days when democracy and democratic institutions penetrated the states where they are now triumphant, the voice of these newcomers was weak and uncertain; now it is vociferous and insistent and has been heard by a tremendous and ever-increasing multitude. These newcomers are socialism and communism. There can be no doubt that they have complicated the situation and rendered the task of harmonizing the German people much more difficult. Communism, with its militant slogans of "class conflict" and "complete abolition of private property," has frightened the people and has actually set them against each other, very often where there was originally no dislike and no consciousness of difference. German social democracy is a much milder thing than German communism, but in the popular mind it is constantly confused with, and suffers for the sins of, the latter.

In the conflict of the two older combatants, democracy seems to be winning, but the forces on the side of the old regime are still mighty. In general, they fall into two classes. There are those who, as a result of sentiment, prejudice, or passion, cannot forget the good old days under the monarchy. They include all those people who are 'die-hards,' who cannot adjust themselves to new facts easily, who believe the clock of history can be turned back, who possessed and are now dispossessed, who wielded power and are now powerless. On the other hand, there are those who come to their conclusions by reasons which command our greater respect. Their arguments must be listened to. It is true that democracy is being weighed in the balance today. In the days when it reached the United States, when it came to England, to France, to the other lands of Europe, the people as a whole received it with open arms. The ruling elements ridiculed it and fought against it, but the man in the street embraced it readily. It was a new religion, a new philosophy, and it was accepted. Its teachings, its value for good, was not doubted; what was questioned was its difficulty of application. But now, today, democracy as a way of organization, a philosophy, an expression of social relationships, an instrument of increasing man's well-being, is being seriously considered and challenged. Wherever we look in Europe, or even in our own America, we see this is true, and these persons who question are by no means all 'enemies of the people' or self-seekers. And the same holds true for Germany. A good many people, out of reasoned, sober reflection, are convinced that the older system, with its firm hand and benevolent despotism, was more conductive to the welfare of the German people, that it kept the nation a close entity, suppressed the preaching — at least openly — of class war and class hatred, assured order and stability, and brought Germany to her enviable peak of national development.

But this is talking in more or less abstract terms. The programs of the different parties touch concrete things; they must, if the average man is to understand. Amid the welter of issues which each party includes in its full program, there are a few that are common to all and over which the German nation has split into so many segments. On external matters, they include the Versailles Treaty, the Dawes Plan, the entrance of Germany into the League of Nations, the Locarno Treaty, and the Eastern Frontier. Domestic issues include the restoration of the monarchy, the character of the republic, democracy, separatist tendencies of certain states (Bavaria and Saxony, for example), the relation of State and Church, socialism, and communism. The leading questions of economic policy embrace the time-hallowed matters of taxes, agriculture, the peasants versus the large landlords, and trade relations with other States.

There is little reason to doubt that it is on the vital economical and domestic issues that the people are in reality divided, not on the problems of foreign policy. In theory, all the Rights stand for the abolition of the Dawes Plan and the whole question of reparations, and for the rewriting of the Versailles Treaty, particularly for the return of the Polish Corridor, in order that Germany might be solidly united with East Prussia. But, as in other countries, the program of a political party may say one thing and the results of their legislation quite another. It is the question of being 'in' and being 'out.' "Theory is gray, but green is the eternal tree of life." Where the Rights participate in the government and have a decisive say, they, too, face reality, shove aside these troublesome questions for future consideration, and turn to the vital problems of everyday domestic life, particularly the economic aspects.

The numerical order in which the six leading parties stood as a result of the elections of 1924 has not been changed by the elections of last Sunday, May 20th, except in the case of the Communists, who climbed from fifth up to fourth place, exchanging positions with the German People's Party. But what did change is the relative strength of the parties. The Social Democrats and the Communists gained heavily, occupying now first and fourth place, respectively, while the German National People's Party lost just as heavily. In the order of their present strength, the six leading parties now stand as follows:

	Reichstag Seats	
	1928	1924
1. Social Democratic Party of Germany	155	131
2. German National People's Party	73	105
3. Centrum	62	69
4. Communist Party	54	45
5. German People's Party	45	51
6. German Democratic Party	25	32

Of the three leading right-wing parties, the German National People's Party is the strongest, polling over a million votes in the elections of 1924 and standing second in point of strength in the State. As a result, however, of Sunday's elections, it lost about one-third of its seats in the Reichstag, though still retaining second place. On the political spectrum, it stands in between the People's National Block, an extreme-right group, and the German People's Party, which is the most moderate of the right-wing groups, closer to the center. Formally, the Nationalists talk of fighting for "faith and home, for freedom, order, and law," for "the protection of German labor and women-labor," for a "Christian national School Law," for a "strong state power," which will make impossible the "party confusion of parliamentarism." It is the party that wants the monarchy restored, that looks back to "the proud glance of the Bismarckian Empire," that wants the "reconstruction of the Fatherland" as it was before 1914, and that agitates constantly for a larger army and navy. But a good deal of this, as I have mentioned, molders in the program and is never brought into serious cabinet discussion. In the last government, which was composed of Rights and Centers, the Nationalists played the leading part and, with surprising acquiescence, faced reality. They spoke softly to France, cast their vote for the League of Nations, accepted the Dawes Plan, and negotiated and consummated trade treaties with France and Poland. But at the same time, the party maintains its theoretical program, and this brings it into conflict not only with groups of the Center and the Left, but with its own right-wing factions. The People's National Block, for example, accuses it of treachery and of deserting its principles in practice, while the other groups pour contempt on it for its opportunistic, wishy-washy tactics.

The second most important right-wing group is Foreign Minister Stresemann's party, the German People's Party. This is more moderate in its views. It doesn't openly ask for a return of the monarchy and is satisfied to let those things alone which are impossible to attain. It recognizes facts and realizes that Germany is in no position to undo the Versailles Treaty, that its sanest policy is to work in harmony with France, England, and the rest of the world. It has entirely accepted the Dawes Plan, the League of Nations, and the Locarno Pacts; it seeks to establish good relations everywhere. On only one important point in foreign policy does it coincide with its more right brethren: in refusing to recognize the Polish Corridor and to sign an "East Locarno" treaty. In this last election it lost considerable strength due to its prominent part in the last government, which met with the people's disfavor.

The strongest of the central groups is the Center, or Catholic, Party. To it is usually joined the Bavarian People's Party, also a Catholic group. In the last government, they had 88 seats combined; now, by the last elections, they are reduced to 78. As in almost every other country of Europe, the Center fights for recognition of the Catholic Church as an integral unit that the State must consider in legislation, and in general for a closer union of Church and State, which in practice usually takes the form of agitation for Catholic teaching to Catholic children, for more spiritual or religious life in the State, etc. But since it is a political party, and seeks like the others to increase its membership, it must take cognizance of other issues as well. The satisfaction of incompatible issues often hinders the attainment of its religious goals, so the party is unable to pursue a single course and constantly oscillates between the Rights and the Lefts. The Bavarian group has nationalist aspirations for Bavaria, is not satisfied with being in the republic, and desires separation. However, because of its great Catholic membership, it votes on almost all issues with the Center.

A left-middle group is the German Democratic Party. This comes closer to expressing our American notions of democracy than any other party of the Reich. It stands for the fulfillment of all Germany's peace-treaty agreements; strongly battles for the maintenance of the republic; rails against the 'particularism' which is everywhere raising its head; stands for a more unselfish spirit in social, economic, and political life; and is an enemy of the older spirit which ruled Germany, with its class privileges and inrooted class institutions. It wants unity and peace among all classes and sections, based on republican, democratic ideals in the best sense of the word. It sees in democracy the only possibility of building a living state-consciousness: "Parliamentarism, insofar as it does not falsify the will of the people, is the best guarantee for the selection of the best leaders." As in 1924 it still ranks sixth, but it has lost representatives, now having only 25 seats in the Reichstag instead of 32. Just why it is not stronger than it is, is difficult to say. The Nationalists will have none of it, while the ordinary run of people, particularly the workers, would rather vote for the Social Democrats, who they believe more adequately represent their interests. The Democrats explain their losses in this last election as a result of the people's resentment against the dominance of the Right, which caused voters to swing in exactly the opposite direction and in doing so, to pass over the middle groups as well.

The first party in the republic is the Social Democratic Party, a member of the left wing. It is one of the oldest in the State, going back to the days of Ferdinand Lassalle and Wilhelm Liebknecht, to the seventies of the last century. As I have already mentioned, it suffers by contiguity with the Communists, and many people — often innocently, but very often intentionally, as in the case of their political enemies — readily confuse them. In actuality, there is a wide gulf separating them. The Socialists are a party of peace, the Communists of war. Both base themselves on the teachings of Karl Marx, but the one sees the process of socialization as long drawn-out; the other is impatient and asks that it be artificially hurried, by force if necessary. The one is the party of evolution, the other of revolution. Again, the Socialists recognize the existence of class conflict but make use of it only as a principle of truth by which to explain history; the other, the Communists, are not satisfied to confine it to academic tracts but want to put an edge on it and use it as a real weapon in the battle for its ideas. In practice the Social Democrats work very closely with the German Democratic Party and, like the latter, fight for the spread of egalitarian notions. It is, however, a more purely workman's party than is the German Democratic Party, and struggles for the economic betterment of the worker's conditions and for his greater role in the management and ordering of the State. In this latter endeavor, it is joined by the Communists, who, however, do it as a means to an end, not an end in itself — the end being the quick and complete overturn of the present State, with its system of private property, and the substitution of their own State and system.

Of the other 23 parties or factions, the most important are the Economic Party, the National Socialist German Worker's Party (the Hitler Movement), the Christian National Peasant's Party, and the German Peasant Party. At present, the Economic Party is almost as strong as the Democratic. It represents the bigger business and industrial people, and it puts the economic prosperity of the groups above everything else. The National Socialists are led by the famous (or infamous) Hitler and may be classed as a Socialist party of the right wing. It is quite anti-Semitic in its tendencies, and in practically all things joins the extreme Right, except on its avowed goal of dispossessing owners of lands and goods by about 50 percent and turning them over to the workers. It avoids conflict with the Catholics, and in this also stands apart from the Nationalists. The Christian National Peasant's Party and the German Peasant's Party fight in the interest of the peasants against the large landlords, particularly the Prussian Junkers, and so displease the extreme right wing, although on all other questions they usually work in harmony together. These 23 parties actually count for very little in determining policies. Altogether they only polled 14 percent of the total vote, and their Reichstag representation is still less, only 10 percent, as a result of their votes being spread to all parts of Germany instead of being concentrated in one or two districts.

The elections of May 20th leave no other conclusion than that the Lefts have certainly triumphed. They lack, however, a majority, and if they wish to participate in the government, they must work in coordination with at least two parties of more conservative tendencies. The entire talk at present in all the papers concerns the "Great Coalition," a government made up of Social Democrats, Communists, Democrats, and members of the German People's Party; and as these four have only a bare working majority, it is to include one or two other parties as well. Whether such a government can long remain in power is very doubtful, owing to the nature of the economic program which the Lefts are sure to put forward and which the Rights are just as sure to refuse.*

---

* It is important to note that Joseph Werlin did not review these comments on the May 20, 1928, German elections after he returned to the States in September 1928. He typed another version, which he submitted to the *New York Times* for publication (too late, he was advised), but that copy does not survive. This transcription leaves ambiguities that only he could have clarified. Political alliances in Germany, of course, changed dramatically with the onset of the Depression. His analysis of attitudes has enduring interest, however, especially in light of the (deceptively) weak showing of Adolph Hitler, a recognized threat, even if on the fringe.

However it may be, a survey of contemporary German politics can judiciously end by saying that the present-day political situation in Germany is certainly unsettled, and the future cannot be predicted.

MOSKAU

by
Alexys A. Sidorow

Published by
Albertus-Verlag / Berlin, 1928

THE FOLLOWING PHOTOGRAPHS illustrate specific sites Joe visited, selected from a prized book he brought back from his travels: *Moskau* (Berlin: Albertus-Verlag, 1928) by Alexys A. Sidorow, who wrote the introduction and curated the photos. *Moskau* was one of a series called The Face of the Cities, which seems to have included Berlin, London, Paris, and Rome. The copyright page lists several names of photographers, but none is identified specifically with a particular image. The seven-page introductory essay by Sidorow, written in (or translated into) German, is dated "Moskau, April 1928." Joe left Berlin for Moscow in early April and returned in early May, so where and how he learned about the book is not known. The limited biographical information about the writer available online mentions his birthplace in Russia and notes that he was an esteemed Soviet art and cultural historian. It would seem from Sidorow's compassionate yet non-propagandistic remarks, documenting parades and protests, beggar children, and women washing clothes amidst ice floes in the "Moskva," as well as iconic buildings and contemporary architecture — "reconciliation of old and new"— that Joe would have admired the writer as well as the photographs. "Among all the cities of the world," Sidorow says, "Moscow triggers the most contradictory feelings. Does it have a face, 1,000 faces, or none at all?" The heart of Russia is "a heart not at rest."

Dserjinsky-Platz mit Wladimir-Tor Place Dserjinsky et Porte Wladimir
Дзержинская площадь с Владимирскими воротами. Dserjinsky Square with Vladimir Gate

Bahnhof Kazan Gare de Kazan
Казанский вокзал. Kazan Railway Station

Meeting am Denkmal Worowsky
Митинг возле памятника Воровского.
Meeting près du Monument Worowsky
Meeting at Vorovsky Monument

Wäscherinnen an der Moskwa
Прачки на Москве-реке.
Blanchisseuses sur la rive de la Moskwa
Washing linen in the Moskva

Der Alte Markt am Ssucharewsky-Turm   Le Vieux-Marché près de la Tour Soucharewsky
Старый рынок у Сухаревской башни.   Old Market at foot of Szucharewsky Tower

Demonstration am Roten Platz   Manifestation sur la Place Rouge
Демонстрация на Красной площади.   Demonstration on Red Square

Theater-Platz

Театральная площадь.

Place du Théâtre

Theater Square

May 16, 1928.

Mr. Joseph S. Werlin,
c/o American Express Co.,
Berlin, Germany.

Dear Mr. Werlin:

The post cards from Moscow and Riga give interesting reports of your trip, although I was a little surprised to hear you express relief that you were out of the Soviet atmosphere. This however is rather usual. I shall be glad to have the outline and shall give it as prompt attention as possible.

I suggest that you keep the books in your own possession until you are through with them. If you send them by parcel post, there is no duty charge unless they are in English. Therefore there is no object in sending them direct to the university. I remind you that I will relieve you of books up to the amount of $100.00. You have probably found that you can buy books as reasonably in Berlin as in Moscow and certainly more easily.

I regret to have to report that I was unsuccessful in the matter of scholarship for you for your last quarters. However I have talked the matter over with Mr. Huth and others and we are hoping to be able to do something, perhaps in the line of paper reading. Again I cannot promise anything definite. I am afraid we shall have to leave the matter thus until you turn up on the ground.

Perhaps it will occur to you to write me briefly your general impressions. When you speak of interviewing all sorts of people I surmize that you established a good many contacts and therefore have some basis for judgement. If you have not done this do not bother to do so. It is often well not to have to commit one's self too definitely in short space, such summaries being rather dangerous.

Yours very sincerely,

SNH/CF

Berlin, Wednesday, May 15th, 1928.

Dear Mr. Harper;

Now that I have returned from Russia and my plan of work has taken more definite shape, I can turn to your encouraging letter of March the 7th and reply to some of its implied questions.

First of all with regard to my Russian trip. I spent exactly 22 days in the Union, 18 in Moscow and 4 in Leningrad. I should have liked to have included other cities, but it was impossible. The weather made travelling very disagreeable, for one thing, and for another, I lacked the time. I wanted to be back in Berlin in time for the beginning of the lectures. On the whole I am quite satisfied with the benefits of the trip. I kept in mind the chief purpose: material and advice on my thesis-problem, but I did not neglect other things on that account. The Bokc was the height of kindness, but I used its services very little except in connection with my thesis. Through its offices the facilities of the Lenin Institute were put at my disposal. I was introduced to Kramolnikov, an old-time party man and a personal friend of Lenin. My thesis-plan includes the third party congress, as I shall explain latter, and for this he was very useful since he personally participated in this congress. Unfortunately he spoke only Russian and I had to use an interpretor, but just the same he was of great help in pointing out the most important works for my subject. He is one of the leading co-editors of Lenin's collected works and was therefore in an excellent position to give me advice. He invited me to write him on any matter that troubled me in the future, which was also a good thing, as you can see. I asked the Lenin Institute to also furnish me a list of the very best sources. They did this and by checking this list with that given me by Kramolnikov as well as with that cited in various bibliographies, I was able as it were to reach an "average," to know what are really the best works. Before leaving Moscow I ordered shipped to me at Berlin practically every good work bearing directly on my interest. I have since received most of them and the balance--a few are out of print--I hope to obtain soon.

I wanted to avoid the limited, one-sided impressions which comes from putting yourself in the hands of official guides, and that is why I used the Bokc as little as possible. Through an address or two that I had in Moscow, I was able to quickly increase my circle of acquaintances and before I was through with Moscow and Leningrad I collected a rather valuable series of notes on a great many phases of present-day things. By working only through private people I believe I obtained a truer and wider understanding of things than most people who now visit Russia. However I didn't neglect putting myself in good with valuable people, such as Mr. Block, now one of the main officials at the Bokc and with the heads of the Lenin Institute. I wanted to leave the way open for me to return, and I believe I have thus far succeeded.

What I shall do with these notes is a question. I do want to write several articles, but for a serious piece of work I haven't the time right now, and for a popular account, as for example for "Asia," I don't feel particularly enthused. Perhaps

Letter from Werlin to Samuel N. Harper, including thesis proposal
Copied by permission, Special Collections Research Center, University of Chicago Library

when I return to America in the Fall I may do something in this connection.

Now as to my university work here. I am taking 13 hours a week in various courses, which is slightly more than 3 full majors at Chicago. I thought it best that I obtain all the information pertaining to Russia that was offered, and for that reason am taking four courses in this field. You may be interested in learning what they are. Under Karl Stählin I am taking his survey course, "Russian History from the beginning until the end of the 18th century." From Zaitzeff, a former private-dozent at the University of Kiev I am taking his " Political-Legal Structure of the Russian State in the 20th Century"(with emphasis on the Soviet period), and "Exercises in Russian Law"(practically limited to the present period). The other course in the Russian field is under Vasmer, "History of Russian literature in the 19th Century). The other courses are in connection with German and general history. Too bad I had to scatter myself to 7 courses but under the German system there is hardly anything to be done, for, as you know, most of the courses consist of only one or two hours of lecturing a week. In this general connection I shall be pleased if you will take up with Mr. Joranson a matter that I am now mentioning. In his letter to me he reminded me of the requirements for the degree and pointed out that as I now have only 19 credits and since 27 are usually required, I shall have 8 to make up whxxx for my doctorate requirements. Now it was told to me by Mr. Huth before I left and thoroughly understood that I was to get credit for all the work that I did at the University of Berlin, that the time I would spend there and the lecture-hours I would take would be equalized with the Chicago system and I would obtain credit accordingly. I suppose Mr. Joranson also understands this but in order to make it positive I am writing to him and I shall appreciate if you will also take up the matter with him.

And now concerning my thesis. It has been far from an easy thing to decide on a subject. There was the material to be considered, the form of treatment, its boundaries and a good many other points. Finally, on the basis of my thinking of the last three months and my conversations in Russia and elsewhere, I have hit on something that I believe will be satisfactory and of this I now wish to speak to you. The exact name of the title doesn't matter but for the present we will call it "The Second and Third Congresses of the R.S.D.P(Bolshevik) On a separate page I am outlining a very rough draft of my plan of procedure. Here are some of the reasons that caused me to look with favor on this subject and I hope it will meet with your approval as well. First of all, as you well know, the Bolshevik party had its birth at these Congresses. All the present-day doctrines and methods are foreshadowed in the programs of this time. This was the period when Lenin came to the fore and wrote the works that have become the constitution of the party since. This was the period when the revolutionary movement really became active in Russia, when it was joined to the economic strikes and grievances of the workers and peasants, when the Russo-Jap War broke out and the First Revolution had its beginning. It was a period of great polemical struggle among the various revolutionary or radical currents,

particularly between the Bolshevik and Menshevik factions. On the whole, therefore, the years in which these Congresses fall are excellent for approaching the history of the Party.

One of the difficult things, as usual, is the mode of treatment. The easier thing is of course to give the theme a purely historical setting, to string along the facts in a chronological order. Inasmuch as the thesis is being written for the history department it is a legitimate form of procedure, but I know you do not relish this sort of treatment and neither do I. For this reason I have decided to take up the subject from an ideological and tactical standpoint, to explain the philosophical viewpoints of the Bolsheviks, particularly Lenin, to state their views on questions of organization, theory, tactics, their clashes with other revolutionary currents and groups, and so forth. On the other hand, in order to meet the requirements of a historical dissertation, I shall couch the whole thing in a historical form. On the whole, therefore, the treatment will be similar to that of my master's thesis. On the basis of this earlier dissertation I believe I am warranted in saying that you can expect a good piece of work from me this time also, in fact, a much better thing, for I am much better acquainted with the literature and vital points of view now than was the case then.

It is necessary in making a declaration of candidacy for the doctor's degree, that is, before it can be formally accepted, that the subject of the dissertation be approved by the professor under whom you are working. I am making this declaration now in a separate letter to Mr. Joranson and I kindly ask that if you approve the subject for my labors you conclude the necessary formalities with him.

Mr. Morrison, as you know, is in the city waiting to hear concerning his visa. He is rooming with a good friend of mine and we see each other quite often. Asked me to mention that he received your last letter and to thank you for your efforts in his behalf. At present he is still marking time. Now that he has the recommendation of Rado (editor of the Guide to the Soviet Union), I believe his outlook is good, but of course Moscow moves slowly. I waited 8 weeks you know and only after I sent a telegram did I get action. Morrison may do likewise if no reply is forthcoming within the next few days. I might also say that once he gets to Moscow I have a good room arranged for him free of charge, and you know what this means in present-day Russia. Saw Mr. Dorn twice but not since I returned from Russia.

I shall be pleased to have a reply from you at some early time relative to my thesis subject and to the two matters which you are to take up with Mr. Joranson. May I also ask what success you had with my application for a fellowship or a scholarship? I don't suppose you will be in residence this summer and as I may want to get in touch with you, I shall appreciate your summer address. Just as soon as I hear from you, I shall inform you of all further developments in connection with my thesis. Permit me to thank you again for all that you have done and are continuing to do for me. Is there anything I can do for you here? I hope I haven't forgotten to thank you for your offer to take books off my hands to the extent of 100 dollars, but I have now come to the conclusion that I shall not take advantage of it: costly as my book investment is I don't see how I can give them up. By the way, bought 3 rather good wall maps of the Post-Revolution Russia; perhaps you would like one or two also for the University?

Sincerely,

Joseph S. Werlin

P.S. I don't mean to burden you with too many things at one time but there is one other matter that I should like to place before you. It concerns the various fields that I must present for oral and written examination in connection with my candidacy for the doctor's degree. It seems no more than right that in view of all the time and labor I have devoted in the general domain of Russian history, that this should count for at least one or two fields in which I should be tested. The university regulations permit the naming of new or special fields when circumstances warrant it, and I believe that my claim is just. You will recall that a somewhat similar exception was made for me in connection with my master's requirements. I have written to Mr. Joranson on this matter too and mentioned that I shall ask you to have a talk with him on it as well.

The Second and Third Congresses of the R.S.D.P.(Bolsh)

I. The Prelude to the 2nd Congress.

   A. General Historical Setting.

      Political, Soc., Econ. Situation, etc.

   B. The "Iskra" Period

      1. Various Revolutionary Currents.

      2. Struggle against "Economism."

      3. Inner-Party Differences.

         a. Development of these differences.
         b. Nature   "   "   "

II. The Second Congress (Summer, 1903).

   A. General Historical Setting.

      1. Strike Movements, etc.

   B. The Sittings of the Second Congress.

      1. The problems: Statement and Analysis.
      2. The Bolsh. proposals and viewpoints.
      3. The Other   "   "   "
      4. The Final Resolutions.

III. The Period Between 2nd and 3rd Congresses.

   A. General Historical Setting.

      1. Russo-Jap War, etc.

   B. Social Currents and Movements.

   C. Sharpening of differences between Bolsh. and Mensh.

      1. Nature of these differences, etc.

IV. The 3rd Congress(London, Spring, 1905)

    A. General Historical Setting

        1. Russo-Jap. War
        2. Worker's and General Social Unrest.
        3. 9th January, etc.

    B. The Sittings of the Third Congress.

        1. The Program; Statement and Analysis.
        2. The Problems, debates, etc.

    C. The Conference of the Mensheviks(1st All-Russ.Conf. of
                                    Party Workers, Geneva, Spring, 1905)

        1. Resolutions, Debates, etc.

Concluding Remarks.

The More Important Sources

Writings of Leaders: and 7
Lenin, Collected Works, Vols 5 & 6 (Years, 1900-5)
Plekhanov, Collected Works, Vols XII-XIII)
Martov and Dan, History of Russ. Soc-Democracy.
Zinoviev, History of the Russ.S.D.Party(Bolsh).
Trotsky, Axelrod, etc, Brochures, Collected Works, etc.

Documentary Sources
1. Full Text of Protocols of 2nd Cong.   (Ordered)
2. Full Text of Protocols of 3rd Congress. (Ordered)
3. R.K.P(B) in Resol. of Congr. a) Congr.
4. How Grew the Bols.Party--Lit.Polemical, 1903-04)
5. History of the R.K.P.(B) in Documents.
6. "Iskra" Nos. 1-52, 1900-03 (Ordered).
7. "Forward" and "Proletarian" Bolsh.Papers of 1905 (Ordered)

May 28, 1928.

Mr. Joseph Werlin,
c/o American Express Co.,
Berlin, Germany.

Dear Mr. Werlin:

I have your letter of May 15th and was glad to hear more in detail about your trip to Moscow.

I think you are wise not to consider writing up your notes for immediate publication in the form of an article until your return.

I shall take up with Mr. Joranson the matters which you mentioned and you will hear from him officially. I have approved the subject of the dissertation. Also I have suggested to Mr. Joranson that you offer Russian history to 1800 as one of the five subjects for the preliminary examination and modern Russian history as the field for the final examination and dissertation. Such an arrangement has been made before so there will be no need of any special decision for your case. You will of course bring back the proper credentials on the work you are doing at Berlin to satisfy the requirements when you make application for credits for this work.

On your preliminary outline the only suggestion that occurs to me is that you do not allow yourself to go too far afield in discussing under each point the "general historical setting." I think it would be well to let me have a more detailed outline in the course of a month or so. I shall be in or around Chicago all summer and in any case letters addressed to me at the University will be forwarded. I note what you say with regard to the books. The hundred dollar offer still holds if you find it necessary to cut the corners and make an economy.

Yours sincerely,

SNH/CF

Stentsch   Grenzbahnhof   Bahnwirt Paul Baer

Dearest:

I was drawn to this city by the remembrance that the great philosopher lived and died here. Nothing could have been more suitable to his memory than his words:

"Two things file the mind with ever new and overpowering wonder and awe, the more often and arrestingly our reflections concern themselves therewith: The bestarred Heaven over me and the moral law in me."

— Immanuel Kant

Return to Berlin in morning.

Königsberg, East Prussia
May 2, 1925
Postcard, Joe to Rose

Der Rote Platz. Parade
Красная площадь. Парад армии.
Revue sur la Place Rouge
The Red Square. Parade

Correspondence

"Deep, deep in the heart of "Red Russia." But Russia is not "red," not bloody but far, far the contrary of what we've been told and imagined. I pinch myself to make sure that it's all reality, that I'm truly in the land where so many weird things have come forth to startle the world."

— Letter to Rose
Moscow, April 10, 1928

THERE ARE CLOSE TO 2,000 photocopied pages of letters from which the following extracts are drawn. Some entries are duplicates — typed reproductions of handwritten letters, copied 60 years later through a secretarial service, reverently commissioned by Ernest Werlin. Whatever the number, this is an astonishing collection, recalling a bygone era when family, friends, and lovers gave each other the gift of time, recording quotidian moments of life, and when postage was remarkably affordable. Sadly, the original correspondence, including postcards and photos, was lost in the course of office and household moves. But there is a benefit in that loss, in that poring over black-on-white photocopies allows objectivity and seems less personally invasive.

The selections which follow were chosen for four primary interests: Joe's changing purpose in keeping the diary; observations and personal experiences that amplify those in the diary; insights into Joe's character, his ambitions and constraints; and progress and challenges in accomplishing the mission of his costly study in Europe.

These letters are especially helpful in filling in missing pieces of Joe's travels to and from Moscow. He offers additional observations about Warsaw, beyond those in the diary pages he sends Rose later from Berlin. On his return travels from Moscow, he sends postcards to Rose from Königsberg and from the rail station in Stentsch. He writes to her from Riga, but he does not write about Riga for the diary. And he mentions writing to her from Leningrad, but either she didn't receive that correspondence or he didn't include descriptions for the diary. There are two explanations: Joe tells Rose that he was worried about Russian censorship of his letters, although he doesn't say what he means by that. Also, Joe expected to write up other impressions from the Soviet Union after he returned to Berlin. For reasons partly explained later, that never happened.

The Diary also doesn't mention Joe's short excursion to Leipzig, the site of the single surviving photo of his travels in 1928. Fortunately, a postcard and letter give us the date and circumstances.

The reader should not imagine that the selected extracts reflect the overall content of the letters. These are love letters! Rarely do the selections reveal a quarter of their substance. Joe is in love to the point of unimaginable distraction from the serious purpose of his travels in Germany and Russia. The letters reveal his cautious but eager overtures to Rose through a progression of increasingly ardent appeals. At the outset, Rose genuinely resists Joe's enticements. Love and marriage were not in her plan when the two were introduced by Joe's classmate from Rice, a Galveston resident, in the summer of 1928. Rose had been accepted into the acclaimed journalism school at the University of Missouri, in Columbia, beginning in the winter term of 1928, and she was determined to follow that path. Gradually, Joe turns to Rose as his confidante. Rose reciprocates with girlish flirtation, yet reveals increasing admiration for her unusual suitor. Soon she offers her publicity skills to promote his scholarly aspirations. He in turn boosts her confidence and supports her ambitions for a career in journalism. By mid-April, they are speaking of marriage. In August, when Joe begins his return voyage home, they have wedding plans for before the year's end.

Neither the Diary nor the letters directly explore the subject of Joe's doctoral studies, but the letters allude to his progress and to frustrations. However, Joe mentions correspondence with his thesis advisor, distinguished Russian specialist Samuel Northrup Harper. (Those letters between "Mr. Werlin" and "Mr. Harper" endure in the Special Collections files at the University of Chicago and are reproduced at the close of this section.) Samuel Harper's encouragement initially fortifies Joe's confidence that with this high-level support and his own rapid progress on his thesis he can count on timely success. The contrast between Joe's optimism in a letter to Rose dated February 26 and his outpouring of anguish on June 20, after he learns that no prospects are materializing, dampens the energy of his succeeding letters. He is comforted only by his joy over being reunited with Rose. He is not prepared for one obstacle after another, which will delay completion of his degree and lead down a very tough road, which they will travel together.

I reserve that story for the Afterword.

À bord De La Salle [ship letterhead], *January 29, 1928*

We must write each other every three days or so. It takes 24 to 30 days to get a letter and its reply from Germany to the United States and back, and probably 35 days from Russia.

I have greatly improved my facility to speak and write German. My Russian has improved too, though, of course, it in no way compares to my German. It is almost impossible to learn two languages equally well simultaneously.

The "diary sheets" which I am enclosing, or else mailing separately, will tell you of practically all of the objective experiences (as well as a few of my subjective emotions that belong to an account of this kind). . . . I have made no attempt to be rhetorical or stylistic, though I have attempted to be somewhat full in treating a number of experiences. I am writing these notes mainly for your information and entertainment, and for my own pleasure in the future. However, it does incidentally serve the purpose of giving practice to my writing facility and powers of description, and a good part of it may serve as a fruitful source of information on European peoples and conditions for my future work. Because of these two factors, I shall occasionally expound at length on various subjects that have caught my attention.

Berlin, *February 4, 1928*

[Rose later notes that this letter was postmarked February 6 and arrived in Columbia, Missouri, on February 17, a much shorter time than anticipated.]

The seminar I am taking has a considerable number of works which are relevant to my thesis subject. From conversations [with professors] I gather that I can get most of the needed material right here in Germany. Whatever is lacking, I can order through one of the Russian bookstores. There are four or five other large sources for books on Russia in addition to the seminar: the State Library, the Socialist headquarters, König (a large Russian bookstore), etc. I haven't visited any of these other places yet, but if it is true that they possess fairly complete stores of information on the Russian Comm. Party, my trip to Russia will not be so necessary. Of course I am terribly anxious to see Russia, but I must consider the expense. Prices in Germany, particularly in Berlin, do not seem much less than in the United States. On the average, they might be 20 to 25 percent less. I had figured on their being at least 50 percent lower and on this basis had calculated my finances. In Russia living is even dearer, I am told. . . .

At the American Express Co.'s office, I found a note waiting for me from one of my closest Chinese friends, Chao-Ting Chi. The note informed me that he was on his way to Moscow, and to be sure and look him up at the Hotel Lux when I got there. . . . This means that I shall have a good friend with me all the time that I am in Russia. . . . I shall write to him at Moscow immediately. More than likely he will be able to help me get in.

I have located a room and have already moved in, baggage and all, with a Jewish family by the name of Kohen. Really an elderly couple, for I believe all the children are married and live elsewhere. I don't know, as yet, much about them, whether I am the only roomer or not, etc. My room is quite large, clean and well furnished. I'd rather it were closer to the University* — about 10 to 15 minutes on the bus and about the same on the *Studebaker* [electric trolley] — but I was told I could do no better.

I fell into luck in meeting a Jewish fellow from California, one Shilkin. I was sitting in a cafe, and recognizing me as an American from my "brogue," he came up and introduced himself. He also came to Germany to work on a Ph.D. thesis, but for one reason or another — I didn't question him closely — he decided to take his time and turn his attention to other things. He is in some kind of business here and is clearly not too well off. The fellow has more nerve — took me into a half-dozen fine cafes and dance places without it costing either of us a penny. He would rush into a place, I at his heels, and pretend to look for Mr. Brown or Mr. White. Thus I was enabled to see something of Berlin's nightlife at no cost to myself. We walked the principal streets together and he explained everything as we went along. He is quite a nice-looking man and I believe we shall get along very well together. He is also very much interested in Russia. Is from there originally and speaks the language.

Berlin, February 7, 1928

My new friend Shilkin is turning out to be quite a find. His adventures of the last 12 years are hair-raising: on the Eastern front

---

* The University of Berlin was named Friedrich Wilhelm University in 1810 and renamed Humboldt University of Berlin in 1949.

in 1914 . . . desertion from the Russian Army . . . wandering through southern Russia . . . arrest in Siberia . . . eight months in prison with death once or twice just at his door . . . journey through Siberia and Mongolia to China . . . interpreter, etc., with American Army in Siberia . . . six years in Philippines . . . America . . . journey through Siberia and Russia . . . Germany . . . say, that man's good! Going to teach me Russian. Knows all about Berlin; in touch with big men all over. He's a find. Hope he doesn't turn out a flat tire.

Berlin, Sunday, February 12, 1928

As to what you have written me with regard to Shirley making a copy of my "diary sheets" and the possibility of some of it being printable, has set me to thinking . . . . Do you think there can be found a paper that would be willing to consider me as a sort of special correspondent and pay me for what might be called a weekly letter, for example, some such headings as "Scenes and Observations in Berlin," "Berlin as It Is Today," "Weekly Letter from Our Special Berlin Correspondent," etc. It would for the most part be light stuff, for instance, descriptions of the people, streets, nightlife, operas, cafes, parks, buildings; amusing accounts of German ways, mannerisms, eccentricities, types; attitudes toward life, toward Americans and other nationalities; effects of the World War; light touching on political, social, economic conditions. I could occasionally bring in descriptions and references to other parts of Germany; perhaps also Russia. In the main, however, I would stick to Berlin. It is true that I haven't too much time, but if I were paid something, I might be moved to do it. . . . There must be thousands of people in America curious to learn how people live and act and think in Germany today . . . . They can't expect me to write just silly comic stuff. Take the note about "begging" in Germany. I have included three instances, but beyond merely describing them, I have touched on their social significance and have occasionally fallen into a didactic view.

Somehow I find the hours moving by so rapidly that I scarcely know where the time is to come from that I must use for the "diary." I have given up the thought that I once had of making each day's incidents and experiences the subject of a complete account, as in the case of the 20 days which I spent on the ship. Then I had relatively plenty of leisure time; now it is impossible. Hence what I shall do is to describe, every other day or so, some little incident or observation in a topical manner, as against an autobiographical or narrative form. What think you?

I am rapidly feeling quite at home in Berlin. My German is getting better all the time; I make my way about from place to place without difficulty; I am learning where to buy everything I want; I have one good friend and a very helpful landlady. In short, I am losing my feeling of strangeness. This week I began taking German lessons from Mrs. Apt, daughter of Mrs. Kohen, my landlady, and Russian lessons from my friend Shilkin. The biggest thing I can do for myself is to learn to use these two languages easily. And that is not such a light task. There are ways and ways of knowing a language. There is the tongue of the man in the street, and the vocabulary and diction of the educated man. Those in America, particularly Jews, who tell you so rapidly and glibly that they know German are to be laughed at. To know a polished, educated German is quite, quite another thing, and that is my problem. As to the Russian, that's a bit more difficult to say. At present I am interested in knowing how to read it well, for it's a tremendously difficult language for a foreigner. Many a time I am almost in despair over my progress. This week I have devoted myself largely to reading and writing exercises in both tongues. Probably next week I shall begin to approach my thesis material more closely.

My plans with regard to Russia have not advanced. I am still waiting for answers from Russia as to whether I can stay with a private family. But even if I go, I shall more than likely not stay long. The money is a very important item with me, and I should like to use some of it to see more of Germany and perhaps Austria & Hungary. However, to be safe, I shall have in my application for admittance into the U.S.S.R. tomorrow.

Berlin, February 19, 1928

I am enclosing a number of "notes" which may prove interesting. As you will observe, they are written in a more formal fashion than the earlier ones. I thought by doing so you could get a better idea as to their printable value. However, in the future, I shall be slightly more personal and informal, and if anything is found of a printable nature, it can be "edited" and fashioned to suit.

Berlin, February 26, 1928

My life here is just settling into routine channels. The surroundings are losing their novelty, the people, their interest to me. That is bad — it will make it harder to endure the five months yet to come. This whole week I spent in book-hunting at various bookstores — on Russian and German history — in attending two lectures, and in my usual reading of German and Russian. By next week or the week thereafter I hope to begin advising on my subject. Until now it has only been practice in the two languages and in orienting myself with respect to sources of information. My best bet is going to be the seminar library of the University, the State Library, and the Russian bookstore, King's [König]. On the basis of the material in these three places, I have to find enough information and nonfiction to write a worthwhile thesis. What I shall lack, I shall try and obtain either from Russia directly or from the various universities and sources in the West European countries.

I wrote letters to two of my Chicago professors last week, asking their assistance in obtaining a fellowship. The three or four fellowships in the department of history are announced on April 1st, so that if they haven't committed themselves to anyone else, $450 to $600 (I don't know exactly) will come in very handy to us, and the distinction is worth a good deal too. If there are more needy or worthy cases than I, perhaps I may be offered a scholarship, which usually pays tuition — about $225. This too would be very acceptable. We mustn't hope too much on either, for the department is a very large one, and I am really known only to four of the professors. Each man usually has a favorite, and besides, the Russian department is considered as a sort of appendix. But we shall see.

I am reading at present a new work that has come out here, *The Strife over the Sergeant Grischa* [by Arnold Zweig]. It is being read and discussed very actively owing to its frank portrayal of the military system with which Germany lived, particularly during the Great War, with which the book deals. If it is already translated, try and read it. By the way, honey, do get hold of Katherine Mayo's book, *Mother India*, and read it. It will make a tremendous impression on you, and while it is certainly a good book for you to read, don't take her conclusions too seriously. She has greatly overdrawn the fiction. I have succeeded in making some good buys in the second-hand bookstores — really not that: either they are called antiquarists in Germany, and mean places that sell rare books or old editions, or they outright sell used books. The books deal with German history and will be quite necessary to me as texts and reference books in the future. To my chagrin I haven't as yet been able to locate such bargains in Russian history, or in fact even new works on old Russia, but perhaps later on.

Berlin, March 18, 1928

Darn, am getting worried about my Russian visa. Now that I've made up my mind to go, I don't want to be disappointed. Can't understand why Chi is delaying to answer me. Perhaps he's too intoxicated with his wife. I told you she was Jewish, didn't I?

Columbia, Missouri, Saturday, March 24, 1928

[Letter from Rose to Joe]

Joe, darling, your diary notes are as interesting as they can be. Really, if I ever go to Berlin, I believe I'll be able to find the places you talk about, or at least point them out, without any difficulty whatsoever. Oddly enough, the very point which you brought out was told to our class in sociology (about Germany's rehabilitation, etc.) and was also pointed out in an article in the *New York Times*. For fear lest you have not gotten in touch with some of the literature about Russia, I am going to enclose some of the things from the *Times*. Somehow, whether it is because I happen to notice it more easily or whether it is because it is so, there seems to be so much material bounding up about Russia and Germany today. You were undoubtedly correct when you said that Russia and Germany were going to be "live historical" subjects.

Berlin, March 25th, 1928

The weather here has greatly improved within the last three days. An overcoat is still necessary, but the sun is undeniably warm and pleasant, and all nature seems to be inviting one to go outdoors. I wrote you that I visited the zoo here Thursday. Friday afternoon I thought I should like to witness a Reichstag [German parliament] sitting before the present session ends, that is, March 31st. A pass or some such formality is required, so I took the opportunity at the same time of calling on Edgar Ansel

Mourer, the *Chicago Daily News* representative in Berlin, partly because he could probably obtain the permission for me, partly because I wanted to make his acquaintance. The *Chicago Daily News* has, in my estimation, with perhaps the exception of the *New York Times*, the best foreign-news service of any paper in the U.S., staff and quality and length of articles considered. Of this excellent staff, the two Mourer brothers are perhaps the best, Paul Scott [Mourer] in Paris and Edgar Ansel [Mourer] in Berlin. I have kept up with those two and always found their articles written as from people who had a good understanding of their subject. I had called on Mourer soon after I arrived in Berlin, but he was away on his vacation and returned only a few days ago. He was consequently quite busy, so I merely exchanged a few words with him. Very friendly and a rather younger man than I had pictured. Apparently had a hard time learning the language, and I gather he still has a weak grasp on it. Said it took him two years to make any headway with it. I thank heavens that I had my ear prepared for it, as well as a small vocabulary, by the Jewish tongue. But while Jewish springs from German and hundreds of simple words are common to both, they are two entirely dissimilar tongues, with German much more difficult to learn owing to its cumbersome sentence structure and certain of its grammatical forms.

Coming back to Mr. Mourer, he was very cordial and got in touch with one of the legation counselors of the German foreign office in order to obtain a pass for me. I shall call on this man tomorrow, not only for the pass but to get a little information about the political leaders here. Possibly I may decide for the sake of meeting such people, and for the information, to interview the leading men of the many political groups. If I do, I shall more than likely submit the results to one of the American newspapers for publication. There is a difficulty, however, that I must go to these men in the capacity of a private individual without the card even of a small newspaper.

I have interrupted the writing of this letter by witnessing the Russian film *The End of St. Petersburg*. It affected me so much that I am enclosing a diary page or two describing the picture and my reactions.

So you like the diary, honey. But honestly, you are too flattering. Just the same, though, your good opinion gives me a lot of pleasure and is causing me to take the diary more seriously. It has become almost a pleasure to sit down and extend myself on my various thoughts and experiences. This you may rely on: that I endeavor to be painfully exact and truthful in my descriptions or accounts. . . . I simply am determined not to be a shoddy, rambling thinker. I want at all times to be precise, accurate, and, above all, truthful. One of my chief desires is to avoid anything that smacks of demagoguery.

One of the things that I consider a great personal achievement and look back to with pride was my decision, several years ago, to ruthlessly disregard or strike out words and sentences that were not relevant to my topic, to emancipate myself from word-idolization, to realize that words are not ends in themselves.

About having my stuff printed — you're a dear for thinking of submitting some of my stuff to certain papers. I'm sorry now that I didn't make arrangements with one or two before I left. But you see, I didn't know just what conditions I would face when I got here. I hadn't decided on my thesis subject and didn't know what hardships I would have to undergo to find and write up material. Not that I haven't now long hours of daily reading that I must do, but I do have an hour or two a day that I can devote to other things, at least until I get deeper into my subject. This latter will be the case in a short while, yet it will not be so bad that I can't find time for an hour or two of diary narration. Regular correspondence writing is another thing. That involves interviews, varied reading, exactness, etc., and I'm sure I couldn't do this.

Berlin, Thursday, March 29, 1938

Chi's letter tells me that he is doing all he can to facilitate my entrance into the [Soviet] Union. This morning I had the Russian Legation wire Moscow relative to my visa, and perhaps a favorable reply will be forthcoming within a few days. If this should be the case, I shall immediately take the train for Moscow. I am anxious now to go, for I want to see the land and have little time to delay, owing to the fact that the spring semester at the University begins April 15th. This is in reality only the official opening day, and lectures actually begin about the end of the month, but I want to be in Berlin in time to adjust myself to the lectures and general routine. If I reach Moscow by the 3rd or 4th of the month, by staying there only ten days and spending a short time in Leningrad with Mrs. Holland's brother* . . . . In this case, I can be back by the 20th in

---

* Mrs. Holland was the wife of Herbert Holland, owner of the Holland Furniture Company; Joe's father worked for Mr. Holland as a bookkeeper.

Berlin, which will be ample time. My "south-German trip" is knocked to smithereens by this delay in hearing from the Soviet Union, but perhaps I can be compensated by weekend trips to various localities of the country.

Sweetness, don't expect me to answer your four wonderful letters at this time. Wait until Sunday, when I shall write in detail on all their points and possibly tell you that I am on my way to "Red Russia."

Berlin, Sunday, April 1, 1928

From my side things are not bad. The weekends are the worst, as you say, but in company with Alex they pass quickly enough. This week I have an extra treat in the person of one Mr. Glusman, a Canadian who is in Berlin preparing to enter Moscow. I am describing him in the diary. We may go together. Perhaps Monday or Tuesday will find us on our way. I told you I sent a letter to the Foreign Office? If they delay much longer, it is very questionable indeed if the trip will be worth the expense. As it is, it is very questionable — 10 to 15 days at a cost of $100 to $125 — if I get by that easily. Saturday I actually was on the point of backing out. I thought it over again and the expense seemed far and above my capacity to pay for such relatively small return. But there returned the argument of the great value of the trip in terms of prestige — to be introduced as having just returned from Russia; in the future as lending insight to my words in a lecture or general address — and this won out again. One good thing exists now that did not when I first arrived: I know exactly what I want to find out relative to my thesis: what advice, information, books, etc. I appreciate your encouragement to make the trip and your arguments along the same line.

Gee, this is a punk letter [referring to his handwriting]. If you only knew what torture it is to hold the pen just now. It's always hard on my hand to write with a pen and sometimes almost impossible, as on this occasion. I've fallen down on you in the matter of the diary this week too. Haven't written a thing so far, though will write you about the Canadian tonight and enclose the sheets in the letter. I have jotted down a brief outline on what I wish to say, and if it's any good in your estimation, I wish you'd send on a typewritten copy to Father so he may turn it over to the *Herald*. On those strictly Jewish topics it may do "our cause" some good to get a little publicity among the Texas Jewish Congregation. But do exactly as you like in the matter: you're my manager — yes, and my self-declared boss — who has all my loyalty and for whom, if need be, I am willing to work day and night . . . .

P.S. Sweetheart, I wrote out the story. Not so good. But if you think it's worthwhile to send it on to the *Herald* you might add a title to it, perhaps "A Jewish 'Innocent' Abroad," in reference to Mark Twain's *The Innocents Abroad*, or perhaps "Epic of an Israelite in a Strange Land."

Possibly once I get into the Union, and the costs are not as high as I expect, I may stay three weeks or so. It is all right with the University if I matriculate as late as May 1st. I won't be missing any lectures, either, for they do not begin in actuality until then. The longer I stay in Russia the better. Three months would be even better. Did I not want the prestige and academic credit of having attended the University of Berlin, I would certainly stay there that long, that is, if the expense could be kept down.

So, dearest, Tuesday or Wednesday, if the gods are kind, may find your "boy" on his way to that mysterious and misunderstood land sometimes called Red Russia and a thousand other similar things. . . . But as a last word, don't be surprised if the next letter tells you that I'm not going: who knows what answer I will receive.

The Inferior Half

Berlin, April 3, 1928

I finally received a reply in the affirmative from Moscow, and tomorrow evening, unless something totally unforeseen occurs, I shall be on my way to Russia. By leaving here 6:18 p.m. I shall arrive in Moscow 2:00 p.m. Friday, i.e., about 44 hours later. My route takes me through Poland and White Russia [Belarus], through such cities as Warsaw, Minsk (White Russia), and Smolensk, and then Moscow. I confess to quite a thrill at the prospect ahead of me. The multitude of fantastic reports about "Red Russia" has affected me too, despite my knowledge to the contrary. How long I shall remain depends entirely on the cost of living. I simply cannot afford more than $100, and with this as a limit I shall do and see what I can. If it will allow me, I shall return by way of Leningrad, Riga, and Königsberg . . . . I shall take as full notes as I can without running counter to the censor, and upon returning to Berlin will round them out and endeavor to make the greatest possible use out of them. Don't worry about me in the slightest. Everything will be all right.

Warsaw, Poland, April 5, 1928

[Postcard: reverse shows view of the "Grand Theatre"]

Dearest one,

I'm going through this city top to bottom. Very, very interesting from innumerable angles. The Jews especially: the home of all the "funny" ones. You should see what I am seeing. I shall do my best to give you a faithful and accurate report of all my chief observations and impressions. But you must wait until I return to Berlin. I can't take a chance with the Russ. Gov., and besides am completely out of the diary paper. Thinking of you every minute. If only Rose was here too!

[Sent from Berlin? For the diary?]

The Jews of Warsaw: really, truly, a non-Western people. . . . With few exceptions, five-foot-six is the maximum, and about five-two the average. The bodies are poor and weak, the chests fallen-in, the shoulders round or bowed, the looks gaunt and heavy, the eyes poor and weak with inflamed-looking eyelids or else burning with an unnatural fire, as though in fever. . . . In clothing, the West has touched most of the younger ones. The "greener" is gone, but in general appearance, carriage, ways of talking, walking, acting, clearly not Western as we know it in America. Adding to this effect are the thousands of representatives of the unadulterated older things: the hundreds of old Jews with the long, straggling, unsanitary beards, the skullcaps with just a faint shadow of a bill, the long, black overcoats trailing the ground, the walking with head and shoulders facing the ground and hands behind the back, . . . the many youths with flapping, curling earlocks reaching halfway to the chin and curling up to meet the brim of the hat, usually set firmly on the ears, the still younger boys with the same black caps as the old men and peculiar little ways.

Stolpce [Stowbtsy], Poland, April 6, 1928 9:00 P.M.

[Postcard: reverse shows churches]

Dearest:

This is the last town in Poland, a customs place, therefore. We are here for two hours, after which we ride to Nieharelaje, the Russian toll-point. Am writing down a full account of everything. Shall send it to you just as soon as I can write it legibly and on the usual diary sheets.

Moscow, U.S.S.R., Tuesday, April 10, 1928

Deep, deep in the heart of "Red Russia." But Russia is not "red," not bloody, but far, far the contrary of what we've been told and imagined. I pinch myself to make sure that it's all reality, that I'm truly in the land where so many weird things have come forth to startle the world. I just can't make myself feel the hero and adventurer, the courageous explorer and self-sacrificing scientist who has penetrated into a fearful land in order that the world might profit from his daring. Such excellent relatives I have, so hospitable and warm is everyone, so many friends I've made, so completely at home do I feel — wonderful, amazing, unbelievable. . . . Had the exquisite pleasure of meeting with my close friend Chao-Ting Chi yesterday. Since last spring we hadn't seen each other, so the meeting, particularly under such strange circumstances, was unusually cordial.

The BOKC* are taking me in hand and have outlined a truly marvelous program of interviews and sightseeing for me. If they live up to their promises, I shall come out of Moscow and Leningrad with a knowledge of the Soviet government, the institutions, and the life and general feelings of the people that very few foreigners possess. For I am in a truly excellent position. Thru the BOKC, I shall see and hear all that the visitor — even the most distinguished — has been allowed to see and hear, but more than that, through my relatives and friends I come into aspects of life and points of view and states of mind that the great majority of visitors never have.

---

* BOKC (VOKS in English) was an acronym for the Society for Cultural Relations with Foreign Countries.

Moscow, Wednesday, April 11, 1928

[Postcard: reverse shows Mausoleum of Lenin]

Dearest:

Here is the mausoleum of Lenin. On certain days of the week it is permitted to enter and gaze upon his features. Terribly cold and disagreeable ever since I arrived, which interferes with my sightseeing. Will write again shortly.

Moscow, U.S.S.R., Saturday, April 14, 1928

I have been unfortunate in only one respect here, the weather. Yesterday, owing to the brightness of the sun, I anticipated good weather, but this morning showed me that I was wrong. All Moscow is under a mantle of white and the snow is still coming down with force and persistence. Typical Russian weather. These seven days of cold and slush have certainly interfered with my sightseeing, but on the other hand I can by no means say that my trip was not worthwhile. On the contrary, I have learned more than a thousand books could teach me. The BOKC continues to arrange interesting things for me to do. Yesterday it enabled me to go through a large textile factory from top to bottom, and the day before, to be shown every detail of the new Lenin Institute, including the original manuscripts and writings of Lenin. The other night I attended the studio of the Little Theater and tonight have tickets for another. I am gradually seeing the most important buildings, streets, monuments, districts, shops, and other things of value in forming an idea of Moscow. I have also spoken to quite a few people and am learning the state of mind and general spirit of the people with respect to their condition. . . .

I cannot begin to tell you how kind everyone is to me. Rebecca [Rebecca Torpisorna, a relative] is a charming woman and the acme of thoughtfulness. Through her I managed to meet another family of relatives, the head of which is a physician and a very intelligent man, who will be able to supply me with considerable information. I have been out in company with my friend Chi on two occasions and plan to spend more time next week. As I wrote you in my card, love, this visit of mine to Europe is performing a sort of pioneer work which will "dot" *our* way half across the globe with friends; wherever we shall go, a warm hand will be waiting to clasp our own. The traditional kindness of the Russian people of which I have heard so much is in every respect being borne out by my own experience. In America we have lost the pleasure which can come from spending the evening in sitting at home and talking and carrying on with friends, but in Russia it is still in vogue — the winter evenings are too disagreeable to be outdoors — and I have had this simple yet exquisite pleasure on several occasions, rendered all the more so by the feel of the hospitable glass of tea under your hands or the experience of the warm liquid coursing down your esophagus. I must confess that the wonderful spirit here — a spirit thoroughly inexplicable to the average American, should he observe the material surroundings — is rapidly capturing me, despite my original great prejudices.

Officially I am treated as a distinguished visitor and shown every courtesy. The newspapers printed an account of my visit and purpose in coming, and I cannot help but appreciate all of this.

Moscow, April 19, 1928

[Postcard: reverse shows view of the Kremlin]

Sweetheart:

Here's a rather good view of the Kremlin, the historic section of Moscow containing the palaces, churches, and government building of the Tsars. Am sending you a letter today also. By the way, discount considerably the beauty of the view; both of us know how flattering pictures can be.

Moscow, Sunday, April 21, 1928

Three of your glorious soul-elevating letters came to hand in this isolated far-off region, where, despite its abundant evidence of calm, order, and civilization, I feel untold miles from you. I could kiss myself for guessing that Russia possesses at least some shreds and tatters of peace and stability, and hence that I could have a few of your letters forwarded in consciousness that their precious contents would not be lost to me. . . . I have to laugh every time I recall your statement in one of the three letters about how "determined and definite and brave" I am for making a trip "into that chaos." I just read it to Rebecca Torpisorna, my relative, and we both went into gales of laughter. If you could only visualize my present surroundings and how much order and "respectability" and tranquility it suggests.

It is Sunday morning and to my ears as I write comes the continuous sound of the chimes in the tower of the church just outside my window, and as my eye sweeps the horizon, I see tower after tower, spire after spire, of the scores and scores of other churches, symbolic — at least so it is commonly thought — of God's grace and benign approval. Even the sun itself, heretofore so terribly frigid and sullen, seems to have reconciled itself to this land and is sending forth kindly rays to cheer the people who for so long have been entreating its favor. Though it is past 10:00, the whole city appears to be sleeping still, seeking to make up for lost sleep or for tiredness from the labor and excitement of the work-a-day week, just like every other city of the civilized world. Indeed, overlooking the peculiar shapes of the church towers and spires which everywhere greet the eye — for Moscow is a city of churches — with their clusters of gilt domes and their minarets, and surveying the panorama of rooftops and upper portions of the dwellings, one might well imagine he is back in some part of America — not Houston, perhaps, but certainly in many industrial towns of Pennsylvania or Ohio. And then you write what a brave, courageous lad I am to venture into this "chaos!" Ha-ha! But really, honey, you are not to be blamed. Nine hundred and ninety-nine out of any thousand Americans or Europeans, probably even a greater percentage, have a similar conception of present-day Russia. I too had it to some extent. But while it is true that this land is not running blood at every foot of ground and that people in Moscow are living much the same sort of life as everywhere else, there still remain countless items which feed our sense of oddness, romance, and adventure.

Moscow is not a fair example of Russia. The real, true Russia lies in the villages and smaller towns and buried in the spirit of the people. I have lots to tell you about them — lots. Most of this you will have to wait for until I return to the States. The more apparent and surface things you shall know from my diary. . . .

Did I tell you I received a letter from Dr. Cohen yesterday? Made me feel good. I feel a bit guilty, though, for while I sent him quite a few postals [prepaid postal cards], I failed to write a letter. He asks me to write again, and I shall do so as soon as I reach Berlin. I sent him a card from Warsaw and also one from here, as I did to most of the other Galveston and Houston friends. . . .

This letter hardly sounds as though I am writing it under fearful or unusual conditions, does it? That's your best proof how perfectly normal life is in Russia.

. . . A whole day has elapsed since the last line. You just don't know what a popular and busy man your future husband is. Everyone wants to meet the American or to invite him to dinner or in some way to show him kindness. Yesterday I had dinner at the sister of Mrs. Holland, while at night I attended for the first time the famous Grand [Bolshoi] Theater of Moscow. No wonder the Russian theater is so celebrated. *The Red Poppy* was a superb spectacle: a ballet in which everything was carried on by pantomime, dancing, and symbol. I hope to describe the unforgettable creation in some detail in "our diary."

So your first attempt with my writing came back with a rejection slip [likely from the *St. Louis Globe*, where Rose earlier spoke of submitting his work]. Really, that's to be expected. No responsible newspaper would print feature articles on political and social matters by a correspondent whose background, personality, and point of view is unknown to them. . . . But my main ambition is not to write for newspapers but for periodicals read by men in my profession. That will be the thing that will give me the publicity I need and help in giving me a good job and, in general, the recognition that I need. I shall very seriously attempt to do this in connection with my experiences here in Russia. But you understand that for serious, scholarly periodicals, it is not enough to have a mass of data or material. It is necessary that this be exact and copiously peppered with statistics and quotations, and for this I am really unprepared. I simply can't afford the time necessary to refer to the necessary works in order to lend a scholarly appearance to my writing. But just the same, I shall gather and edit my present material in some fashion and shall set it down in the diary. If time permits, I shall prepare some of it for immediate sending to a periodical for consideration; if not, I shall wait until I return to America and there at more leisure couch it in an acceptable form and endeavor to have it printed.

You were right: this trip to Russia, though only for three weeks, is of incalculable benefit to me, not so much from the standpoint of my thesis, but from the fact that it has given me an understanding of both the old and the new Russia which no amount of reading could have done. . . .

Today — it is now 6:00 p.m. — I spent most of the time getting visas from the different consulates through whose countries I must pass on my way back, and in having certain books that I purchased forwarded to me at Berlin. Everything takes time in these European lands, particularly in Russia. Oh, I have a long and bitter story to tell you of European procrastination and general inefficiency. Tomorrow night at 11:30 I take the night train for Leningrad. I may stay there until Thursday or until Saturday, depending if I receive free lodging at one or another of the people for whom I have regards [one is Mrs. Holland's brother]. Leningrad is an exceptionally modern city for this part of the world and equally beautiful, so I am told. I shall then leave for Riga, arriving there about 24 hours later. . . . On an extra page I am attempting to explain this schedule and this map. Try to follow progress on the map. Whenever time permits, I shall send you a card or letter, and in this way you will be able to check my wanderings. . . .

And now, my sweetheart, you must permit me to say adieu for this time. I have quite a few more letters and postals to write and a large number of thoughts to develop for the diary. As I mentioned, I leave here for Leningrad tomorrow, that is, Tuesday, the 23rd, at 11:30 p.m., arriving there at 10:00 a.m. Shall stay there for one to three days and then go farther . . . .

Moscow, Wednesday, April 24, 1928, 11:00 p.m.

[There is some confusion in the date of this letter. Joe says he hopes to be in Berlin by the 28th.]

I'm certainly lonesome for you just now. Perhaps it is due to my conversation with Chi, my Chinese friend, whom I left just a few minutes ago. We sat in a small "cooperative" restaurant not far from his hotel and talked for two hours or more on various subjects but in the end returning, as we invariably do, to our respective affairs of the heart. So similar they are in many ways! I told you he is married, to a Jewish girl from New York City. Too bad she left for New York sometime before I arrived in Moscow. . . .

Moscow is a terribly long way from home, but do you know, honey, that despite the many, many strange things about the place, I frequently lose consciousness of the fact that I am not in familiar surroundings. Seems as though the human mind has the faculty of quickly adjusting itself to a new environment, or rather, the imagination ceases to work. It ceases to compare, and hence the new environment loses its novelty. For instance, in the last two or three days when I spent so much time at the Hotel Europe in company with Chi. Just like old times back in Chicago, where of a winter evening we would spend hour after hour in the most absorbing conversation, very, very often with the love motif.

Monday I expect to leave the city for Berlin, unless something unforeseen arises to interfere. My trip to Nizhny Novgorod did not take place. It would have meant two nights of traveling, coming and going, and would have been made under terribly disagreeable weather. I have certainly been unlucky in the latter respect. Continuous snow, cold drizzle, slush, and general unpleasantness. You can't imagine what an uninviting sight Moscow presents in such weather. The pavement in most of the streets consists of rough brick or cobblestones, which are now in a terrible state of dilapidation, so that mud and deep puddles of water and filth and slush greet one everywhere and must be traversed in order to get anywhere. For the most part, it has been no pleasure whatever in going to various sections of the city to visit the places of interest; in fact, it has been responsible for considerably limiting my sightseeing. Another phenomenon checking any tourist enthusiasm is the crowded condition of the streetcars. I have never seen anything like it before. This is due to the fact that the trains, aside from a few dozen buses, are the only means of transportation in this city of almost two million inhabitants.

Day Later

I've got lots of diary material. Not nearly as much on Russia as I should like, yet fairly ample and exact for the short time I am here. Everyone is kind and helpful to me, and only the terrible weather and the shortness of my visit prevents me from obtaining full information on every topic in which I am interested. Just as soon as I reach Berlin, I shall begin developing the notes to a complete form and send them on to you. I hope to add a considerable mass of interesting material during my return trip home, particularly in connection with my contemplated stopovers in Leningrad, Riga, and Königsberg. A sample of the kindness which I continually meet up with took place this morning at the Lenin Institute. One of the leading scholars there, a personal friend of Lenin, gave me gratis a fine-bound volume of the Lenin work that is of particular interest to me, autographed it, and promised me every type of assistance, including a copy of a new volume of Lenin just as soon as he finishes editing it and it comes from the press. I am enclosing for your benefit a copy of the newspaper announcement dealing with my arrival, which someone was kind enough to give me. Please save it, as it is the only one I have and may come in useful one day should I desire to return to Russia.

If I can get away, I desire very much to leave Moscow on Monday. By spending five or six days on the way, as I plan, this will put me in Berlin by the 28th. But I fear that I should be delayed. Visas from the Russian govt. to go out, visas from the consulates of the different countries through which I have to pass — four (such is the curse of boundaries in Europe) — etc., all take time, much time, in these European lands.

Leningrad, Saturday, April 28, 1928

[Postcard]

Am here for the second day already. Will leave for Riga on Sunday, and shall spend Monday there. Leningrad a great improvement over Moscow, but seems to be deteriorating rapidly. Too bad I can't find better cards. New ones not being made. You shall have a card from Riga.

Columbia, Missouri, Sunday, April 29, 1928

[Letter from Rose, mailed to Joe care of American Express Company in Berlin]

I am enclosing for you the surprise — it is some of your diary extracts which were published in my paper! To think, darling, you rated the University of Missouri magazine section! There's some advantage in having a sweetheart who is a journalist. Now, isn't there? 'Fess up. You see, this was the travel edition, so of course your travel notes were timely. You are the only one, however, who had anything in it outside of the school or school connections. They cut it down some, but at that you got a whole page in.

I've just been thinking. Now that you are back from Russia, I wonder if it would not pay you to rent a typewriter and try to send some articles in for publication. . . .

I am anxious that you do some writing. Am glad that you got this in the *Missourian*. Of course they do not pay, but it rates very well and that helps some.

Riga, Latvia, April 30, 1928

Dearest,

I am writing this from the Imperial Hotel, where I shall stay for the night. I've written you a postal already, but I know you won't mind if I supplement it by a letter.

I have spent the whole day rambling through a large part of the city. This is one of the finest and most interesting towns in Europe that I have seen. As clean as you could desire, excellent shops crammed with first-class merchandise, remarkably up to date yet preserving withal such a charm and impression of bygone times that I have experienced delight after delight and my wanderings have given me untold pleasure. . . . Just coming from Russia, this seems Paradise itself. Nowhere in Europe have I seen such well-dressed, smart-looking people. The up-to-dateness of the girls is astounding. Such clothes and makeup is not to be excelled in New York itself.

Not the least prosperous-looking are the Jewish people. Almost every other store is Jewish-owned and I am glad to say that they are about the best-looking type of Jews that I have observed in this part of the world. I have seen some quite pretty girls among them, and from the standpoint of clothes and general appearance they certainly match our best in America.

The influence of German culture is very apparent. Riga is a meeting point of Teutonic and Slavic influences, and exhibits traces of both, with the former predominating. The admixture seems a very happy one, if I am permitted to judge hastily. The cleanliness, efficiency, and general solidity and worth of the German is combined in the people with the lighter disposition and more mobile features of the Slav.

Such a charming city, so clean, so many remains of an ancient past, such a beautiful river as the Dvina, such an interesting waterfront, with ships every few feet, a market crowded with booths that has not changed its appearance since the days of feudalism — at least, not very much — such winding, twisting streets, with the upper stories of the houses almost touching . . . .

The Latvians are all but an unknown people to me. The upper classes, as I said, are a mixture of German and Slav, or else Jewish, but the peasants are a distinctive people, neither German nor Slav yet possessing features of both. The Latvian language stands out almost by itself in Europe and is next to impossible to learn because of this. In my diary I shall write down a few common words just to show you how entirely different it is from anything you know or have some inkling about.

The total number of Latvians is very little. About six million, I believe. Riga is about the only large city and is the heart and core of its life. If Riga dies, the country dies with it. Actually, there is some fear that this will be the case. Riga's trade and industry has been built up in connection with Russia; now that they are separated and only a small trade relation exists, the industrial life of Riga has greatly slowed down. Unless trade connections are restored, or a substitute is found, Riga must die.

These little Baltic states are very interesting. So little is known about them except that they exist. Tomorrow I shall pass through another – Lithuania. Sorry I couldn't see something of Estonia too; didn't have time. All three countries speak totally separate and distinct languages. Lithuanian is even more unrecognizable than Latvian, I am told. It is closer to the Slavic than the latter, I believe, Latvian having some connection with Finnish. One thing is sure: neither a Russian nor a German can recognize any of the words except those of recent borrowing and international usage. I am enclosing part of a Latvian newspaper, that you may have a better idea of what the language looks like. What Estonian is like I do not know at all.

Tomorrow morning I leave for Königsberg. Unless I change my mind at the last minute, I shall remain over for 24 hours. I want to see the city, of course, but my money is running so low and my expenses have been so heavy that I hesitate about adding to my already large debts.

Königsberg, East Prussia, May 2, 1928

[Postcard: reverse not copied, presumably showing a statue of Immanuel Kant]

Dearest:

I verily believe that I was drawn to this city by the remembrance that the great philosopher lived and died here. I know of nothing that could have been more suitable to his memory than these own great words of his:

"Two things fill the mind with ever new and overpowering wonder and awe, the more often and arrestingly our reflections concern themselves therewith: The bestarred Heaven over me and the moral law in me." [Immanuel Kant]

Stentsch [Szczaniec], Wednesday, May 4, 1928, 10:30 p.m.

[Postcard]

Honey:

At the last town in Germany — stopped for an hour preparatory to passing the Polish Customs. Stentsch is just a little place. Sitting in a little restaurant along the R.R. track — drizzling and quite cold — dark as pitch. Reach Warsaw 9:00 tomorrow morning. Will stop a day. Getting farther from you. Watch my progress on a map.

Tenderly, Joe

Berlin, Monday, May 7, 1928

Returned from Russia on Thursday to find six letters from you, and on Saturday received two more, making eight in all. . . .

We both have heavy responsibilities on our shoulders. Friends, admirers, and well-wishers are sometimes a great burden, that's clear. But one thing I believe we have the right to comfort ourselves with: the world must allow us a reasonable length of time to show it our worth. Furthermore, that this "worth" is by no means to be translated as being achieved by screaming front-page headlines. Very often this latter is accomplished at the sacrifice of what is truly precious or noble in human nature.

I want to write you lengthy letters, to tell you everything, but that's so hard to do with pen and I'm so pressed for time these next three months. I must have that thesis all but completed when I return. I shall have all I could do preparing for the many examinations that await me in the spring. . . . I now have most of the material I need; the task now is to go through it, organize my thoughts and notes, and whip the dissertation into some sort of shape. This would not be so bad, did I not have 10 or 12 lectures to attend every week, which, in coming and going to the University, in actuality means twice that length of time. One thing is good: I need only listen. As far as I know, there will be no reading or reports required of me. Then too, spring is here and summer will soon follow. On the whole, I am relatively immune to their solicitations, but occasionally I yield, which means the loss of several more hours weekly.

I confess to a little disappointment in not hearing from Chicago with regard to my scholarship. That in itself does not mean a negative result. I should be answered either way. But just the same, would like to know positively at an early date. Don't say anything about the matter at all; we'll see what the future brings.

Berlin, Sunday, May 13, 1928

Now, as to myself: First of all, while not officially enrolled as yet, I am sitting in on various lectures at the University. As a foreigner I was compelled to take an examination to test my knowledge of the language before being allowed to register. I did this this week, passed all right, and on the 21st will be matriculated. The system here varies in many details from America. There is no roll call, no examinations. A man may sit in to all the lectures or not to any; no one cares or is the wiser. At the end of two years, however, he must present himself for "test" examinations, while at the end of four years he takes examinations for his degree. Officially, classes were supposed to begin on April 15th; actually they began in the first part of this week. Frankly, I don't like the lecturing methods here. It's next to impossible to learn anything from them: whatever you know at the end of this university career comes from your own reading and thinking. As soon as I have a little time, I'll write in the "diary" some account of the university system here.

The fact that I shall get very little out of the semester here is not bothering me. I didn't intend to originally. I was mainly interested in getting the credits for the semester's work on my Ph.D. requirements and for the prestige. As far as I now know, I shall continue with the following courses: Russian History through the 18th Century, Political-Legal Structure of Russia in the 20th Century, Seminar in Contemporary Russian Law, History of Russian Literature, German History 1815-1917, Comparison of French Civilization and German Culture. No studying is required, no written work, merely to come and listen. This being the case, it won't interfere with my special interest. The titles look impressive, I know, but mean very little. I repeat: the lectures give you next to nothing; only self-reading and thinking will profit one here.

. . . I shall outline this week to Harper, my Chicago professor, my definite plan of procedure, telling him just what I'm doing and just what I want my thesis to be. His approval is necessary, but I'm sure he will agree to my outline: he accepted my master's thesis with hardly an alteration.

Now, about the "diary." After much exasperation I finally received a good typewriter and am beginning to type the notes. I shall enclose the first batch in this letter. Here's my plan, dearest. I shall type and send you the notes almost word for word as I have written them originally. I want to be honest with myself, to have my thoughts and writings in the original form. Then I am natural and true to myself, and in later days this will be interesting to have in order to observe what changes my opinions or points of view have undergone. I don't know what to do about the Russian notes. But I believe I shall type them almost the way they are written too. I shall save the original notes here, and later, if I have time, I can expand and embellish them as may be necessary, depending upon the type of magazine for which I am writing or the sort of article that I may be interested in. I also want to write three or four articles for the *Herald* [the *Jewish Herald*, Houston]. This I shall do soon, since for that purpose no quotations or statistics are required and it doesn't have to be anything elaborate: just a change of phrase here or there, or a little decoration of the notes as they are now written. If I only have the occasion, dearest, I shall obey your suggestion about the Russian articles, but as I've explained to you, it would be next to useless [unless] to write for a periodical that will bring me credit from men in my profession, and for this, a serious, carefully prepared article or two is necessary.

I believe I shall divide my writings into two categories: for popular appeal and for "professional" appeal. The former can be achieved by writing an article or two or three for such a magazine as *Asia*, and this I may do before I leave Berlin, if only I have the time, or else when I return to Texas. The latter will have to wait, I'm afraid, until a more future time: that's a much more serious thing. What do you think of the plan? To give us "local reputation," I'm considering at least three subjects for the *Herald*: "The Jews of Warsaw," "Jews and Jewish Situation in Present-Day Soviet Russia," and "Jews in Latvia and Lithuania." What think you? Dad wants me to take a few weeks off and make a trip to Palestine. Sounds interesting, but it's impossible. I can neither afford the time nor the money. . . .

Alex Shilkin and I are together as usual. Mr. Glusman, the Canadian, is still here, poor fellow. He has been definitely refused admittance and is now waiting to hear if the Soviet government will permit his mother to leave the country in order to visit him in Berlin. A fourth man has joined the group, one John Morrison. Morrison is also from U. of Chicago. We sat in classes together. He is also interested in Russia, though from a geographical standpoint, and is waiting for a visa in order to go into the country and obtain material and information on certain phases of Siberia. Was rejected once, but is trying again. In that, he and Alex Shilkin are interested in allied fields. It is a tremendously difficult task to obtain a visa and it's quite unlikely, even if both should get permission, that they will receive it at the same time. Morrison is quite a fine chap. His father is one of the professors of education at the U. of C., and Morrison has the post of instructor in geography waiting for him as soon as he returns in the fall. That's what comes of being a "faculty child."

Berlin, Thursday, May 17, 1928

What else to tell you? Sent off a long letter to Mr. Harper, the man at Chicago under whom I am working, and one to Mr. Joranson, the secretary of the department. I gave the former a short account of my trip to Russia, a tentative outline of my thesis subject, and a statement of my plan of treatment and procedure. To the latter I made formal application to candidacy for a doctorate and took up certain matters in this same connection. If Harper approves my choice of subject and is satisfied with my plan of work, this is all that is necessary. As I mentioned in my previous letter, I feel sure that his approval will be forthcoming on the basis of my experience with him at the time of taking my master's degree, though he may have a few suggestions to make. I also asked him to inform me what success my application for an award has.

I am enclosing a second batch of notes of my Russian trip. As you can see, they leave off where I arrive in Moscow. The question of treatment arises. So far I have copied the notes practically word for word as I wrote them originally. You thus obtain a true picture of my impressions and moods at every particular moment, as well as a sort of sense of rhythm and naturalness. You will observe that once I reached the Russian border I began writing only in headings, as at Nieharelaje, or very skimpily. This was because I was afraid of censorship. Later on, most of this fear passed away, but I continued to write down brief notes, for there were so many things to be seen and to be heard and I was so pressed for time that I could not afford to describe everything in full. Besides, at all times I remained in slight fear of the censor. It was impossible to continue the chronological narrative for the 22 days that I was in Russia, and I therefore cast my writings in a topical form, just as I did in the case of my Berlin or Warsaw experiences. As much as possible I shall adhere and send you an almost verbatim copy of my notes of Moscow and Leningrad as I originally wrote them down, but in several cases, in order to make them intelligible or interesting, I shall expand them somewhat, particularly in all those cases where I wrote with my eye on the censor.

In respect to my experiences after leaving Russia, I shall transmit almost an exact duplicate of my original notes. The notes in general would have been much fuller and probably more interesting if I hadn't written them from a moving train for the most part. It is so hard to write when the train is in motion, particularly when you are using your knee for a pad, not to mention when you have neighbors at all sides of you who are crowding you or else disturbing you by their talking or movements.

What more, dear? Guess there's nothing else. Besides, the servant girl just came in to tell me my bath is ready: running hot water is all but unknown in these parts; baths have to be specially prepared.

Berlin, Monday, May 21, 1928

I'll tell you what kept me busy these last two days and prevented my writing the customary Sunday letter or sending you some more Russia notes. The Reichstag elections — the first in four years — were held yesterday, and the different programs, campaigning, and general significance was so interesting that I determined to write something on them and send it in to the *Houston Chronicle* for publication. At first I thought I'd make it short and humorous, then I decided to do the job more thoroughly — you know how these things go — with the result that I've bought every paper I could get hold of. Attended political gatherings, watched the excitement yesterday — election day — and spent quite a few hours working the material over. I'll have it finished in a day or two, just as soon as I get a little spare time and the election results have been decisively established, and will send it to Father to turn it over to the *Chronicle*. May make a copy for the "diary."

What do you think of my present idea in connection with the notes on Russia, to have them printed in full in the *Chronicle*? This won't hurt my chances to make use of them later on, to develop the material for one or two magazines, and will give us local rep. I've written Dad I shall do that. But you'll get the notes just the same — can't cheat "our diary," can we.

Berlin, Monday, May 28, 1928

[Typewritten letter]

Rose, you must forgive me for using the typewriter this time, for I fully know the greater sense of warmth that self-written characters contain, but I have a really good excuse. I have been using the typewriter so much during the last few days that my right thumb has become very sore and it is next to impossible to hold a pen. This a German-made machine, by the way. Don't like it so very much. For one thing, the y and z are just reversed from the American keyboard, and a few of the other characters are also transposed. I really need a Russian keyboard. I'm forced to take quite a few notes on my Russian reading, and since the characters are quite different from the Latin, I must either translate at once into English or use equivalent sounds, which is not very satisfactory.

I just got through writing a letter to Dr. Cohen. Gave him a short outline of my work and experiences of the last few months and reminded him about his promise to endeavor to obtain a gratis passage for me on the return trip. I assured him that whether he succeeded or not, my high respect and admiration for him would remain unaltered. The boat that I shall take is the *Niagara,* a sister ship of the *De La Salle,* on which I came to Europe. It leaves Havre on the 7th of August but unfortunately does not arrive in Galveston until the 2nd of September. You know, sweetheart, how badly I want to get to you and therefore what this delay of a week or two, as compared with the time schedule of other ships, will mean, but I'm afraid it cannot be helped. I cannot forego the possibility of a gratis passage. It means about $100 at least, and such a sum at the present time means a lot to us. I wonder if I couldn't get on a German boat at Hamburg. There is a German line that has direct connections with Galveston, same as the French lines. . . . I'll look around and see if anything else can be done.

Just got through with an afternoon with two of my friends. One was Alex Shilkin, the other was John Morrison. I told you of the latter, did I not? He is also from the University of Chicago. His father is professor of education there, and he is in Berlin preparing to enter Russia. He is also working on a doctor's dissertation and has chosen a certain section of Siberia as his subject in the field of geography. I knew him from Chicago, while Shilkin met him here. The two are now staying together and we see a good deal of each other. He had been turned down once for a visa, but now I believe he has succeeded. He heard indirectly to this effect and will probably leave for Russia within the next two weeks.

I met still another man from Chicago, a Jewish fellow by the name of Robbins.* Robbins is a good friend of Saul Weinberg, but we met quite by accident. He is a very cultured fellow and has spent considerably more time in Europe than I. He was in law practice in Chicago for three years after graduation, made considerable money in that time, and then tired of the practice and determined to go into the teaching field. As a consequence, he is in Europe now for the second year. Has attended five different universities so far: Oxford, the Sorbonne, the Universities of Heidelberg and Freiberg [both in Baden, Germany], and now the University of Berlin. Once in Europe, it is a relatively easy thing to go from one university to another — a semester here and a semester there — for no examinations are required, and it has a lot to recommend it, particularly where universities are in different countries. It brings you into contact with different educational institutions, different cultures, different peoples, and different lands, and so enriches your experience very much. Its value is particularly great in that it enables you to compare, to set off the one against the other, and so obtain finer standards for evaluation.

Speaking of friends reminds me that Friday I was with still another from the University of Chicago. Quite unexpectedly, Urban Westenberger dropped in on me. He is a young German fellow whom I met in Chicago almost the first day after his arrival from Germany. He could hardly speak the language then. We spent considerable time together last summer and came to know each other quite well. In fact we corresponded for a time after I returned to Houston. Then I lost his address . . . . Imagine then my surprise when the door opens and in walks Westenberger. He lives in Mainz, one of the fine old Rhine cities, and begged me to pay him a visit, but I have determined to wait until I leave the University. My route lies through this region, and I shall therefore spend a day or two with him without the additional expense that would be the case otherwise.

Remember Mr. Glusman, the Canadian whom I mentioned several times? Well, his mother finally came last week. They were together

---

* Albert Robbins, in later years, was one of the most dearly held friends of Joe's lifetime.

until today, and now Glusman has left for Canada and the mother leaves tomorrow for Russia. The old lady, in point of fact, left yesterday for Russia, but owing to the fact that she did not have a Polish visa, she was turned back at the Polish-German frontier. A dirty shame, but such is Europe today. It is impossible to imagine what needless hardship and often real suffering this stupid system of passports and visas causes. Shilkin, Morrison, and myself all saw Glusman off at the station, and it was with real warmth that we shook his hand goodbye. In fact the old fellow kissed each one of us. Nothing particularly impressive about him, just a businessman like thousands of others of our Jewish people, but there was something about him that we all liked. Often on a Saturday or Sunday, or even weekday, we would drop in at his hotel and sit in his room, drinking tea and listening to him damn the Russians. There was something very comical about him, and often we would almost split our sides laughing at his attempts to give full expression to his feelings about the Russian government and the Communists, all because — at least, largely — they wouldn't let him in and made so much hardship for his mother to get out. In a way, there is something quite saddening about leave-taking, especially under circumstances like these, where the possibility of meeting one another is so very remote. When one is traveling, he meets so many people with whom he often becomes very close, only to bid them goodbye, knowing that they will never see each other again. It's not like traveling in one's own country, though even that often presents the same situation.

The three of us this afternoon, after seeing Glusman off, visited a Chinese restaurant in one of the neighborhoods and had quite a good meal. Was very tasty for a change. Then we called at Roberts, a sort of combined ice cream parlor and sandwich shop operated on the American plan and owned, if I am not mistaken, by an American. It was my first taste of an American sundae since I left the States, and let me tell you, it felt fine. At the Von Humboldt house, a sort of meeting place or clubhouse for foreign students, we snapped pictures of one another and in groups . . . .

I mentioned that we are having a ten-day holiday from school, did I not? This is in connection with *Pfingstfest* [Pentecost/Whitsuntide], the holiday that is in progress since yesterday. Really, I am beginning to be very dubious about the value of the German university system. Here lectures officially are supposed to begin April 15th. In actuality they do not begin until about May 10th. Courses have not been in progress for three weeks, and here they declare a holiday for ten days. But worse than all is the fact that next to nothing is gotten from the lectures. Imagine a system where most courses are only one "hour" a week, and this hour is in actuality only 40 minutes, and furthermore, this 40 minutes is consumed not in attempting to explain or teach but in reading from a prepared paper, often a verbatim copy of a textbook, or at best written in a textbook style? Thank heavens I am not here to learn anything directly from the university. Incidentally, I might mention that I went through the formalities in connection with matriculating and listened to a representative of the rector welcome the incoming students in the most approved style — which means extremely dry — that is in vogue in our American universities. Also, I was presented with an impressive-looking Latin document which certifies that I am a student of the Friedrich Wilhelm University and looks like an American diploma. Well, it will look good in a glass frame, anyway.

I believe I shall take advantage of this holiday to spend two or three days seeing Leipzig and other nearby cities, such as Dresden. They are only two to four hours' ride from Berlin and it would be a pity if I were to leave Germany without seeing more of the country. . . .

Hon, guess you think it funny that I should be again writing you on Monday. The explanation is that today being a holiday, no mail would leave the city. Another reason is that I spent a good part of yesterday typing out some more notes, which I am now enclosing. You will observe that one set is in connection with the German Reichstag elections, which I mentioned in my last letter. Honey, will you please do this for me. In as much as Shirley has to make a copy anyway for the other "diary," it will be the same work if she makes a duplicate. I want you to send this duplicate to Father and ask him to turn it over to the *Chronicle* for publication. I feel sure they will be glad to print it, as it is something that is not easily obtained in America: an analysis of German politics. You might give it this heading, if they should desire one: "The German Elections of May 20th." Will you please see that Shirley copies my notes exactly and that no mistakes are made? I would do it myself, but somehow I hate to take the extra time that is needed for this work.

The other set of notes are the first batch in connection with my experiences in Russia. Some of them are elaborated a bit from the original writing, others are about as I wrote them the first time. I shall touch part of them up a bit — I made a duplicate

— and turn them in to the *Chronicle* for publication, just as I told you. I shall have one article for the *Herald* on the Jews of Russia and one on the Jews of Latvia and Lithuania. In the latter connection, I shall so write the notes that they will be fit for immediate publication, and when I send them to you shall ask that Shirley make a copy and send it to my father for publication in the *Herald*. With regard to the Jews of Warsaw, notes on which I already sent you, I shall touch my copy up and send it on to Father directly, and he can also give this to the *Herald*.

In taking up time to type my experiences of the trip, I am neglecting Germany, but I hope that in a few days I shall catch up with everything and send you thereafter my impressions of this country, as has been my habit in the past. By the way, honey, I have just been thinking: wonder if it would be too much trouble for you to retouch my notes on Russia and turn them in to the *Chronicle* for publication. This would save me so much extra time. It is such a job to have to type all these things over again. I believe that the form they are already written in is almost suitable for publication; in any case, they could pick out what they wanted, just as in the case of the University of Missouri magazine. This would be so much of a help. Then I could devote my spare time to writing up fresh impressions and so avoid the gap of time which would otherwise result. Write me what you think about all this, darling, and I'll act upon your suggestion. . . .

P.S. Next morning. Got to thinking last night that it might be a good idea to send in this article on the German elections to the *New York Times Current History Magazine*. This afternoon, therefore, I shall make a few alternations in my copy, double-space it, and send it in. If they print it — which I am rather inclined to think will be the case — it will help the "cause" considerably, for this is the most popular magazine among the men of the history profession that we have. But you send your copy to Father just the same for publication in the *Chronicle*.

Columbia, Missouri, Saturday night, May 1928

[Letter from Rose to Joe]

Dearest:

By the time you receive this letter, I will be on my way to Galveston. Intend to leave here on Sunday, June 3, and stay in St. Louis until the following Sunday. And then Homeward Bound!

Read your diary notes with interest. They are typewritten exceptionally well. . . . You mentioned something about writing some articles for the *Jewish Herald*. My suggestion would be that you send those very same articles to the *Jewish Tribune* of NY, the *Menorah*, or the *Jewish Forum* . . . . I think your work is too good for such a comparatively local and mediocre sheet. No, sweetheart, your better half's judgments point to the fact that you try for bigger and better newspapers. Now that you have a typewriter, it would not be difficult to whack off about 1,500 words. . . .

Surely am sorry to hear about Mr. Glusman. I cannot understand why the Russian government would be so strict about allowing visitors in. Surely there is nothing to guard themselves against. If anything, they ought to be willing to allow visitors to come in and spend money.

Berlin, Sunday morning, June 3, 1928

[Typewritten letter]

I don't know how to describe this past week. From one angle it has been unusually happy: I received five of your letters and many clippings, the program of Journalism Week [at the University of Missouri], and many other things which you sent me; from another, not so good, owing to trouble with my right hand. You remember I referred to the latter as the cause of my typewritten letter of last Tuesday. Well, the trouble continued and has been an inconvenience in many ways. Darn if I know what's the matter. Seems to be a slight sprain of one or two of the muscles leading from my right thumb to my right wrist, but small and insignificant as it is, it is sufficient to make writing very disagreeable. I have been rubbing it with stuff and have avoided writing ever since Tuesday in the hopes that it would pass away. This morning is the first time that I touched the typewriter since then, for it seems improved today. As I say, this minor ailment has been quite inconvenient. For one thing, it prevented me from writing you my usual mid-week letter, as well as letters to many other people. For another, it has kept me from sending in that little contribution to the *New York Times Current History* that I mentioned in my last letter, and from writing up more of the notes that I took on Russia. Let's hope the thing disappears entirely in a day or two, then I shall work hard to catch up with neglected tasks. . . .

What to tell you about myself? It has been a holiday all week — *Pfingstfest* — as I mentioned last time. I didn't leave the city as I intended, except to go to Potsdam. Was expecting a check from Houston and didn't want to cut myself too short until it came. But I shall be able to visit Leipzig and Dresden during one of the later weekends. The trip to Potsdam was very interesting. As you know, it was the residence city of the former Prussian kings and emperors (like Versailles for the French kings or Tsarskoe Selo for the Russian) and contains, therefore, their palaces and grounds and other items of historical interest. There are two palaces in Potsdam where the kings lived, one called Sans Souci ("without care" or "without anxiety"), the other, the New Palace, both built by Frederick the Great in the 18th century. I mailed you a picture the other day showing myself standing with a group of tourists before a wing of the palace Sans Souci. Some professional photographer snapped it as we were going down the steps leading to the gardens. . . .

Monday, that is, tomorrow, lectures begin again. It is really a matter of indifference to me. I got nothing out of them anyway. Perhaps I shouldn't say that. The fact that I at least know how German lectures are conducted is worth something, and the outline that I obtain on two or three of the subjects should also be of some value in the future.

Weather hasn't been particularly good this last week. Cool, and intermittent rain. In fact the whole spring has been a very poor one. . . . My thesis is coming along, though slowly. This Russian reading is very slow going, particularly the type of stuff I have to master. But as I said before, I hope to have the first draft well on the road to completion by the time I return. . . .

Do you realize it's June? June 3rd, to be exact. In a little over two months I'll be on the ship wending my way homeward — a sort of Enoch Arden. Better still, our old friend Odysseus. I hope, though, that unlike Penelope, you won't be surrounded by a lot of unwelcome suitors whom I shall have to kill in order to get to you, as Odysseus did of old.

Awfully sorry about the lack of diary notes for this week. At the moment my hand doesn't feel particularly bad, but a little while ago it was complaining, and I don't dare risk bothering it too much. I shall be forced, therefore, to delay sending the next batch of notes until next week, perhaps only until my mid-week letter. I believe I have about 30 or so more pages of notes on Russia and about the same amount on my return journey through Lithuania and Latvia and East Prussia. Quite a few things have come up in connection with Germany since I returned. Some of these I shall develop for you. The balance will have to be dismissed to make way for new experiences or impressions when I turn to Germany once more.

Berlin, Thursday, June 7, 1928

[Typewritten letter]

I'm going to the opera tonight, sweetness. My first German opera. Going to witness *Rigoletto*. Didn't want to leave Germany without seeing at least one of its operatic renditions. Would give an awful lot if you could accompany me. I shall be in the second or third gallery and it will be very lonesome up there all by myself. Hon, if I develop an interest in operas, then we'll go to lots in Chicago. How do you stand on them? We are matched on so many points that it's almost superfluous to mention still another: our lack of enthusiasm for music. But I sometimes wonder if we are not neglecting what so many people claim is a tremendous source of indescribable pleasure simply through a sort of laziness or inertia which keeps us from giving our "souls" a fair chance, as it were. . . .

Thank goodness I finally got that article off to *Current History*.

My thumb is all but well now, and so yesterday I typed the thing and sent it away. Cut it down considerably. Rather doubt whether they will print it. For one thing, I hear that they are rejecting all contributions for the next six months because of superfluity; again, owing to the range of authors from which they are able to pick, they give preference to those who have already made their mark, as it were: professors, diplomats, officials, etc. Thirdly, the *New York Times* has its own correspondent in Germany and may not care to publish something that belongs to his domain or else that might contradict his statements. Anyhow, it was worth taking a chance. We'll see what happens.

P.S. I hope to have all the Russian notes finished within the next few days so that I can "start back" on Germany.

[Galveston,] Monday, June 9, 1928

[Letter from Rose to Joe]

My most Beloved One and Would-be Husband:

If I am not making my letters as lengthy as formerly, I am writing more frequently. It is rather warm for long dissertations. The heat is the humid kind which makes you restless, oh so restless.

I went to town today to get my salary. They may use me a little later on for about a month on a special edition which they are going to put out. This is not definite, however.

Received your wonderful letter today, dearest, the one in which you and Alex went to the dance with one of his girls. It seems funny to think they even have dates in Berlin. It sounds so American, doesn't it? But of course I am just kidding. Surely, do they not love and live like we? It must be difficult indeed for you to be refraining from girls' company, not that I would not trust you. I *would*. The moment we cease trusting each other, then our lives are not worthwhile. Really, I'm mighty glad that the Almighty saw to it that you had found a friend as fine as Alex upon your immediate arrival in Berlin. After all, it is hard to find pals and especially in a faraway land. Too, we must admit that Americans have to be even doubly careful abroad, with so many people trying to exploit them at every step and turn. I hope someday we will have the opportunity of showing Alex a real time at our home. Dearest, all of your friends will always be treated in the most royal manner possible by your wife. We are going to make our place a literary center, Joe. . . .

When do you intend to finish, June or August? Either way it is O.K. Boy! Howdee — what are we going to do with all of those grand diplomas. Gee, I am anxious to see the Berlin one, and of course it goes without saying, the Ph.D. and the others. The future generation will have a lot to live up to with a dad like that. Say, Joe, so long as we have everything else decided upon, what shall we make out of them — before they attain the presidency. Al Smith's nomination* has caused a lot of religious comment, with prohibition as the ruse.

---

* Alfred Emanuel Smith, a Catholic who opposed Prohibition, was the Democratic candidate for US President in 1928.

Berlin, Sunday, June 10, 1928, 6:00 p.m.

[Typewritten letter]

Am enclosing another batch of notes. Seems as though I'll never get through typing that old stuff. My finger, you know, was the cause of some delay, and now, owing to the fact that I want to give as much attention to my thesis as I can, I can't find the vacant time. Sweetheart, I've determined that, tempting as it is to sit down and write out several articles for the various magazines, the thesis deserves first call, that every spare hour I have must be devoted to it. It's a long and very slow thing and I simply must have it well in hand by the time I return. You can do with the notes what you will. One thing, dear, that I should like to do is this: this last batch contains my notes on the Jews in Russia. It is in almost complete shape for printing, and if you would have Shirley make a copy of it, and then perhaps you would touch it up a bit and send it to Father, he could turn it over to the *Herald*. I observe what you wrote in the last letter about sending the stuff off to some of the better Jewish papers. I agree with you, but as I've explained, sweetheart, I just can't afford the time for polishing the material up. If you think this thing on the Jews in Russia is suitable for publication in these other papers, why, just send it on to them. But I would like to have it in the *Herald*. We need that local publicity, as it will probably do us more good than an article in the better journals, which are not in Texas. You recall that bit of description on the Jews in Warsaw and Poland? If you like, retouch that too and send it to Dad to put in the *Herald*. But I believe it would be better to have the Russian thing first sent in — it's more complete.

What else? Running out of thoughts. I gave Alex your regards. We're always talking about you. Believe I'll have him with me for a couple of weeks this fall; who knows, perhaps he'll be in the bridal party. Would like to have him: really a fine man. About 30 now but acts often with the jolliness of a kid.

Let me tell you about John Morrison, the "faculty child." Poor fellow, after all this waiting and hoping, he was finally turned down flat by the Russian government. Received the definite notice Thursday that he could not be admitted, and so Saturday, that is, yesterday, left for Sweden. Alex and I saw him off. It's too bad. His purpose in going to Russia, as I believe I told you before, was to obtain material for a doctor's thesis, just as in my own case. His intention was to visit various parts of Russia and Siberia and obtain various data and material in connection with certain geographical and railroad problems which he wished to develop as the subject for the dissertation. This was the second time he was turned down. The trouble lay with his first application, made about two or three months ago. Gave so many references from well-known people that he probably frightened the authorities rather than helped his cause. Well, once they refused him, it probably was too severe a thrust to the prestige of their foreign office to alter their first decision. It is bad, of course, but then not as severe a blow as it might be under other circumstances. As a "faculty child," Morrison has had it relatively easy. He goes back to the University this fall with a job as instructor awaiting him and doesn't have to worry like myself to get a doctor's degree in order to obtain a job — at least a worthwhile one. So it is largely a matter of good use of his time as possible, and accordingly worked out a very interesting trip. It was all I could do to keep from going with him — but of course I am only talking; it's impossible for me to get away. The trip he has outlined includes traveling through the northern part of Sweden and Finland, spending a while in Lapland among the Lapps, which means going up into the Arctic Circle, and visiting various interesting points in all these regions. Then he plans to return to Berlin by the first of the month to meet his brother, who is coming by ship to Bremen, and from Berlin will wander through various parts of Western Europe and then, on the first of September, meet his parents in Scotland.

One of the reasons why I am disappointed along with him for his having failed to obtain a visa is that now my poor cousin Rebecca Polsky will again have waited in vain for the articles she wanted so badly from Germany. As you know from my letters, it is next to impossible to buy some of the most necessary things in Russia: either they are not obtainable or else the price renders them prohibitive. I bought her considerable stuff when I went and made her very happy, and I promised her when Shilkin or Glusman or Morrison would go, they would also bring her stuff. Well, as you know, the latter two were turned down, while the former has delayed his plans for going.

I told you I was going to witness *Rigoletto*. Well, I did, and enjoyed it immensely. Watch my smoke from now on — yes, and *our* smoke when we get to Chicago. Just cross out that part of my last letter where I went into a long complaint about the present standards of culture.

[Galveston?], June 13, 1928

[Letter from Rose to Joe]

Your folks brought a big pail of tomatoes, great big red ones that came from your garden. Your mother surely is a marvelous gardener. She said that her flowers were beautiful this year, and I can well believe her.
Your dad invited me down to spend a few days and offered me the "finest Bellaire pure air," the finest red tomatoes and green cucumbers right off the vines, all the roses and flowers that you care to enjoy. . . . He also says that if I'm in need of a real writer's exercise to prepare me for my golf championship, he can offer me a full free course in hoeing corn and strawberries. . . .

Berlin, Thursday night, June 14, 1928

Since I wrote you Sunday it has been a routine trek from the University to my room. I'm hitting up the thesis work to a very active pace now, and it leaves me with almost no time for anything else — not even to write up the balance of the notes on Russia and the return trip, let alone new experiences. In connection with the latter, I must say that I regret the fact. The "diary" has really come to mean something to me, aside from your own feelings toward it. Has become a sort of register not merely of my external experiences but my internal reactions and thoughts. I believe that in later life I shall at times return to it with interest as a record of my impressions and standards of judgment at my present age. Because of this, I shall try hard not to give it up. You shall certainly have the balance of the old notes, which I shall try to finish in the course of the next week or two.

Spent several hours this afternoon with Alex Shilkin. He felt unusually prosperous apparently and invited me to a picture show. I've seen about four in the whole time that I am in Berlin, and after the last one — an old picture with Vilma Bánky — I vowed not to go again, but I accepted Alex's invitation anyhow and witnessed again the embodiment of trash.

I told you that I intended to take in more operas, but so far I haven't. For one thing, I hate to give up an evening; for another, I must watch my funds. Some very good pieces are playing this week: *Madame Butterfly, Boris Godunov, La Bohème,* and several others.

Six more weeks now, my sweetheart, and your boy will be leaving Berlin. Then seven more days and he shall be on the water, and

26 more days (unless "the Doc" fails me: frankly, I half wish he would) and . . . . Boy! But I really must work hard these next weeks. By Saturday I shall have completed the first chapter of my dissertation, I mean, in its rough form. There is to be four chapters in all, and the last three I want to have finished in the draft form when I reach Galveston. I shall then touch it up at various points and do whatever extra reading I need and have it all ready for submission to Harper when we get to Chicago. As a matter of fact, if I don't have time to work on it when I am home, it will hurt nothing in particular, for I don't have to submit it until sometime in the spring.

Galveston, Friday afternoon, June 15, 1928

[Letter from Rose to Joe]

Excuse stationery, sweetheart, but it is the only thing I could find around here. Just finished typing off that May 20th election article. As soon as I get through with this letter, I shall begin typing off the other on Russia. I hope to have both ready for your dad when he comes Sunday. My typewriter is about as bad as yours. It had been neglected during my absence and it became rusty and clogged. Anyway, I did the best I could under the circumstances.

Next week, sweetheart, when I begin to work. Yes, my love, I have a temporary job for the next week in a dentist's office, which will probably pay $10 or $12 per. For the following week I have a job on the *Galveston News* as an extra reporter for the [Democratic] Convention. A large mass of the conventionites will land in Galveston, so they think they will be able to use me. There is no opening on the *Tribune* side. You see, they took a girl, and naturally I would not expect them to be firing her for me. The *News* side means working until 11 o'clock at night, and I myself am not overly anxious to work that late should there be a permanent opening. For the week or so, however, I will not mind it.

During that time Mr. Will H. Ford will have returned from Alabama, where he left. Mr. Ford and Mr. Shaw are to consult each other over employing me as their publicity man for the American National Insurance Company. (This is a Moody* concern and was the place I once wrote up and griped so much about.) Mr. Elbert,

---

* The Moodys were a prominent family in Galveston since the 1800s. William Lewis Moody Jr. founded the American National Insurance Company, along with two banks and other ventures. He bought the *Galveston Daily News* in 1923 and the *Galveston Tribune* in 1927.

general manager of the newspaper, thinks I am quite capable and is going to use his influence in getting me that job. I am not going to ask more than $25 a week, as they don't know what it is all about and probably would not pay more. It will be worth it to me, rather than doing just plain office work or going out of town. I got two letters of introduction from the man Shirley writes for, Mr. Perkins of the *Houston Press*. They were written to the *Chronicle* and to the *Press*. But it would be foolish of me to work in Houston. I could have just as lief worked in St. Louis. Well, darling, at any rate, I am in better spirits.

Berlin, Sunday, June 17, 1928

[This letter is not included here because it does not relate to the diary but to Joe's joyous anticipation of marriage. It is noteworthy that Joe, during these final days in Berlin, takes eight pages to review for Rose the progression of her attitude towards him: from cooling their friendship to rejecting his proposal, to accepting an engagement ring, to planning a wedding. It is addressed "Dear Wife."]

[Berlin,] Thursday afternoon, June 21, 1928

The experience [of being content with my own company, to study] certainly comes in useful now, now that Rose Ella has entered my life and all but shattered this ability to find the "ego" sufficient company. My spirit is always revolting now. When I should be studying, it insists on bringing Rose Ella to me. It does the same thing in the classroom, in the streetcar, at a cafe, at night when I should fall asleep, at any and all times. But just the same, the old "experience" is of some value still, and helps make things easier than would be otherwise.

The play, *La Bohème*, is the only other opera besides *Rigoletto* that I shall have seen in Germany thus far. Don't know how I shall like it. Will write you about it. Witnessed the welcoming of the *Bremen* trans-Atlantic flyers yesterday.* Happened to be in the downtown section and decided to wait until they rolled by. Don't advise you doing this stunt. A wait of two hours or more, all for the pleasure of a momentary glance at fleeting figures.

---

* See "Diary," p. 152.

Galveston, June 19, 1928

[Letter from Rose to Joe]

My Most Beloved Sweetheart:

[Long section not included here, in which Rose reviews her early, unfavorable(!) impressions of Joe and how her opinion has changed.]

Listen, Joe, after going through what you did in your travels through Russia and Poland, it is even lucky you got out alive. From your letters while in Moscow, I thought I was sailing under false colors when I said you were "entering chaos." From your diary notes, which I take to be a typical picture, I am convinced that the place is in pretty poor condition. No, sweetheart, I am afraid you would have to do some tall convincing to ever get me to visit those dumps. And your *dad* agrees with me.

I hope that your wrist is fully recovered to its normal state by the time this letter arrives, and that my suggestions will not be needed. But be careful, dear, about any drafts. Whoever said that a Ph.D. was easy to procure (that writing up a dissertation on how many ham sandwiches can be gotten out of a hog is all that is necessary) — well, I would like to tell them a few things.

Your folks had not received a letter from you in two weeks. They little realized it was your wrist which caused the delay. Your dad said he would have worried otherwise but is not now, since he knew I have heard from you.

Berlin, Saturday night, June 23, 1928

[Eight-page typewritten letter, most of it impossible to read, as it was written on two sides of thin paper and did not photocopy well]

It is almost midnight at the moment. Have just returned from a cafe dance with Alex and one of his girls. As the evening is unusually warm and agreeable, we decided to take a walk through the Tiergarten, a large park in my neighborhood. All the while I thought only of you — wondered — with an ache — whether you too were looking up at the stars at this very time and also wondering — with an ache. This separation is so hard. . . .

Monday Morning

Apologies, sweetheart, for interrupting the letter. Came Sunday and something else arose to interfere. I chanced upon an article written by a traveler among the Lapps of Northern Sweden and somehow it set my wanderlust to working. The thought came to me that my time in Germany was drawing short and here I hadn't seen Leipzig or the other cities yet. Impulsively I made up my mind, rushed over to the station, and purchased a ticket for Leipzig. I planned to spend the day and night there, then take a train for Dresden and return to Berlin either Monday evening or Tuesday morning. But somehow, when I got to Leipzig my enthusiasm waned. I thought of my studies and my funds and several other things, and besides, my romantic ardor, the curiosity to see new places and things, has cooled. I did manage to visit the most interesting thing in the city, however: the monument commemorating the Battle of Leipzig, or Battle of the Nations, as it is often called (*Völker-Schlacht*). I sent you a postal from there, and from this you can get an impression of the monument. It was a beautiful day and the grounds in connection with the memorial were especially lovely. A guide took a party of us visitors into the _____ and endeavored to impress us with the _____ size, cost, and symbolic value of the site and even sang a song in order to show the _____ of the property.

[Leipzig,] June 24, 1928

[Postcard: reverse shows *Völkerschlachtdenkmal* (Monument to the Battle of the Nations), Leipzig]

My Dearest:

Spending the day here. Have decided not to stay overnight, and am on the point of returning to Berlin. Most interesting thing here is the monument erected in memory of the Battle of Leipzig, 1813. You have the photo on the reverse side. Will write from Berlin tomorrow.

Berlin, Monday, June 25, 1928

[Typewritten letter, again on thin paper; photocopy is difficult to read]

I rather hoped you wouldn't consider a job at all during these extremely hot months and would take a rest. . . . But Rose, I shall insist that you keep your promise and stop working before the wedding (Oh, Glory Be!). You said a month, but since I'm your equal half (you said I could be, didn't you?), I insist upon being accorded my rights, and since you took a month, I want a month too, and therefore you must stop *at least* two months before the glorious day.

It should be very interesting, this covering of the Democratic Convention. I should have put that in the past tense, for the thing is over now. At least it must be. I haven't kept up with the Democratic debates very much this time, but I do know that Al Smith is nominated as the presidential candidate and Joseph Robinson as the vice-presidential. I should like to know how Texas and the other Southern states voted. I'm really surprised that Al Smith received the nomination. . . .

So Doctor Cohen came over and mentioned that he had everything arranged for my return trip, in accordance with your former conversation with him. As I wrote you last time, my appreciation for his kindness is unbounded. But there is one person I omitted to thank, and that is my soon-to-be sweetheart-wife. I well know to what extent you made this kindness possible. After all, it was the rabbi's friendship and affection for you that dictated his generous conduct on my behalf.

Berlin, June 30, 1928

[Nine-page typewritten letter, on both sides of thin paper; much of the photocopy unreadable]

Harper's letter (of which I wrote you quite a while ago), which I received from him immediately after my application, was very encouraging. He did not know about a fellowship (as I told you, the Russian department is sort of auxiliary to the history department in general) but believed he could do something for me with regard to a scholarship (which makes cancellation of the tuition, about $200, whereas fellowship earns about $450). When I returned from Russia I received a letter from him in which he devoted just a brief line or two to the effect that he regretted to report that he was unsuccessful on my behalf but believes he can arrange for me to be a paper examiner, which, while in the end would probably amount to tuition, is not easy work and would only interfere with my studies. Now, all this is quite puzzling in view of Harper's very encouraging letter, seen after the application and the acknowledgement of failure thereafter. On Harper, I can depend. He is quite a real friend, and has in the last month written me four letters and has _____. Something has happened at the faculty deliberation that Harper did not foresee _____. I don't believe it can be due to my grades. While it is true I never worked hard for the department, for I wasn't interested in grades and preferred to do independent thinking and work, I am still a B student, which of course is not bad, and therefore I didn't think that the matter would be decided on this basis. I thought for a time it might be due to my "communistic interests." American professors are very timid on many matters, and they have feared to encourage one who manifests _____ in the subject. I have rejected this as a possibility. I don't believe the Jewish question has anything to do with it, for few know my background, and if they did, I don't believe that would [count]____ against me at this university, for it is _____ liberal.

There remains only one other possibility, and this I believe is the cause. Along with my letter to Harper asking for his _____ word on my behalf, I wrote one to Mr. Thompson, head of Medieval Studies, asking a similar favor. Now I _____ if you knew Thompson well, why a politely written, perfectly proper letter of this kind should arouse his ire would be inexplicable to you, but Thompson is a person all to himself. A very good scholar in a certain sense of the term, but possessed of many peculiarities and prejudices. He has absolute standards. It is very easy to "rub" him the right way, and it is just as easy to "rub" him the wrong way. Woe betide you if you do the latter. Now, he and I have had many long talks together and were very friendly. Last fall he was one of the honor guests of the American Bankers Association in their annual meeting in Houston, and there I listened to his lecture and afterwards had a long talk with him in the lobby, where I outlined my plans for next year and received his advice and approval. Now, it is well known that Thompson is one of the most difficult men to satisfy on the doctor's examination. He is an extremely hard worker himself and prizes only similar types of men. In line with this general nature, he makes a practice of _____ with any of his students aside from his office hours. . . . [Long, unreadable sentences] . . . very touchy on the question of private feelings to interfere with official duty. [In my last letter?] I was careful _____ but it was quite frank and it is very likely to have [provoked] just the thing I wished to avoid, for I never received an acknowledgment, and the same held true for several postals that I sent him subsequently from Moscow and other points. The more I think the matter over, the more I am convinced that Thompson is at the root of it. When I return to Chicago I will ask Harper for an explanation, but until then am saying absolutely nothing. . . .

Concerning the _____ the department has been more than kind. The four letters of Harper and the two from the secretary of the department [Mr. Joranson] and from Mr. Huth, the former secretary, all are in this connection. Harper has approved the subject of my thesis on the basis of the outline I submitted, and I am now formally admitted to candidacy. This was quite good, for very often the thesis subject is not accepted or must undergo various changes, and in my case, [this] would have been almost calamitous, seeing that I bought books on this subject and have been doing so much reading in anticipation of its acceptance. The hundred-dollar offer for books still stands and has been repeated, even after I wrote that despite their heavy cost to me I don't believe I shall give them up. Concerning the credit for my work here, they have been very liberal and tell me that on the basis of the outline of the courses that I am taking at Berlin, which I submitted to them, they believe I shall be excused of all further courses at the University of Chicago excepting three courses . . . . [Remainder of this page is illegible.]

The question then is: what to do about them. I certainly don't want to delay my degree just on account of two courses, but of course it is impossible to be in Chicago in the fall. Harper will do all he can for me, I know, but he tells me, as does Joranson, the secretary, that it is difficult to get out of them. They have both asked me to be sure to try to get them in Berlin, but unfortunately, their exact duplication cannot be had. However, I am taking one course here which I believe will pull the trick for one of them. Besides, [illegible].

Berlin, July 5, 1928

[Typewritten letter on light letter paper, both sides; photocopy is very blurred. Reverse page is missing, which from context refers to continuing problems with Joe's painful finger.]

Rest and movement is all that it needs. But it is not going to let me do much by typewriting. I am writing this somewhat gingerly, using four fingers of the right hand and of course my left hand. I might say, sweetie, that this has been responsible for the lack of further notes for the last six or seven weeks about Germany and my failure to finish the rest of the notes on Russia and the Baltic states, of which I still have a good many.

Spent yesterday afternoon and night — that is, the Fourth — rather hilariously with the boys; that is, they did, while I, as usual, was asked why I don't "live up more." Never could drink and never was much of a hand at cabarets, and now, of course, still less so. Were five of us. John Morrison had just gotten back from his trip through northern Sweden and Finland. By the way, he got into Russia — six feet and ten inches, he measured: crossed the border from Finland (that is, just took two steps across in order to say that he had actually been in Russia) and then hurriedly stepped back as the Russian guards came running down. His brother [joined us], who has just arrived from America. The fifth member was Albert Robbins. I wrote you about Robbins before, a good friend of Saul Weinberg, whom I met quite accidently at the University. Well, the boys were all for having a grand time. The ambassador held a reception for all Americans in Berlin at the embassy, and we thought of going to it first, but when we got there, the boys decided it looked too tame, and without even going in, we went elsewhere. I would have really liked to have gone, but I had to do as the crowd wished. Well, not to prolong the story, it began with the cafe, where the boys did some dancing, but then, as this wasn't wild or exciting enough, continued with a cabaret, where the boys drank their liquor [illegible]. I don't exactly [approve of?] the drinking, but that is a matter of individual preference and may or may not hurt character. By the way, Alex does not drink either. The management found out that we were Americans and put itself out in various ways to please us, playing American national airs, etc. The boys cut up a good deal and gave the crowd a great time. Albert and Hugh (John's brother) can really sing quite well and have a wide repertoire of selections. We are quite an academic bunch. Hugh is teaching history of art, etc., at Amherst next year; John, geography at University of Chicago; while Albert is offered a job on the law faculty at the University of Berlin.

Friday Morning

Excuse the interruption, dearest, but couldn't be helped. Another acquaintance of mine from Chicago just dropped in on me. He is a young, quite brilliant chap by the name of Leon Depres, a Jewish kid of French origin. I knew him very well at Chicago, though was never intimate with him: is a bit too young. . . . I wrote him, at a Paris address, where to find me. He's quite an old hand at traveling (though like so many travelers, he makes a point of giving the impression that he is more extensively traveled than is actually the case) and has been to Germany twice before, though never to Berlin. Though I am quite busy, there was of course nothing else to be done than to spend the afternoon and evening with him: as the opera season ends for the summer this week, I took up his suggestion and witnessed the piece *Boris Godunov*, which, as you know, is an entirely Russian thing, done up with great elaborate sets.

You asked how friends find me so readily here: is not Berlin a large city? For one thing, there has been only two or three who have looked me up directly, and that has been through more or less the same method as Depres, that is, learn from friends in the States where I am and how to get hold of me. Besides, one learns quickly who is in town, because for one thing, not so many Americans come to Berlin; for another, visitors usually register at the consulate or American Express Co., and one often finds out in this way.

P.S. At Leipzig, before the monument erected to the famous Battle of the Nations, one of the photographers there "caught me off guard" and persuaded me to take my picture with the monument in the background. That's a typical embryo tourist _____, and I try to avoid all that "show," but I was "caught" that time. There is nothing else to be done but send you the photograph.

I am also enclosing a letter from *Current History* concerning my article on the German elections. This was my very first attempt at submitting anything to a large journal, and though I failed, you can see it was not because of the merit of the article itself. You might save the letter.

Berlin, Sunday night, July 8, 1928

So I look great in the picture? Somebody's "weakening." I am beginning to have confidence that in the end I shall persuade you that I am a handsome man after all. As to my looking "solemn," that is merely a natural look, except when I am around you, and then my face brightens up like Apollo's itself at midday of the summer solstice. . . .

The thumb is thoroughly healed, so far as I can tell. You see, it has the bandage on, and as this covers the sprain, I have no way of knowing whether the thing is cured or not. I'll know definitely by Thursday, when I remove the bandage. If it is, and I'm quite sure it will be, I'll say "Hallelujah," for it has kept me back in many ways. I've lost, or rather you've lost, five or six weeks of diary exercise.

Berlin, Thursday night, July 12, 1928

Thank heavens, Al Smith was nominated on an early ballot (the second, was it not? Or was it the first?), otherwise your night job would have prolonged that much more. Wouldn't be at all surprised, however, to learn in your next letter that you've decided to accept the night job as a permanent thing. Just wait till I get home. . . .

I should confess that last night, or rather, this morning, I got to bed at three. Had my first contact with American girls since I left the States. A group of eight Vassar girls and their chaperone came into the city on one of the tours, and Hugh Morrison, who traveled with them on the same boat across the Atlantic, asked the "gang" of us to help him entertain them. There were six of us fellows: the two Morrisons, Shilkin, Robbins, Depres, and myself, and the eight girls. The affair consisted of a sort of supper dance, along with an exhibition of fireworks, and I must say that it was a really enjoyable evening. The group was splendidly congenial — each girl dressed well, danced well, and looked surprisingly well. The girls with their evening gowns were a sensation to the Germans. It was impossible to avoid noticing the superiority in dress of the American girls over the German girls, not merely in quality (which is understandable) but in taste; not merely in dress, either, but in general carriage and deportment . . . .

Hon, I've been thinking about the desirability of giving a few talks in Houston and Galveston when I return. I shall not have time for anything as complete or serious as I should like (that is the only sort that satisfies me) — I refer to the time required for preparation — but I could give a few "popular" talks on my knowledge of present-day Russia, Baltic states, and Germany. I want to do this for two principal reasons: local reputation and practice in addressing the public. In Galveston a group about the size of the Temple Society and about that type would be the right sort of audience. What do you say to your sounding out Dr. Cohen on this matter? I believe that many people there would welcome an opportunity to get a little more information about these lands, particularly of Russia, especially if the information came in a more or less informal manner and in a place where questions could be freely asked and answered. In Houston I shall take the matter up with Dean Caldwell of Rice Institute, and he may arrange a talk or two under the auspices of the college. I am not exactly overeager for this sort of thing — that is to say, I don't consider it a matter that will give me special disappointment should I not talk in public now — but I feel that if I am ever to amount to anything as a public speaker, I had better take advantage of all opportunities to address an audience. Of course, you are not to tell Dr. Cohen all this, merely to put the question to him whether he believes the Temple Society would be interested to learn a few things about present-day Russia, as well as of the other states. With regard to Russia, the contents of my speech could be in line with my diary notes, and if he likes, another talk explaining the rise and character of the present government. It would be carried on in an informal, conversational tone, as a sort of discussion.

Got lots of work. By the 20th I want to have finished reading most of the necessary material for my second and third chapter, and from then to about the 3rd of August, when I shall leave for France, to have typewritten it as the first draft of these chapters for my thesis. The reading for the fourth chapter (the last) I shall do on the boat and cast it in draft form after my arrival.

Berlin, July 15, 1928

Received two letters from Father yesterday. Tells me that the family expected you that week. Certainly hope that you finally came and spent a few days resting up from your exhausting labors of the Convention week . . . . With us is almost like living in the country. Would be nice if your mother could enjoy the family's hospitality and the Bellaire breezes for a time too.

Four days after you receive this message, I shall be on my way home, not with the wings of Mercury, to be sure, but on my way nevertheless. And when that glorious Moment will finally have arrived, Past Time will have lost all meaning to us, and only the Present and the Future will be intelligible concepts.

There is much more to talk about here, but I want to get to some reading, and besides, I want to give my hand as much quiet as possible. Had the thumb-wrist bandage removed, and though the thing seems far better, I am told to give it complete rest.

[Galveston,] July 16, 1928

[Letter from Rose to Joe]

Now, about your letter [referring to June 25]. Honey, what do you mean writing me a little letter of 12 pages. Gee willigens, that's not so very much at all.

Was glad that you told me about the outcome. I sensed it after I did not hear anything about it. Don't worry, dearest. I know it will all come out all right in the end. No, I should say not, grading any papers. I would not give them any satisfaction. If you ask my opinion, dearest, I will not let you do anything of the kind. You deserve a marvelous fellowship for the work you did. When you return, do not "play" that you are piqued at them at all for it. The profs will see where they are wrong. At any rate, it will pay to let the matter drop for the present. You may need them for recommendations when you finish. . . .

So, dearest, we'll just "swallow" it and let it go at that. You need their recommendation, and perhaps they may even secure your position for you. The University of Chicago rates very high in the scholastic world, so of course they can do things for you. Well, from now on we'll let the matter drop. S'alright, dearest, do not worry.

Your dad had a fine article in the *Houston Post Dispatch* which was reprinted in the *Herald*. Frequently he writes rather long, involved sentences. But this time the little article was dramatic and as vivid a piece of writing as could ever be. I am sending you a clipping of it. Really, with your dad's knowledge, he could easily teach in some college.

Berlin, Wednesday, July 19, 1928

My Beloved "Better Half":

On the basis of that overwhelming pile of clippings representing your activity during Convention Week, which I received yesterday, justice compels me to acknowledge you my "better half" . . . at least for this "round of exchanges." You're setting a hard pace for me not merely to surpass but even to keep up with. . . . More seriously, sweetheart, that was certainly splendid work you did. All my great love and admiration goes out to you. . . . I have no end of love for you for your thoughtfulness in the matter of your correspondence with me. I well know under what great difficulties you must occasionally write, yet you forget self and write me anyhow. For instance, the letter you dashed me off from the *News* office during the small hours of the morning when the Convention excitement was at its height. . . .

About the kitchen, my likelihood of trying to "domesticate" you, my endeavors to interfere with your desire for a career — to all these things I plead not guilty. I should like to open my thoughts to you on this subject, but it would fill many pages and this I am not in a position to do now. One thing you can rest assured of, beloved: I shall never stand in the way of any of your ambitions. I may express my opinion and offer my suggestions, but that is all. This is to be an equal, lifelong "partnership" of two fully free and equal individuals who have entered into the relationship because they are convinced they will immensely enrich their own lives, and they hope, others, by so doing, but who, while willingly being ready to renounce a certain share of their individual desires, tastes, ambitions, and the like as the necessary "working capital" of the partnership, retain for themselves full and complete freedom of action in all other matters.

About Riga, you are right: it is in Russia, at least belonged to Russia until 1919. . . .

In two weeks I shall be departing from here. Two or three days in Paris, then Havre, then home! Could anything be more wonderful, more glorious. . . . I wish with all my heart that I could take a faster boat, but that extra two weeks is very necessary to my thesis (you know how little occasion I shall have to do anything on it when I return home), and the $100 is also valuable. . . . In the next letters I shall tell you definitely of my plans.

[Galveston,] July 19, 1928

[Letter from Rose to Joe]

[Rose reports she has received encouraging recommendations and promising offers of newspaper jobs.]

Well, my dear boy, I want to tell you that you only wrote 38 letters, 15 postal cards, 1 cablegram, 1 telegram, and lately you have only been sending me one letter weekly. And here I have been sending you on the average of two to three weekly. Now is that fair?

[Galveston,] Friday night, July 20, 1928

[Letter from Rose to Joe]

Gee, dearest, I just got through writing up an article for Doctor Cohen. I have one more to write before showing them to him for his final approval. I had to ferret out the information from a pile of papers he gave me on the prison system here in Texas. Say, darling, if I ever decide to go to jail, I'll wait and commit the crime out of Texas — more likely in California. The system here is almost barbaric.

Dad read in the papers today that the temperature in Berlin is 112. Poor boy, I hope you have been able to go out to the country. After all, Texas isn't half bad in that case.

Your dad had another article in the *Herald* this Friday. He writes excellently. (You have some stiff competition, with a father as brilliant as yours and a sweetheart . . . Oh well, I'll let you finish that part.)

Berlin, July 26, 1928

Little wifie, all your dreams about the future — about making our home a literary center, about your plans for leading an ideal life — these are things that are just what I dream about too.

The inevitable trouble with regard to packing has begun. I have about 90 pounds of books to ship off, which is doing its share to make things uncomfortable. I shall ship them by international parcel post, the cheapest way. The trunk goes with me. I have pretty well decided to go by way of Brussels, for, including a transit visa, the difference over the direct way is only two dollars.

I shall write you Sunday again, the last time from Berlin. You will hear from me right along, from almost every place that I stop. I shall write you from Vigo, Spain, from the Canaries, and from Cuba, so that you will have letters from me until almost the last moment.

Berlin, Sunday, July 31, 1928

Little one, do you realize this is my Last Letter from Berlin! Last night I walked through the Tiergarten and as I walked, I looked at everyone I met and everything I saw with an intensity, as though I wanted to literally burn their images in my memory. A sort of sadness came over me, the feeling "we have met but we will probably never see each other again. We live in two separate worlds, separated by incalculable distance. I go but with happiness awaiting me, such bliss that I dare not even picture it for fear it will vanish." . . .

I saw Alex for what will be the last time until probably December. Alex and I have been very close since the day I met him — my second in Berlin — and I have a lot of admiration and liking for him. He has his faults like all of us, but essentially he is an excellent man. For one of his age, 30, he is unusual: traveled and unusually experienced and has a capacity for getting around little obstacles that is nothing short of remarkable. He has an unusual command of languages, speaking four very well — Russian, English, German, Spanish — knows French fluently, and has a smattering of Latvian, Chinese, and of one of the Philippine tongues. Very finely built and nice-looking. I am quite sure we will have him in the bridal party.

Well, I finally got off my books, fun yet exasperating. One characteristic of the Germans is that they are very faithful to the letter of a regulation or a law and seldom have the courage or fertility of mind to go beyond it. The American postal regulations say that packages to America must be either in wooden boxes or sewed in cloth. Now, since four pounds is the maximum that can be sent, the wooden box in itself will almost take up that weight, while to have packages sewed up in cloth — really a sort of burlap — is putting a lot of hardship on an individual, particularly where, as in my case, I had already packed the books in good, strong cartons. I had been told I could do this by one post office, but upon delivering them to another post office closer to the house, they were refused. The next morning, however, when I brought the packages down and the afternoon clerks were not there, they were accepted just as they were. Another instance was in connection with a book I sent to Russia. One postal clerk refused to accept it as second-class mail because the string was not tied with a bow so that the contents could be easily examined. At another post office, where I took it for the fun of the thing, the clerk took the package without saying a word. These are only a sample of what is characteristic of Germany and which slows things up so badly. . . .

There are a number of other things to be done, but these I shall have completed by tomorrow. One is to ex-matriculate at the University. This I have done and await only the return of my papers. The semester ends Tuesday or thereabouts, so that I am leaving technically at just the right time. So far as learning things are concerned, I could have left a week after the semester began, to have stayed merely long enough to learn how little one is advantaged by the majority of lectures here. The system is good only in so far as it compels the student to depend practically altogether on his own initiative, resourcefulness, and energy to get what he wants, and from this standpoint it justifies itself. But one can well ask, "If this is the case, why go through the motions of lecturing?" If self-initiative is a good thing, why not have all of it possible, and therefore do away with those miserable remnants of what a real lecturing system ought to be. . . . To this I can only answer that there is no reason whatever why a lecture, if it is given at all, should not be as complete, as instructive, as useful, and above all, as inspirational as possible . . . .

I leave Europe having accomplished the principal thing for which I came: to find a subject and the necessary material for a doctor of philosophy dissertation. I came away with the thesis, as it were, in my pocket. I have almost finished the reading for the third chapter. The reading for the fourth and last chapter I shall finish in the 26 days that I am on the ship. I shall try to spend a month of odd hours during the fall getting it in more or less complete draft form. Whether I shall hand it in complete in March or in May (that is, the winter semester or the spring) depends on how much preparation I shall have to do for the written and oral examinations. The secondary things for which I came to Europe — or rather, that I hoped would result from my trip, for the determining reason was the thesis — to see Europe with my own eyes and learn it by myself and not through the agency of others, has also been satisfied. That I could have undoubtedly gotten fuller results than I have goes without saying. I see now how inefficient and wasteful of time and opportunity I have been. Yet I think it can justly be ascribed to the mistakes all "greenhorns" make, and that if I had to do it over, I would do much better.

Düsseldorf, Germany, August 1, 1928

[Postcard: reverse shows photograph of Heinrich Heine,* a poet Joe deeply esteemed]

---

*   A monument to Heine by sculptor Ernst Herter was meant to be erected in Düsseldorf in 1897 for Heine's 100th birthday, but the installation was cancelled due in part to widespread anti-Semitism. The monument was instead installed in New York City in 1899, where it is known as the *Lorelei Fountain*. A Heine memorial was finally erected in Düsseldorf in 1981.

Dearest:

Too bad it is raining and I won't get to see much of the city. Should like to see the houses in which Heine has lived. Also the Rhine. This is an important industrial town of almost 400,000 inhabitants. Too late to see anything, however. Almost seven o'clock. Leaving for Cologne, where will spend the night.

Paris, Saturday night, August 4, 1928, 12:00 a.m.

Have been in so many strange cities these last six months that it's becoming a sort of second nature with me to find my way about. Let's see, what did I do today? Sorbonne, Senate building, Notre Dame, Latin Quarter, Louvre, Palais de Justice, Place de la Bastille, Garden of the Tuileries, Place de la Concorde, most of the important boulevards and — last but not least — the Folies Bergère — just returned from the performance at the latter. But let me go back in time.

The last card I sent you was from Cologne. I left that city at 4:30 Thursday the 2nd and arrived in Brussels that same night. I left there, saw the most important points of the city, and left Friday at 4:00 for Paris. Got to Paris about nine o'clock last night.

Hon, you have my earnest word that these last few days of wandering have not been a pleasure, simply because there is always that ache for you — loneliness. I see what I can. I get momentary pleasure, but it's all mechanical, empty. Always there is with me the thought, "If only Rose was at my side, if only she were here to see these many things and exchange reactions with me!" . . . This separation has been cruel — *cruel* for both of us — but thank goodness the thing is drawing to an end.

Paris, Sunday afternoon, August 5, 1928

Darling, the letter I am enclosing was so poorly written that I simply can't send it off without a few supplementary words. Since writing it I have gotten a good night's sleep and done quite a few things. Had my trunk transferred from the Gare du Nord, where it arrived from Berlin, to the Gare St-Lazare, to be sent on to Havre; visited the Triumphal Arch; saw the grave of the Unknown Soldier; climbed to the top of the Arch to view Paris; inspected the church of the Madeleine (dates to the 18th century); walked along some of the boulevards; and then returned to the Hotel

Royal, where I've since been. Don't know what I shall do tonight. Probably stroll along one or two of the boulevards and watch the people and sights. I am quite accustomed to the open-air cafes, but Paris is remarkable in this extent. On the whole, they are not very clean and not pretty. Germany is the place for elegantly appointed cafes.

There is much to be seen here — much that affects the sense of beauty and the desire for variety. Yet there is no place like your own. Paris is for Parisians, for French people; for us it is interesting for a week, two weeks, no more. . . . I expected to find a good many more Americans here than is the case. Met one of my professors from the U. of Chicago in Berlin just before I left, and in the course of the conversation, he mentioned that this appears to be the case this year — fewer Americans.

Things on the whole are cheaper than in New York, yet you must watch your step. The tipping system is very much in evidence, just as the last time I went through, but I've gotten on to the ropes better. However, have been "caught" several times just the same, if not in tipping then in other forms of knavery or graft.

Le Havre, August 7, 1928

Here I was, fondly anticipating that by this time I should have left the French coast far behind. The French lines seem to be far from reliable. True, this time they claim a good excuse — that a strike among the seamen (a certain division only, apparently) is in progress, which prevents their leaving in time. As things now stand, we are to leave for certain Thursday the 9th, two days behind schedule. I imagine the lost time will be made on the way, as they think now, which means that instead of arriving in Galveston the 2nd as I had planned, I will arrive the 4th, if not later. Honey, this is what I have just thought of. The boat should arrive, in accordance with the revised schedule, on the 31st of August in New Orleans. I can take the train from New Orleans and arrive in Houston the 1st of September. This I believe I shall do. The 4th is almost too late for New Year cards, and if it isn't, I shall lose a good portion of my regular business. This being the case, it is entirely advisable to spend the $10 or so and take the train from New Orleans. I am writing to the family and shall tell them the same thing.

From every angle except one, this seems the advisable thing: that my fond anticipation of seeing you at the dock — having you there to greet me — will be shattered. But then — I'll be with you two days quicker. I'll let you know in some way from New Orleans of my plan — will telephone you (I'm broke). Anyhow, will probably telephone the folks, and they can telephone you. And just as soon as I catch my breath in Houston and kiss the folks, I'll hurry on down to you. Or maybe you'll be a grand little girl and be in Houston for my arrival. . . . Then we can both go back to Galveston together, and we can be alone all the while. This solves lots of problems. . . .

Wednesday

I arrived in Havre in the afternoon. Imagine my perturbation upon learning that the ship is delayed two more days in her schedule. I wracked my brain for a plan whereby to avoid this horribly long voyage, but always returned to the conclusion that there was nothing else to be done. Any other way would cost me no less than $150, which at the present time would be foolish. And then there was the thesis. I know how completely occupied I shall be when I return, and I don't want to take chances. The 26 days will just nicely serve to let me finish the reading for the last chapter and round off some additional reading for the thesis as a whole.

The ship company is feeding us free for the extra days and also furnishes lodging, but the latter is so bad — the whole crowd en masse in one large ward or dormitory — that I decided to stay at a private hotel.

I have had little direct experience with France, as you know, but what I have has revealed the French as lacking the preeminent virtue of the Germans: cleanliness. This is a country where one should avoid looking too closely at his food or the plates if he is to be happy — or at the rooms, courtyards, general surroundings, or anything else. Friendly, agreeable enough people — I like them better than the Germans in this respect — but in disaccord with our American notions and standards in *many things*.

Curious to know what the other passengers will be like. According to a list that I hastily read, there seems to be quite a large number going on to the States. Whether these are Americans or foreigners I didn't have the opportunity to notice. I hope it will be an interesting group.

One could find excellent material for a study of European peoples merely by associating with the third-class group that is now eating at the Company's expense, waiting for their respective ships to sail. Most of them are going on to New York, others on the *Niagara,* and still others in various other directions. They represent Europe in miniature, and on the whole not a flattering picture. It is easy enough to take an attitude — to be the epitome of generosity and beaming brotherliness and sing, "Come one, come all, brethren and sisters, we greet and welcome you all," or to take the opposite attitude, [to insist upon?] the 100-percent type — but to consider the imaginative question unsentimentally, "constructively," is a much more perplexing thing. I confess I'm at a loss for a standard test. I can't say, "Let them all come," for many are in reality very, very sorry people, and if not that, then so hopelessly different in color, type, language, tradition, and above all, "capacity for Americanization" that our national life can only be made more complicated than it already is. On the other hand, these are the opposing viewpoints. Who is to judge what are right and wrong? What is Americanization? If America had come about on the basis of present appearance and present education, most of our present-day so-called valuable citizens would still be unborn, or at any rate, serving with their virtues in some other land. Should you apply a professional, intelligence, physical type, general appearance (clothes, manners, etc.) test? One of them, all of them, none of them? A complicated question, truly.

You've had sociology, my dear: I wonder what your idea is? But I warn you, sentimentality won't do. Wait until we get to Chicago. One of the most interesting things I look forward to is going with you through the various colonies of the city. Incidentally, it should offer you good material for stories or even a book. In the future we shall — at least *should* — do a lot of just such things. Observe and study the different people; something very fascinating about it. And when we get to Europe, we'll find it even more interesting.

We leave at 11:30 in the morning — i.e., Thursday the 9th. In accordance with the revised schedule, we should progress as follows: Vigo, Spain, Aug. 11th; Canaries, Aug. 15th; Havana, Aug. 28th; New Orleans, August 31st. You shall have mail from all these points. This is goodbye for the last time from France.

À bord le Niagara [ship letterhead], *Havana, Cuba, Monday, August 27, 1928*

Getting closer and closer. Won't be long now! This is the first letter I have written you since leaving Havre. The boat failed to stop in Vigo, and from the Canaries it would have served no purpose to write, for I will arrive before a letter could reach you.

Have really had an unexpectedly fine trip. Were it not for my anxiety to be with you and to be home, this might be considered a wonderful trip. For one thing, the weather has been delightful. Fine, balmy nights, with the heavens showered with stars and the sea as smooth as a lake. For another, there is a group of Rice students aboard, a few of which I already knew and the rest of whom I became acquainted with. There has been dancing every night, a concert, a masquerade ball, and swimming every day. The quarters have been none too good, but livable nevertheless, and the food has been good. . . . The Canaries were very interesting. We stopped at three of the islands on three successive days (Las Palmas [on the island of Gran Canaria], Tenerife, and Santa Cruz de la Palma [on the island of La Palma]). These islands are of volcanic origin and consist of one mountain ridge after another. From the sea they present one of the grandest sights I have ever witnessed. The worst part of the voyage lay between the Canaries and Havana — 11 days — but at that, not at all bad.

Today is Monday, the 27th. We shall leave here tomorrow and are due in New Orleans Thursday the 30th. If a check awaits me at New Orleans, I shall take the train from there. If not, I must stay on board and go on to Houston — *nicht anders zu machen* [nothing I can do about it]. By the way, the ship will not stop at Galveston at all. But I am quite sure that Dad will not forget my request and that either Friday morning or Saturday will find you in my arms.

My darling, I'll try writing you another letter tomorrow. At least a postal. At the moment, I can write no more, for it is almost one and the boat will be here to take us ashore. This is necessary, for we are to sleep in the city tonight — disinfecting of the quarters makes this necessary.

[Finis]

No further letter tells whether Joe left the ship in New Orleans or sailed on to Houston. Joe's next letter to Rose is dated September 11, 1928; it was sent from Houston. He had been to see her in Galveston the previous week and was now missing her terribly. They had had a quarrel, for which each apologized, and they agreed they would not let quarrels build resentment between them.

Afterword, 1929–1934

Germany is quite literally in the throes of hysterical lunacy. It all seems rather incredible to me . . . and my literal account of what is going on in Germany must surely sound incredible to an outsider.

— Frederick L. Schuman
Letter to Joseph Werlin
Bolzano, May 23, 1933

Joseph S. Werlin, PhD
University of Chicago
June 16, 1931

Wedding photos of Joe and Rose
December 23, 1928
Matching bronze frames were
a gift from Chao-Ting Chi

IT IS TEMPTING TO TITLE this five-year stretch "A Texas Greenhorn at the University of Chicago." The bright future Joe and Rose envisioned after their marriage on December 23, 1928, soon began to fade. Not that they weren't deeply in love and devoted to one another, but the letters that Rose saved from this period reveal one setback after another.

The newlyweds honeymooned while making their way by train from the breezy warmth of Galveston to the frigid Windy City in January 1929. Their meager resources for living expenses included cash received as wedding gifts and accumulated savings from various temporary jobs. Rosella (as she now identified herself professionally, blending Rose with her middle name Ella), ever ambitious, soon landed a beat as a pennies-a-day cub reporter for the *Chicago Journal*. Right away she achieved some small notoriety when the newspaper sent her to the city morgue with a photographer to count bullets in the bodies of Al Capone's victims following the St. Valentine's Day Massacre. She did not receive a byline this time, but her scrapbooks, compiled in later years, include numerous clippings of feature stories, interviews, and public-relations stunts she initiated once she had established her worth. She was especially proud of her interviews with Golda Meir (then Golda Meyerson) and child prodigy Yehudi Menuhin. Although she was fulfilling her ambitions, the work she loved paid very little.

Joe had confidently drafted much of his PhD thesis while in Europe, since his topic and candidacy had been approved, and he returned to Chicago imagining that he could complete his doctorate by the end of 1929 or the spring of 1930 at the latest. And then, he expected, there would be many job openings. Reality set in right away. He took a risk and sat for the PhD qualifying exams that spring, but he didn't pass. He acknowledged that he had been unprepared, but he hadn't anticipated that the History Department review committee would deny him credit for most of the courses he had taken at the University of Berlin and that he would have to fulfill two more course requirements. We know from his letter to Rose of June 30, 1928, that he had been turned down for either a fellowship or a tuition scholarship and that his History Department advisor had never responded to his letters. He hoped other opportunities would surface once he returned to campus, but it appears no one was in his corner. His thesis advisor, the esteemed Russianist Samuel Northrup Harper, who had been so encouraging and solicitous, mysteriously kept his distance. Joe was on his own. He couldn't fathom the politics behind the indifference confronting him.

The explanation which follows no doubt is missing key factors. But there are two forces to consider: those that Joe understood and those he couldn't comprehend. Joe

Afterword | 213

had explained to Rose that the History Department at Chicago was very large and that only four members of that faculty knew him by name. He also pointed out that Russian history, under the direction of Samuel Harper, was "sort of auxiliary to the history department in general," with the effect that Russian studies was in separate territory. Still, he was baffled: "Something has happened at faculty deliberation that Harper didn't see . . . I thought for a time [the change in attitude of the History Department] might be due to my 'communistic' interests." He rejected this possibility and added: "I don't believe the Jewish question has anything to do with it, for few know my background, and if they did, I don't believe that would count against me at this university, for it is very liberal."

Joe was naive on the last two counts. Apparently, he was so distracted by his immediate concerns, he didn't ferret out, or have informants to illuminate, the background of the situation, which was, as later revealed, quite treacherous. Added to this was the October 1929 financial "massacre"— the beginning of the Great Depression — which Joe and Rose would feel with lasting effects.

Insights into that ugly period are offered in Erik Larson's brilliant historical narrative, *In the Garden of Beasts: Love, Terror, and an American Family in Hitler's Berlin* (New York: Broadway Books, 2011). The American family through whom this tale is told is that of Ambassador William E. Dodd, who was the chairman of the University of Chicago's History Department during all the years Joe was a graduate student there. Joe had never met him personally; Dodd only aroused his special interest when President Roosevelt appointed him ambassador to Germany in June 1933. Joe's friend Frederick L. Schuman, who was in Berlin working on a book for which he had hired Joe as research assistant, wrote on June 20, "I have no enthusiasm for making contacts with lunatics and scoundrels, and all Germans in official positions are now one or the other. I am enormously interested, of course, in Dodd's appointment as Ambassador, and that future contact should lead to some interesting results." By 1933, Joe was well aware of the Hitler menace and Stalin's machinations, but it seems he still didn't know the backstory on Dodd's attitude towards Jews, the several reasons for Samuel Harper's ambiguous attitude in helping him find a job, or the malevolent, if indirect, influence that one Charles R. Crane might have had on his opportunities for teaching Russian history or aspiring to any serious support at the University of Chicago.

Charles Crane, scion of a well-established, wealthy plumbing family, was not a name that Joe ever mentioned in later years, although he would have known he was a prominent advisor to presidents Wilson and Roosevelt. William Rainey Harper, Samuel Harper's father — founding president of the University of Chicago —

accompanied Crane to Russia in 1900, where both men met with the Tsar and influential nobility, fostering their deep interest in Russian history and politics. Erik Larson writes that Crane was a "generous supporter of Dodd's department at the University of Chicago, where he had endowed a chair for the study of Russian history and institutions" — this was the chair held by Samuel Harper. But more ominously, Crane was "no friend of Jews" (to put it mildly). Larson cites chilling advice from Crane to Dodd: "The Jews . . . are deluging the world — particularly easy America — with anti-German propaganda . . . . I strongly advise you to resist every social invitation." Dodd, Larson goes on to say, "partly embraced Crane's notion that the Jews shared responsibility for their plight."

Dodd's outlook towards Jews showed more compassion as the horrors mounted, but his earlier attitude and its expression on campus at the University of Chicago in 1929 was revealed forthrightly by his daughter Martha Dodd in her memoir, *Through Embassy Eyes* (New York: Harcourt Brace, 1939). She described "subtle and undercurrent propaganda among the undergraduates that promoted hostility" and noted that "even many of the college professors resented the brilliance of Jewish colleagues and students." Those words are also quoted in a biography of prominent California Supreme Court Justice Stanley Mosk, a Texas native and Jewish undergraduate at Chicago in 1929. Among countervailing influences for Mosk were his studies in the social sciences under a "truly outstanding faculty of accomplished scholars," including Frederick L. Schuman (*Justice Stanley Mosk: A Life at the Center of California Politics and Justice*, Jefferson, NC: McFarland, 2013).

Larson's book of course centers on Dodd and his family; Samuel Harper is not in the picture. But an online profile of Samuel Harper by the University of Chicago Library ("Guide to the Samuel Northrup Harper Papers 1891–1943," University of Chicago Library, 2007, www.lib.uchicago.edu) alludes to conflicts Harper faced at the University during these years. To oversimplify, Harper was accused of being both a Communist sympathizer and a bourgeois reactionary, which antagonized various departments through which his Russian studies program operated, and risked the loss of his support from Charles Crane.

On January 15, 1931, Joe wrote to Rose:

> *I am to meet Harper at 2:35 Sunday afternoon at the "Proletarian Forum." This is an organization of apparent extremists on Russia, something which Harper didn't know, he told me, at the time he accepted the invitation. But he is mortally afraid of heckling and jeering and wants moral support.*

The following Sunday, Joe described the meeting:

> This afternoon I went downtown in order to attend the lecture at which Harper was speaking and had invited me to give him "moral support."... At the entrance to the "Proletarian Forum" I waited for Harper, and when he arrived, [he] got me in free, just as promised. The man was quite worried for fear of what the world would say when they learned he had addressed such a radical audience. He is a real case. At heart he well understands that all is not too rosy with the world, but out of fear for his easy birth, he plays "safe" with the most consummate caution. His statements are nothing but a mass of qualifying adjectives; he neglects no opportunity, whether called for or not, of telling you he is no Communist. The man is very intelligent and has an unusually intelligent understanding of what is taking place in Russia, but the excessive caution and fear of his own shadow constantly drives away all tendency toward sentiment or emotion toward his subject; as a result, his speeches are cold, factual, soulless. . . . The hall was packed, about 300 people anyway, each paying 50 cents. Harper was mortally afraid of the Fish and other investigating committees, and insisted upon a good proportion of the net receipts in order that it might not be said — at least, this is his reason — that he enabled the radicals to make money for their nefarious undertakings. When he finished, he was given thirty dollars, which he took with alacrity. Not bad for two and a half hours of talking, eh? Which merely recalls the old saying about selling your soul for a mess of pottage. What was uppermost in Harper's mind when he accepted the invitation: the money or simply inability to resist?

It isn't clear that Joe had a full grasp yet of his own precarious situation. By the time he sent Rose the letter describing Harper's talk to the Proletarian Forum, he had surmounted the initial hurdles in his way to receiving his degree: completing the required coursework and passing the PhD qualifying exam. The full force of the Depression had not yet hit, but Rose had returned to Galveston earlier in January, where she could save money by living with her parents and have the benefit of working again for the nationally esteemed Rabbi Cohen and covering assignments for the *Galveston News*. Joe, it appears, only had income from the small holiday card imprinting business run off of his father's press. In letters to Rose, he claimed he was leaving no stone unturned in trying to scope out every job possibility. His reports reveal conflicting information. One week he would be told there were good job opportunities for new PhDs, the next that job announcements were scarce. One week he would optimistically confide that he wouldn't look at unknown colleges in remote locations, the next that he might have to consider anything that came along. On the one hand, he would be a rare find for an institution looking for a historian of Russia; on the other, jobs for Russian specialists were few and far between. Sometimes he was encouraged by meetings with professors in his department; other times, he felt a cold shoulder. Harper, in particular, was warm and friendly; yet Harper sidestepped conversation with him about jobs.

Joe's letters to Rose in the spring of 1931 don't seem truly downhearted. He expresses constrained resentment that a number of PhD candidates who had not yet passed the qualifying exam were given faculty assistantships while he wasn't, but he assigned that to the fact that they had prior teaching experience at other institutions. He never suggests, so it is unsupportable to question, whether their surnames, Cate and Johnson, might have worked in their favor too. One colleague called him a "lucky dog," and others concurred, for having his thesis and likely his PhD so soon in hand. Another of his cohort who held a teaching assistantship had flunked the PhD qualifying exam and was preparing to leave Chicago. But assistantships were only one-year appointments in any case. Joe was excited for Rose to return to Chicago in April and was looking for a suitable apartment for the two of them. "Won't be long now and all our troubles will be over," he wrote. "My little girl won't have to be able to work any more and will be able to finish what is so close to her heart, a college degree.... She is going to get all that or my name isn't 'Success Bound Joseph Sidney Werlin.'"

The ordeal which will follow over the next two years, exposed through letters Rose saved, is painful to read about, so this is a good place to step back and inquire into how "Success Bound Joseph Sidney Werlin" might have been seen by his professors, his colleagues, his friends, and his family. At this stage, there are no encomiums to cite, as there will be in later years. Photos show him to be physically trim, average in height: a nice-looking man, even handsome, some would have said — and so his Rose and her sisters thought. Observers with sophisticated tastes and comforts would have noticed his bargain-store clothing and neckties, not unlike what a rural Texas congressman or a city schoolteacher might wear. He rarely dressed casually, and throughout his life maintained that on Sundays in particular, one must not be out in public unless appropriately attired — meaning, appropriate in the eyes of those attending church. He strongly adhered to notions of acceptable, middle-class, white Protestant culture. His language was always measured. He never was heard to curse, and certainly never raised his voice in public. He didn't have a noticeable

Texas accent. His speech included so many words reflecting a highly educated background, it is hard to know how he might have come across when he was a younger man.

As for "the Jewish problem," there simply was no way any Jew could be indifferent to how he represented himself. That would have been true of any of the non-privileged minority populations of the United States, although some were affected less than others or felt fortified by norms of behavior within their own communities. Joe was unapologetically Jewish, but he resisted cultural markers and religious observances. Having spent his formative years in Pearland, an hour by train from Houston, he hadn't been exposed to a wider Jewish community beyond his own family circle in Texas and Philadelphia. Before he attended Rice, he rarely encountered Jewish youth of his own age. Yet he appreciated "tribal identity," and for the most part, the friends to whom he gravitated were Jewish. He was popular with the mothers and families of Jewish friends at the University (the Rosenbergs and the Halperins), and he enjoyed their hospitality. Even so, he didn't join their fraternal, political, or religious groups. He measured himself, and others, by some inchoate educated, humanist, middle-class ideal. His personal fraternity admitted anyone of any background, so long as that individual could meet his standard. His measure was not always endearing.

Understandably, a question would be asked in these years and later: Was Joseph Werlin a Communist or a Communist sympathizer? Most emphatically, he was never a Communist. His experience in Russia and subsequent observations dispelled any illusions others might have held. While he was repelled by radical political and labor movements, he sympathized with their struggles for reform. But he was cautious in his associations. He added in his letter to Rose following the Proletarian Forum, "You needn't fear, my girlie, I am playing his own game with him. I can't prostitute myself to the extent of uttering violent diatribes against the Communists, but at least I am keeping still." Harper, no doubt, had taken good measure of his graduate student as well. It appears he was comfortable in their association, but he wasn't inviting Joe into any inner circle.

Photos of Joe and Rose taken at Joe's hooding ceremony in June 1931 show a proud but serious Joe and a very pretty, happy, stylish Rose. However, this was far from being the end of their troubles, which were mounting. Joe had found a satisfactory furnished apartment for them, but they moved out not long after, to a place where rent was cheaper. Rose undertook a job with the *Chicago News*, although it paid little. She was soon pregnant, but she had to face the bitter winter of 1932 while commuting to the *News* office or pursuing stories via public transportation out of rather dicey Hyde Park. She never forgot walking past long bread lines. Meanwhile, Joe sent out one job application after another, to no avail. Rose went through a very arduous labor and delivered Herbert Holland Werlin by emergency C-section on May 23, 1932. She was hospitalized for more than a week and continued to be under physician care for some weeks after.

The succeeding chronology of troubles is not simple to reconstruct, although Rose preserved debt notices and anguished letters from friends and relatives, and she recorded angry calls over unpaid bills, leaving one to wonder if she was preserving this record for some future purpose — perhaps a feature story recalling these difficult times, or a memoir? In June 1932, Joe wrote a letter to his Aunt Annie in Philadelphia, thanking her for a baby gift:

> *I needn't tell you people what hard times are. . . . It is a safe bet that you too have felt the general business depression. Dad's financial position is abominable, and the sad part of it is that all of us children are no better off. . . . Certainly my own position is about as unenviable as anybody's, what with a mountain of debts and with the Chicago school system four months in arrears with salary.*

At some point during this bitter year, a close friend of Joe and Rose, owner of a manufacturing business, jumped to his death from a window of his Hyde Park apartment building.

A hero saved Joe and Rose from total despair in the fall of 1932: Frederick L. Schuman. Fred Schuman was almost four years younger than Joe, but a wunderkind: he had completed his PhD at Chicago in 1926 and was already on the faculty in political science. They had met when Joe was studying for his master's degree. In May, Fred and Lily gave the new parents a baby gift of five dollars, which Rosella said later was "like $500." She told that story often and wrote about it in a letter to the Schumans' son Don after his father's death. Most remarkably, Schuman went to bat for Joe in the Political Science Department, obtaining for him in fall 1932 a research grant of $250, increased later to $300. The grant was for his help with a book Schuman was writing on the rise of Nazism, for which Joe compiled the bibliography. Some of Schuman's correspondence with Joe survives in letters Joe preserved. One in particular, handwritten from Bolzano on May 23, 1933, is chilling to read. Schuman was sounding an alarm as loud as he could, warning of Hitler madness: "Germany is quite literally in the throes of hysterical lunacy!" Curiously, he never uses the word "Jew" in his long account of the evils being perpetrated against minorities in Germany. Hard to know whether he was sensitive to his friend's background or whether he understood Joe could read between the lines.

Joe had other part-time jobs, including one teaching in night school through the Chicago public school system. However, that wasn't enough. Bad news came from every direction as the Depression deepened. In early September 1932, Joe's father reported that his salary at the Holland Furniture Company had been reduced by $25 per month, and then by $50 per month. Not long after, he wrote to say the bank had given notice that the Bellaire home would be seized if the past-due mortgage was not paid by December 25. Jacob does not say what Joe knew: that his mother would be especially devastated by this turn. The Bellaire homestead, on the outskirts of Houston, where she cultivated her tomatoes and vegetables and grew the beautiful flowers the city relatives enjoyed, was the center of her world after the death of her eldest child, a daughter, and periods of deep poverty. Jacob added, "All I get now is $35 per week and it melts away." He is disappointed with his other sons in Houston: "Gene refuses to participate in selling Christmas cards. Don't know if I can find the money to help Sam attend Rice. Up to Gene and Sam to pay full interest due between now and Dec. 25 or we will lose the house."

Jacob asked whether Joe knew anyone who could extend a loan. On December 12, Rabbi Cohen wrote to Joe that the US National Bank "insists I pay the sum of $135 which I had guaranteed. . . . They can get no satisfactory reply from your folks in Houston. . . . Please see what you can do in the matter." Joe received a harsh note from his dentist after repeated extensions on an unpaid bill. The People's Bank in Chicago called for repayment of a $52 loan (possibly for Rose's hospital expenses; the reason is not stated).

Perhaps the bitterest exchange came with the best man in Joe's wedding, a former classmate from Rice who, having earned his MD in 1926, was well established (through the benefit of substantial tuition subsidies for medical students, granted by Texas lawmakers, which Joe resented as an inequity in education financing). Joe asked him for a loan, apologizing for an earlier letter in which he had chastised him over an unsuitable courtship that had fueled Galveston gossip. Dr. Diamond claimed his practice was not doing well and turned Joe down flat, although soon after, Rose spotted him driving around Galveston in a new Chevy Roadster. Their friendship never recovered.

Right after New Year's 1933, Rose returned to Galveston with baby Dutchy (a nickname based on his middle name, Holland). The baby was a hit with both families, the first grandchild on the Horowitz side and the second on the Werlin side. Rose sent ecstatic accounts of every adorable baby antic to Daddy, trying to cheer him up. The length of separation was uncertain, but it also was humiliating to the new father, who could not be a proper provider. Rose wasn't just in Galveston for family comfort; she had newspaper and business connections and was looking for ways to add to their income. It isn't clear she was successful, but she reported to Joe on an encouraging conversation with her former employer, Silas Ragsdale, editor of the *Galveston Daily News*. His name is honored in the Werlin family.

The debts didn't go away, and Joe still didn't have serious professional prospects. But it appears the outlook after the presidential election in November must have increased optimism. Rose wrote in mid-January, "Somehow I feel that we have weathered the worst." She ordered a surprise gift for Joe, subscriptions to *The Nation* and *Current Affairs*; the total was $6.50, on which she paid the first installment of $2.00. She also provided detailed accounts of expenses for the baby and herself and reminded him to send a check (it came soon after: $10). Her next letter offers Werlin family updates. She and the baby went to Houston, where "your folks gave a lovely gathering . . . . The home looked lovely, the flowers were growing in full force . . . . Sam is going to Rice . . . . The Christmas card business hardly made expenses . . . . Gene spends most of his days at the club."

It is hard to reconcile this January news with the miseries of autumn 1932, but clearly spirits had lifted. In early March 1933, Joe sent Rose a book of poetry. She replied that "Sunny Beebie has already tasted its contents . . . . He wanted a taste of its beauty in one setting." She signed the letter "your little girl, Rosella," returning to a playful term of the sort she and Joe had used for one another during their courtship. Also in March, Joe's father sent him a 16-page typed article he had authored, titled "Farmer's Holiday — As a Remedy, Not a Menace," responding to crop-management challenges and arguing for a sabbatical year for farmers during which their fields would lie fallow. He also sent a long commentary that had appeared in the *Houston Chronicle*, "A Call to Pen and Pencil Workers to Unite." It included a very amusing poem, "Men of the Pen Unite!" Jacob kept busy writing, but he was discouraged that he couldn't find publications that would pay him for his articles.

Rosella (as she signs some letters now) tells Joe how relieved she is that he is able to pay off some of the debts. She is contemplating when she and the baby will return to Chicago. They miss one another (Joe more so, it seems), but there is no hint that she is overly eager at the prospect. The weather in Galveston is beautiful, and her family is very happy to have the baby nearby. She doesn't admit to Joe in words what she would say so often in later years: she hated living in Chicago.

Rosella and Dutchy returned to Chicago on March 20, 1933. Joe had been renting a single room in various locations and had not yet settled on a good arrangement for the family. Rosella had written that it would be fine to stay temporarily in a hotel with an "in-a-door" (a Murphy bed), but she wanted an apartment with at least two bedrooms, one for an office where Joe could work, away from the baby. She really wanted a home with furniture of their own, not another furnished apartment. That dream, ultimately realized in three fine homes successively, would be a driving force throughout their lives together, no matter what other debts they might carry.

They reviewed Joe's job prospects in their exchange of letters. An article in the *Houston Chronicle* dated December 14, 1933 (placed by Rosella) announced his appointment as "Registrar of the People's Junior College of Chicago," where he also was "professor [sic] of history and head of the department of social sciences." In addition, he was teaching a course in twentieth-century Russian history and social development for the University of Chicago's home study program. But nothing permanent was on the horizon that he could see, so he had obtained certification to teach high school history in the Chicago public school system. That was a hard letdown for Rosella, who continued to believe that her accomplished husband must have better opportunities; she hoped he would turn his PhD thesis into a book, to increase his appeal to major universities. Joe hadn't abandoned serious academic aspirations. In addition to his work with Fred Schuman on Schuman's book, and in spite of rampant anti-Russian public sentiment, he pursued his own investigations into Russian and German political developments. Joe's spirits were raised by a new mentor whose name surfaces during this time: Professor Ferdinand Schevill, who had returned to the University faculty in 1930 to teach humanities. He later mailed Joe a prospectus of his 1936 book, *The History of Florence*. A signed, framed studio photo of Schevill would always hang in Joe's home office.

In July 1933, a flicker of light appeared out of the gloom. Joe's father wrote,

> *Here is something that may be news to you and perhaps of some value. The Houston School Board, with Dr. R. K. Daily as the moving spirit, are seeking to secure Government money with which to convert the Houston Junior College into a major university. It seems that the chances are very bright for it. . . . You might try Dr. Daily for a place on the Junior faculty with the ultimate chance in the major one. Let me know if you are interested. . . .*

Were they interested? Rosella got on the case right away, working her connections in Galveston and Houston. It isn't certain how Dr. Dailey might have met Joe, but she was well known in Texas. She was born Ray Karchmer in Lithuania in 1891. Her parents left to escape the pogroms, emigrating to Galveston, where Rabbi Cohen was instrumental in resettling Jewish families. She was the first Jewish woman to graduate from the University of Texas Medical School at Galveston, after which she set up an ophthalmology practice with her husband. Her public service began in 1921, and by 1928 she had been elected to the Houston Independent School District board, with a very distinguished career to follow. There is a family memory that Dr. Daily wrote a recommendation for Joe to the University of Chicago when he graduated from Rice. She would have paid attention to a man with Joe's record of scholarly achievements, as their subsequent relationship would show.

Not surprisingly, the proposal for the new university in Houston was not a done deal right away. That story need not be retold here, but sometime in the summer of 1934, Joseph Werlin was appointed to the first faculty of what was to become the University of Houston. Joe and Rosella were headed back to Texas. They couldn't have been happier.

This happy ending, however, came about with sour notes that would be hard to dispel. *Ten years* had passed between the time Joe earned his BA at Rice and the moment he finally landed his first full-time job! A full decade, almost half of it during a period of severe economic suffering that was felt deeply in Joe's family. Joe had managed to earn degrees from the finest of America's universities, but nearing age 34, the best position he could get was a low-paying post at what would be reputed in Houston for some years to come as a "junior university." Joe's parents never lost pride in their eldest son; his father championed him in spite of their disagreements on religious and political issues. His youngest brother and sister looked up to him. Rose's parents and siblings admired and even idolized him. But Joe had been a scold, especially hard on his two immediately younger brothers, both of whom also had graduated from Rice — one as an engineer, the other an architect. He argued that they weren't pulling their full weight in the family, that they were not communicative enough, not respectful or responsible enough. True, Joe had willingly given all he could when he was younger, but he had been far away in these years when his family needed help.

Throughout their lives, the siblings remained a unit out of family loyalty, but resentments lingered. Brother Gene — later a prominent architect — threw a stinging bromide in Joe's face: "Those who can, do. Those who can't, teach." Rosella never forgot the insult.

The University of Chicago Press
5750 ELLIS AVENUE · CHICAGO ILLINOIS

Please note:

ewith the proofs of your thesis

RUSSIAN SOCIAL-DEMOCRACY IN THE PERIOD
OF ITS FIRST THREE CONGRESSES
(1898–1905)

JOSEPH SIDNEY WERLIN

The first period of Russian social-democracy is synchronous with the decade 1884–94. In this period the "Emancipation of Labor," the original Russian social-democratic organization, was founded (1884) in Switzerland by G. B. Plekhanov and several other former members of the Populist circles of the seventies. Within Russia a number of social-democratic circles also sprang up at this time in all the important cities; but they were, without exception, small and short-lived, had no organic connection with each other, and exerted virtually no influence on the Russian labor movement.

In the second period, 1894–98, which coincides with an epoch of rapid industrial development and extensive social unrest in Russia, the social-democratic movement experienced its first real awakening. New and larger groups made their appearance, and the relations between them and the workers became more intimate and consequential. The St. Petersburg "Union of Struggle for the Emancipation of the Laboring Class" and the other social-democratic organizations of this period began to play an active rôle in the creating and guiding of strikes among the industrial workers. Certain of the organizations then commenced to look favorably on the idea of merging themselves into a comprehensive, all-Russian party, and, with this purpose in mind, came together at the first Congress, held in Minsk, March, 1898.

The Congress was composed of nine delegates, representing six organizations. A program and a constitution were formulated, a central committee was elected, and the name "Russian Social-Democratic Labor Party" was adopted. But hardly had the Congress ended, when a wave of political arrests swept the country, resulting in the imprisonment of the Central Committee and the temporary disruption of the constituent organizations. While the organizations continued to refer to themselves as "local committees of the party," and to speak of the party as though it actually existed, in reality the social-democratic movement continued to have its former disorganized character.

Following the First Congress there developed two conflicting ideological currents in the movement, the so-called Economic and Political tendencies. The followers of Economism maintained that the Russian workers could be won to the banner of social-democracy only if the social-democrats studied the workers' material needs and their grievances arising out of their working conditions, and sought to satisfy these by leading the workers to strikes and demonstrations against their employers. They contended that the Russian worker, owing to his cultural backwardness and political inexperience, was unable to appreciate the connection between his political "rightlessness" and his material and spiritual debasement, and would not follow the social-democrats if they attempted to lead him to battle for political reforms. Besides, they argued, a specifically political struggle was unnecessary. The profound disturbance in the country which would result from an intensified economic struggle of the workers against the employers would compel the autocratic government, in the interest of "peace and order," to undertake political measures for the protection and satisfaction of the workers. One political concession would lead to another until, eventually, Russia would attain democracy without having had to resort to revolution.

The arguments of the Economists proved very appealing, and for the period 1898–1902 their views remained dominant in the social-democratic movement. The most ardent supporter of Economism within the empire was the St. Petersburg "Union of Struggle for the Emancipation of the Laboring Class," which propagated its views through the journal *Rabochya Mysl* ("Worker's Thought"). Outside of Russia the principal exponent of the tendency was the "Union of Russian Social-Democrats Abroad," the literary mouthpiece of which was the journal *Rabochee Delo* ("Workers' Cause").

The Politicals argued that the methods and ideas advocated by the Economists were those of "trade-unionism," not social-democracy. They maintained that the Russian workers were "historically ripe," as they termed it, to undertake an immediate struggle from the whole tsaristic system, and that they were fully cognizant of the importance to them of acquiring certain political reforms at once. Hence the tactics of the social-democrats should be to utilize every instance of workers' discontent for the purpose of weakening the autocracy; on the occasion of every strike against their employers for economic concessions, the workers should be encouraged to demand simultaneously political reforms from the state.

The current represented by the Politicals remained very weak until around the end of 1900 when the journal *Iskra* ("Spark") was established at Stuttgart as a result of the collaboration of N. Lenin, Yu. Martov, and A. Potressov with the "Emancipation of Labor." The force and clearness with which *Iskra* expressed its opinions, the general respect which its editors, such as Plekhanov, Lenin, and Martov, enjoyed among the social-democrats, together with the zeal and ability of the "network of agents" which distributed the journal and propagated its views in Russia, contributed to the success of the Political tendency by the beginning of 1903. An even greater factor explaining the triumph of the Politicals was the largely spontaneous or untutored action of the Russian workers in raising demands for political reforms during various strikes in the period 1901–3, particularly in South Russia. This beginning of a mass movement convinced most of the social-democrats of the correctness of *Iskra*'s contention that the Russian workers were class-conscious and prepared to do battle with the autocracy, and brought them to the banner of the Politicals.

Encouraged by their successes, the Politicals who gathered around *Iskra* began to make preparations for the calling of another congress, in order to establish unity in the party and secure official sanction of their views. Considerable difficulty was experienced in this attempt; but finally, after a series of preliminary conventions, the Second Congress was convoked in July–August, 1903, at first in

Proof of thesis abstract

Brussels, and later in London. The party program and the constitution adopted by the Congress were in complete accord with the principles for which the *Iskra*-ists stood, so that the latter were completely victorious over their old enemies, the Economists.

But before the Congress adjourned a serious quarrel broke out among the editors of *Iskra*. This led to the division of the delegates of the Political wing at the Congress into two groups, which soon came to be spoken of as the Bolshevik, or Majority, faction, and the Menshevik, or Minority, faction. Lenin was the leader of the Bolsheviks; while Martov, Trotsky, and Axelrod were the leaders of the Mensheviks. Plekhanov sided with Lenin at the Congress but shortly afterward went over to the Mensheviks.

At the Congress itself the points of disagreement appeared on the surface to be quite trivial; they were, for example, whether the *Iskra* editorial staff should be re-elected intact, and whether the party should admit to membership only those who personally joined one of the party organizations. After the Congress, however, the differences came to involve basic questions of party organization and party tactics. The period between the Second and Third Congresses (August, 1903—May, 1905) was marked by a bitter polemic between the respective leaders and by a determined struggle for control of the three chief executive bodies created by the Second Congress. The split became increasingly wider until finally, by the end of 1904, the two factions had become virtually independent parties, each with its own leadership, executive centrals, constituent organizations, and press.

This cleavage into two independent fractions received official sanction when, in April–May, 1905, largely under the influence of the events of the revolutionary year of 1905, the two fractions held separate conventions (the Bolsheviks in London; the Mensheviks in Geneva). The two meetings adopted mutually opposed resolutions relating to questions of organization and tactics. The Bolsheviks carried out completely the ideas of Lenin. The party organization was to be strictly centralized. The workers were to be prepared to engage in an armed uprising that was to be called at the first favorable moment. In the event of success of the uprising, which was expected to develop into a mass revolution, the social-democrats were to force the other classes to agree to the establishment of a provisional revolutionary government and were to participate in such a government in order to insure in this way the calling of a constituent assembly and the creation of a democratic republic.

The Mensheviks, on their side, adopted the views of Martov, Plekhanov, and other members of the *Iskra* editorial staff. The organization of their fraction was to be constructed on democratic principles. Preparations were to be made for an armed uprising, but this was not to be declared until the greater part of the nation had shown itself unmistakably willing to engage in the revolution. The social-democrats were not to participate in any future provisional revolutionary government, because they could insure greater success of the revolution by remaining a party of the opposition.

Following the conventions, each fraction went its own independent way and sought to realize its principles in practice. Despite numerous attempts at integration, the Russian social-democratic movement continued to remain split into the two divisions of the Bolsheviks and the Mensheviks.

Proof of thesis abstract, continued

HOUSTON MAN GETS DEGREE AT CHICAGO U.

Special to The News.

Chicago, Ill., June 16.—Joseph Sidney Werlin of Houston was among those receiving the degree of doctor of philosophy from the University of Chicago today.

Dr. Werlin is the son of Mr. and Mrs. J. B. Werlin of Houston and was graduated from Rice Institute in June, 1924, with the degree of bachelor of arts. He will receive his doctorate in history, a study in which he took an interest during his undergraduate days at Rice Institute. He specialized particularly in studies relating to modern Europe.

In June, 1926, he received the master of arts degree from the University of Chicago. Three years ago he left for Europe to secure material for his dissertation, spending six months at the University of Berlin and two months in Russia.

Dr. Werlin has financed himself since the age of 14. He never even finished high school, family financial difficulties having obliged him to seek employment. In 1919 he passed the entrance examinations to Annapolis, to which he had received an appointment as second alternate. The following year, however, he decided to give up his military schooling. He returned to Houston, where he prepared himself and successfully passed the necessary entrance examinations to Rice Institute.

Dr. Werlin is one of the few Rice Institute graduates to have received his doctor of philosophy degree from the University of Chicago. He is 30 years old and is married to Miss Rosella Horowitz, daughter of Rabbi and Mrs. H. J. Horowitz of Galveston.

Chicago News
June 16, 1931

THE UNIVERSITY OF CHICAGO

ON·THE·RECOMMENDATION·OF·THE·FACULTY·AND·BY
VIRTUE·OF·THE·AUTHORITY·VESTED·IN·THEM·THE·TRUSTEES
OF·THE·UNIVERSITY·HAVE·CONFERRED·ON

JOSEPH SIDNEY WERLIN

THE·DEGREE·OF

DOCTOR·OF·PHILOSOPHY

DEPARTMENT·OF·HISTORY

AND·HAVE·GRANTED·THIS·DIPLOMA·AS·EVIDENCE·THEREOF

GIVEN·IN·THE·CITY·OF·CHICAGO·IN·THE·STATE·OF·ILLINOIS
IN·THE·UNITED·STATES·OF·AMERICA·IN·THE·YEAR·OF·OUR·LORD
ONE·THOUSAND·NINE·HUNDRED·AND·THIRTY-ONE·ON·THE
SIXTEENTH·DAY·OF·JUNE

Harold H. Swift, President of the Board of Trustees
Roy W. Bixler, University Registrar

Robert Maynard Hutchins, President of the University
Donald Slesinger, Dean

HOUSTON CHRONICLE
Thursday, December 14, 1933

Houstonian Named Registrar of Junior College in Chicago

DR. J. S. WERLIN

Dr. Joseph Sidney Werlin of Houston has been appointed registrar of the People's Junior College of Chicago. He has been professor of history and head of the department of social sciences since the opening of the institution in the fall.

Doctor Werlin is the son of Mr. and Mrs. J. B. Werlin of Houston and was graduated from Rice Institute in June, 1924, with the degree of bachelor of arts. He attended the University of Chicago for post-graduate work, receiving his degrees of master of arts in 1926 and doctor of philosophy in 1931. He also spent a year abroad carrying on research for his doctorate.

In addition to this work at the People's Junior College, Doctor Werlin is a member of the faculty of the home study department of the University of Chicago. He is 33 years old. Doctor Werlin is married to the former Rosella Horowitz of Galveston, daughter of Rabbi and Mrs. H. J. Horowitz. They have one son.

Bolzano (Bozen) — May 23, 1933

Dear Joe —

Greetings from "Austria Irredenta"! I arrived here a few days ago with my mother en route from Berlin to Rome on a short "grand tour" (3rd class) of the continent (Fascist). I've been meaning to drop you a line ever since I reached Germany, but with one thing and another I haven't somehow found the time. No — I'm not working already. That makes it worse. It's bad enough to spend all of this time on a job which will have some sort of result ultimately. But to spend it just fooling around is really deplorable. My two weeks in Berlin were largely consumed in discovering how little German I really know and in the delightful(!) occupation of flat-hunting. After much agony we finally rented a modern two room furnished apartment in Wilmersdorf, near Hindenburg Park. It's far from the U. and from Wilhelmstrasse but it's pretty good — and it's cheap — only 80 marks a month. The original lessee — a Frau Goldenweiser and a cousin of the American anthropog — is still in its spare room but she plans to join her daughter in Italy shortly.

I have not fled to Italy to escape Nazi persecution, but merely to have a brief vacation before returning to frau and kind (and to work) in Berlin. But it was a relief to get out of the "Third Reich" — even though I have come to another Fascist state. Here at least, Fascism is 10 years old and has had time to cool a bit. Germany is quite literally in the throes of hysterical lunacy. It all seems rather incredible to me (which only proves that I'm not yet a good political scientist) and my literal account of what is going on in Germany must surely sound incredible to an outsider. There is no disorder or disturbance to public peace — would to God there were — then we might still have some hope and some respect for the Germans! What is most astounding is not the Hitler madness itself, but the complete inanity with which the entire populace apparently to a man has been terrifyingly befuddled, bamboozled, and bewitched by the extraordinarily astute Hitlerite demagoguery. All opposition has completely disappeared. Violence has played its part in this of course but violence and terrorism are much less than half of the story. All of the Communist leaders and many of the Socialist are in jail, all Communist and Socialist papers throughout the country, as well as many "liberal" papers have been permanently suppressed and such non-Fascist political groups and journals as remain alive do so only by licking the Fascist boots. Incidentally, the sniveling cowardice of the German academic intelligentsia is equaled only by the raving lunacy of the German U. students and by the nauseating spit-licking tactics of the Socialists in the face of their destroyers. They actually voted "confidence" in the Hitler cabinet in the farcical Reichstag session of last Wednesday!

Letter from Frederick Schuman, May 23, 1933

What has taken place however, has really assumed the proportions of a "national awakening" — a phrase constantly in Nazi mouths. I should characterize it more accurately as a violent (and seemingly chronic) attack of national insanity. The opposition (which is not perceptible to the naked eye) is less terrorized than hypnotized. There is no doubt whatever in my mind but that the rank and file of all the middle and left parties — even including the Communists — has been wheedled into the Nazi camp by the most clever and unscrupulous demagoguery I have ever beheld. "Big Bill"[Kaiser Wilhelm II?] was a piker by comparison with Adolph. Hitler and 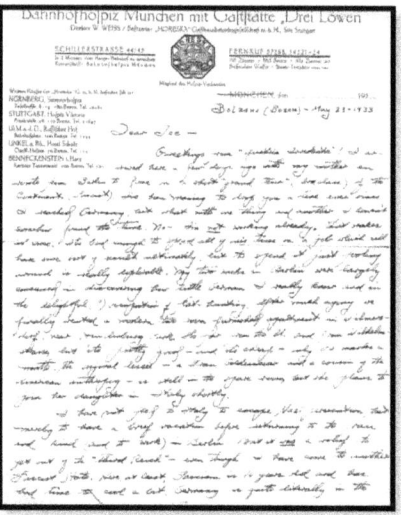 his colleagues know their Germans much better than anyone outside of Germany could ever know them. And believe it or not, it has become my conviction that 99.44% of allied war propaganda against Germany was gospel truth: Here is a people of State-worshipers who understand only the cult of violence and of war. They trust and hunger after despotism and the more that government kicks them in the face and beats them with lashes the better they like it — provided they are given circuses and parades, sword-rattling and goose-stepping, and an opportunity to vent their spleen on helpless minorities within their frontiers and imaginary national "enemies" and "oppressors" _____ their frustration. All of this Hitler has given them — and they are in a wild frenzy of joy — for behold! — again they have flags and idols and war symbols, again heroes and martyrs of national megalomania, again (and more than ever before) a tyrannical régime which turns them all into cannon fodder, again songs and banners and ceaseless incantations, cursings, moanings, and beating of tom-toms — and again charades, parades, parades...

"National labor day" (May 1st) in Berlin was a most disheartening spectacle — a million workers joyously and spontaneously turned out to parade and cheer Hitler and hear speeches and see fire-works. The next day the trade unions were suppressed — without the slightest resistance, the least whimper of objection. The German labor movement, built up painfully, through half a century of struggle has been wiped out overnight — because the Nazis are clever knaves and the German workers are after all, fools ... The dictator-demagogues of reactionary German capitalism and of revitalized Prussian militarism hold the nation in the palms of their hands, and this regime will, without question, continue until the next war. That war is now more "inevitable" that 1914 ever was, whatever words Hitler may utter to gain time for "preparations" this regime lives and breathes only by virtue of the immense popularity of its creed of force and its cult of ceaseless anti-foreign incitement. No man in his senses can spend two weeks in Berlin without despairing completely of the future of Germany — and of Europe — and of peace — and of all hope of a rationally orderly civilized world community. Heil Hitler! [author draws in swastika]

Letter from Frederick Schuman, May 23, 1933

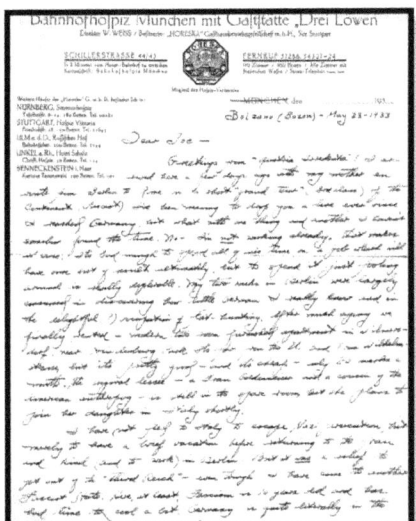

Well Joe, I could go on raving endlessly but I'll write you more later. The grievances of the Germans in this corner of Italy seem now of negligible importance by comparison with what is happening in Germany itself. This is an almost solidly German-speaking community (except soldiers, policemen and school-children), but no effort has been spared to "Italianize" it forcibly. All street names, hotel names shop signs etc. must be in Italian and almost all of the external indices of Germanism have been liquidated. But I am more interested at the moment in the marvelous climate and in the inconceivable grandeur of the Dolomites, which surpass anything I have seen in Switzerland. Tomorrow we are leaving for a few days in Venice, then a few more in Florence followed by a week in Rome and a return via Switzerland and Alsace-Lorraine.

    Hope you and Rosella and the bambino are well and are in the inflationist (anticipatory) prosperity I have been reading about. I am losing money on my £s, though not seriously yet. I should have lost much more if I had carried my money in dollars. It's a god-dammed crazy, cock-eyed world, nicht wahr?

        With warmest regards,
                Fred

P.S. Drop me a line when you get time —
Permanent address —
92 Hindenburgstrasse (Wilmersdorf)
Berlin

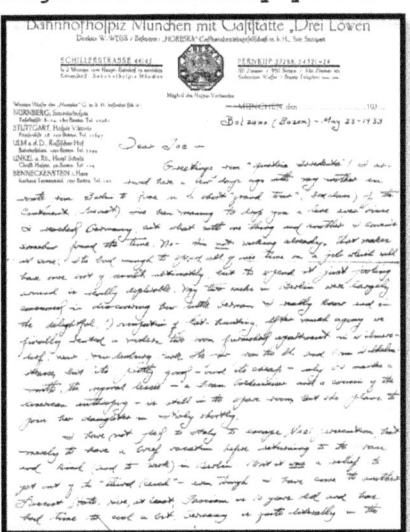

These three images are transcriptions of a letter from Frederick Schuman dated May 23, 1933. The original is in the Frederick Lewis Schuman Papers, Williams College Archives & Special Collections.

At this time, Schuman, a faculty member in the Political Science Department at the University of Chicago, is in Germany conducting research for his first book, *Nazi Dictatorship: A Study in Social Pathology and the Politics of Fascism* (published in 1936). Werlin, who had received his PhD in 1931, had been given a research assistantship from Schuman in the fall of 1932 to help compile the bibliography for his book. Werlin had spent the better part of 1928 in Berlin and Moscow, conducting research for his doctoral thesis, "Russian Social Democracy in the Period of the First Three Congresses, 1898–1905."

The letter was preserved by Rosella Werlin and transcribed by Joella Werlin in December 2018.

Berlin, June 20, 1933

Dear Joe:

Just a note to acknowledge your letter of May 30th. I presume that you have long since received my first letter from Eisenach- or wherever it was that I wrote it from. I have really no news of any great interest at the moment. I cut my vacation tour with my mother short in order to get back to my family and to work the sooner. I had already convinced myself that the Russian tour was off, that I would spend the summer really learning German properly, and then get to work in earnest on my project with perhaps a week or so in Moscow on my own in September. But no such luck! I have just had word that my tour is completed and that I am to leave with the party from Hamburg on July 15 as scheduled. I gather from this and from your letter that my fame (?) has been spread far and wide by Intourist advertising. Think of my feelings when the tourists discover that I know no Russian, have never visited most of the places on the tour, and am really densely ignorant of many important phases of Soviet life! Well...we shall make the best of it and perhaps it will be rather fun if the crowd is reasonable and tolerant. I shall have more to write you after I come back. I have been home a week and have done nothing except bask in the sunshine of domestic felicity, contemplate ruefully my inadequacies as a German conversationalist, and think vaguely about the Russian tour. Quite a contrast to the good old days, eh wot?

If we find a reliable person to take care of Karl- and if Lily can bring herself to part with him for three weeks or so (I doubt it at the moment)-she will accompany me on the second part of the tour and we shall go back to Moscow for a few days in mid-August. In that event I shall surely look up your Rebecca and do all in my power to get you the coveted bibliography. The latter sounds to me like a big order, but perhaps I am wrong. I will do what I can in any case.

Re W. Dodd

As you can well guess, I have no "progress" to report on my project here-and probably will have none to report until late summer or fall. Shameful! But, somehow, I have lost my zest for it. I have no enthusiasm for making contacts with lunatics and scoundrels, and all Germans in official positions are now one or the other. I am enormously interested, of course, in Dodd's appointment as Ambassador- and *that* future contact should lead to some interesting results.

Well, so long for the present. Lily and I send regards to all of you and Karl joins in with "Bah, bah, blah!!!" I suppose he doesn't really mean it, however. One can't tell. Will send you more news later. Cheerio!

As ever,

Fred

Letter from Frederick Schuman, June 20, 1933
Original is in the Frederick Lewis Schuman Papers,
Williams College Archives & Special Collections

Berlin – August 27, 1933

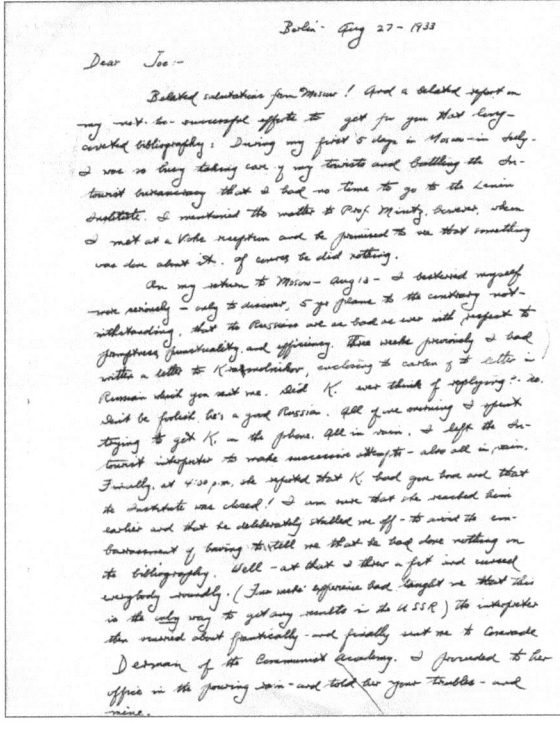

Dear Joe –

Belated salutations from Moscow! And a belated report on my not-too-successful efforts to get for you that long-coveted bibliography: During my first 5 days in Moscow in July, I was so busy taking care of my tourists and battling the in-tourist bureaucracy that I had no time to go to the Lenin Institute. I mentioned the matter to Prof. Mintz, however, whom I met at a Vohs[?] reception and he promised to see that something was done about it. Of course he did nothing.

On my return to Moscow – Aug 13 – I bestirred myself more seriously – only to discover, 5 yr plans to the contrary notwithstanding, that the Russians are as bad as ever with respect to promptness punctuality and efficiency. Three weeks previously I had written a letter to Krasmilnikov[?], enclosing the carbon of the letter in Russian which you sent me. Did K. ever think of replying? No. Don't be foolish, he's a good Russian. All of the morning I spent trying to get K. on the phone. All in vain. I left the In-tourist interpreter to make successive attempts – also all in vain. Finally, at 4:00 p.m. she reported that K. had gone home and that the Institute was closed! I am sure that she reached him earlier and that he deliberately stalled me off, to avoid the embarrassment of having to tell me that he had done nothing on the bibliography. Well – at that I threw a fit and cursed everybody soundly (Four weeks' experience had taught me that this is the only way to get any results in the USSR). The interpreter has scurried about frantically and finally sent me to Comrade Derman of the Communist Academy. I proceeded to her office in the pouring rain – and told her your troubles – and mine.

She had a number of interesting observations to make. One was that you had made a mistake in writing to K. personally instead of to the Lenin Institute impersonally. Another was that K. could not possibly supply you with a bibliography of party history – 1905-1917 – because he has never done any work in that period and knows only the period before 1905. (Why didn't he write you to that effect long ago? Well – that isn't the Russian way of doing things!) She presented me gratis with the bibliographical volume on the "First Russian Revolution" which I sent you from Berlin. She said it covered everything in party history from 1901 to 1906. Perhaps you knew it – or had it already. But since it was the only tangible thing I was able to get, I thought I'd better send it on. She said further that if you would address her directly, she would be happy to prepare for you a select bibliography of the type you want. I tried to persuade her to get to work on it and send it to you, but that, too, is not the Russian Way. You must write at length – and then (maybe)!) she will send you what you want. She speaks English fluently and impressed me as a fairly competent person – and much more reliable than the elusive K., of whom she seemed to have no

Letter from Frederick Schuman, August 27, 1933
Original is in the Frederick Lewis Schuman Papers,
Williams College Archives & Special Collections

very high opinion.

So you see for all my efforts, I can only advise you to start all over again by writing to

Mrs. Derman, Director
Library of the Communist Academy
11 Ulitza Frunze
Moscow, US:S.R. [sic]

As for the tour, it was fascinating and fatiguing. I am writing up my impressions in my spare(!) time and will arrange it so that a copy reaches you eventually. Best wishes from all of us to all of you.

In haste,

Fred

Letter from Frederick Schuman, August 27, 1933

The Nation
20 Vesey Street
New York

Jan. 11, 1933

Miss Rosella H. Werlin
2002 - 31st Street
Galveston, Texas.

Dear Miss Werlin:

Thank you very much for your check for $2 which we are crediting as a first payment on a year's combination subscription to The Nation and Current History, at the special price of $6.50, to be sent to Dr. Joseph S. Werlin, Snell Hall, University of Chicago, Chicago, Illinois.

We are making note on our records that the remaining $4 will reach us on February 1st.

Sincerely yours,

[signature]

The Nation

G/1

Depression financing! Rosella, ever working angles to pick up Joe's spirits and encourage new opportunities, ordered for him a combination subscription to *The Nation* and *Current History*, for a total cost of $6.50. She saved this letter acknowledging her initial payment of $2.00, noting $4.00 due February 1. Did she save it for historic curiosity, or to prove their assertion that she owed 50¢ less than the special price?

As Life Turned Out

It is the urge of a civilized people to know who they really are – their ancestors, their origins, history and vicissitudes.

Joseph S. Werlin
From his book manuscript,
"Mexico Today"

Joseph Werlin, c. 1949
Preparing students for Mexico

Honored by Mexico's Federal District (Mexico City), June 1951
(*back, L-R*) Joseph Werlin, M. M. Feld, R. E. "Bob" Smith
(*front, L-R*) Dr. E. E. Oberholzer, Hugh Roy Cullen

THERE WERE MORE THAN a few among Joe and Rosella's family and friends who barely concealed their dismay, or maybe even gloated, over the news that this overeducated outlier with such high expectations was returning to Cowtown for a faculty post at a junior college masquerading as a university in the making. The original location for the new institution dramatized his fall. Initially, administration and classes were scattered downtown, principally in an old Baptist church within view of the stately Rice Institute, where the four Werlin brothers had received their education. Prestigious Rice didn't yet deign to call itself a university, as this upstart was doing!

Joseph would not let himself be made a victim of schadenfreude. True, this move was not what he had visualized, but he was energized to be back in Houston after his lost years in crowded cities of the big world. Family ties and responsibility had always pulled him towards home, as they had for Rosella. He likely harbored doubts as to whether he was ambitious enough to become a top dog in a very competitive academic circus under any circumstances.

It was no less astonishing, however, that he wasn't offered a job teaching European or Russian history, for which he was so highly qualified. (Perhaps there were historians in the junior college who had those positions locked up?) Instead he was invited to teach sociology, one of those new, less highly regarded social sciences, in which he had no formal education at all!

My brothers and I recall our father saying that a condition of the Houston offer was that he never acknowledge that he had any academic association with Russia. Mother disputed this memory. She claimed that they were so happy for this job opportunity, he maximized his qualifications for teaching sociology instead. Whichever was true, Houston was reactionary and demonstrably racist in that day; touting his authority on the Communist Revolution would not have enhanced his reputation or helped the University appeal to millionaires, brew companies, and cattle barons for support. Joseph Werlin was no greenhorn in Texas!

The transition from historian to sociologist was an entirely natural one for him. His credentials from Chicago carried weight, no matter what the granting department, as the University had famously cultivated and attracted many of the preeminent names in the social sciences. He may not have studied with them, but he had always been drawn into their orbit. In particular, he admired Robert Redfield, an anthropologist who became dean of social sciences at Chicago. A University of Chicago website cites a lecture Redfield gave, titled "Anthropology: Unity and Diversity," in which he spoke to the "breach" that separated historical and scientific inquiry. Instead,

5414 Leopold Street, c. 1940

he argued for a common purpose, an understanding of "people in general." Joseph looked out to the horizon from that intersection.

Redfield had done his PhD fieldwork in Mexico and had published comparative studies of four communities in various stages in their confrontation with modern society. It is hard to say whether Redfield had any direct influence on the newly minted sociologist who would later bring distinction to the University of Houston for his work in Mexico. Mexico was a neighbor, a magnet for someone interested in cultural history.

As a faculty team member, Joseph's priority was to help establish sociology on a solid footing within the University. Sociology was dropped into the general category of "liberal arts and culture." It was later made a department within social sciences, and Joseph assumed the chairmanship. His immediate challenge, however, was preparing to teach four basic sociology courses in subject areas which he himself had never formally studied. In his home office, two full shelves of carefully organized course notes in separate 5" × 8" binders, plus a tall file cabinet loaded with articles and other resource materials, were testimony that he continually worked on revisions. A retrospective on his career, published in the student newspaper the *Cougar* in 1968, cites his other activities in those initial years as well:

> *Dr. Werlin immediately began to play an important role in civic and cultural activities in Houston. Among his earliest projects was the establishment of a Round Table Forum in which leading citizens of the community and faculty members participated. Despite a heavy teaching load, he never rejected speaking engagements to organizations throughout the state.*

Catherine Bateson called her biography of her parents, Margaret Mead and Gregory Bateson, *With a Daughter's Eye*. I beg to use her lens, adding a caveat from Isabel Allende: "All biography is fiction ... what you put in, what you leave in the shadows ... because life is not like that." My filter is this: "Who do I see of the 27-year-old who wrote a travel diary in 1928 in the later life story of Joseph Werlin?"

There is no easy path to answers. "Incongruous" is my operative word, illustrated by my unconscious trail linking "Cowtown" and "schadenfreude" (a word I learned from my father) in successive paragraphs.

I will garble my voice by remembering my father as "Joe." It was unthinkable for me to address him by his first name. Unthinkable for students, for any casual acquaintance, to call him Joe. He wasn't arrogant, but he expected and taught respect. And it's reasonable to argue that he exhibited Southern manners, still practiced in Texas in these decades. Rosella didn't expect such formality, but so it was for women, especially for a woman journalist proud of her byline.

Rosella is central in this story. With two-year-old Dutchy in tow, or in the care of one of her aunts or a babysitter, she began freelancing for various newspapers as soon as she and her "hubby" returned to Houston. I was born four years later, in January 1938. I have the vaguest memory of the duplex where we lived then (on Sul Ross Street, near the University's temporary location in a Baptist church on Main Street). But right away Mother was on the lookout for a home of our own. Four years later, these parents in their forties scraped together a down payment on our first house, on Leopold Street, a little street that dead-ended on the south side of Bray's Bayou (pronounced "bye-oh"). The bayou would routinely flood, occasionally sending baby water moccasins and coral snakes into pools of mud by our driveway or into our victory garden. From the outside, the two-story house looked rather grand, with a cyclone fence enclosing an extra lot. Inside, it was cramped for space. The downstairs

Werlin brothers Joe, Reuben, Eugene, and Sam, c. 1956

porch was converted into a study for Dad, with knotty pine shelves to hold his Russian and German books, which he anticipated he still might need. Mother converted the screen porch upstairs into her office, where her Underwood typewriter sat on an old desk beside stacks of blank newsprint trimmed into legal-sized paper. Later, she squeezed a playpen for baby Ernie into a passageway where she could watch him. Neighbor kids and I played outdoors all day long. Mostly happy memories of Leopold Street conjure up for me now the incongruities of our family life.

My account of my father's experiences in the early years of the University of Houston is based on recollections, not formal inquiry, so parts may not be accurate. However, around 1940, my father was given an office in the first building on the new campus, southeast of downtown, financed by self-made oil millionaire Hugh Roy Cullen. Mr. Cullen's name stands out not just as the principal benefactor of the University but for his ultra-conservative politics and aggressively anti–New Deal attitude. My father, and no doubt other members of the faculty, navigated carefully to avoid his unsettling shadow. However, Rosella, whose real calling was publicity, found opportunities to ingratiate her husband with him and bring credit to the University.

The war years brought out internal struggles and external conflicts for my father that would characterize his life. If he had looked back at his diary, he could have felt proud of his remarkable descriptive powers and insights, befitting a sociologist. More likely he would have cringed, reflecting on what he missed, what might have been beneath the surface that he hadn't seen, at times his unconscious posture of superiority. It is only a diary, after all. Recorded spontaneously and unedited, it doesn't warrant judgment in light of future events. But that is not how he would have read it. Five years after he sent his diary pages to Rose, his friend Frederick Schuman — born into a German Lutheran family — had written him that four-page letter depicting a horrifyingly different Germany. True, the fascist, xenophobic Berlin of 1933 was a different place than Berlin in its cosmopolitan heyday five years earlier. But had "the light that will come from the West" (in Joe's words) really darkened that much? Or had he missed ominous clues?

While the war was in every family's consciousness, it is astonishing how many among my friends say that their families weren't really cognizant of the tragedy emerging in Europe, that they had no hint of the Holocaust. That was not true in our household. Daddy's study was stacked with foreign-language newspapers and magazines. He led and participated in anguished group discussions, often in our home, engaging his youngest brother, Sam, Mother's brothers, and mostly Jewish friends. I would crouch on the staircase landing in my pajamas, trying to listen. The

Joe and Rosella
Guatemala, 1947

discussions were scary. I wrote "Dear Mr. Hitler" letters ("I'm Jewish but I'm really a very nice girl . . .").

Daddy got into disputes with his family, especially with his normally reticent brother Reuben. I recall a meeting of "the Nameless Society" at the home of my parents' friends Chickie and Chuck — a larger discussion group that had a core of regular members but drew in others for a particular focus. Our highly respected (and very handsome) rabbi, Rabbi Robert I. Kahn, of Congregation Emanu El, who had been an army chaplain in New Guinea and the Philippines, sometimes participated. I was older; this occasion must have been in 1951 or '52. The topic was the new state of Israel. My father always had that "third eye" open, looking out from the inside and in from the outside at the same time. He interjected, "What about the Arab point of view?" Reuben blew up: "Millions have died, hundreds of thousands are still displaced, and you sit there, professorially, asking a question that is not our problem!" Mother was furious too. Uncle Sam came to his defense, or at least tried to calm the situation. Dear Uncle Sam, eleven years younger than Daddy, was peacemaker among the four brothers. Behind his disarming smile he revealed a serious, non-dogmatic intellect. He shared books and took long walks with Daddy, but he played golf and met up at weekly Rotary meetings with his other two brothers. Uncle Gene, who had drifted socially towards the Presbyterian church, where his wife was active, was not a participant in these discussions.

Daddy kept his Jewish concerns separate from his teaching at the University (although articles and speeches from the war years, which I haven't read, may reveal otherwise; they are listed on the University of Houston's Special Collections website). As one of the few Jews on the faculty, he was also sensitive to how he reflected Jews in the eyes of his colleagues. There was a lesson for me and my siblings: others would judge every Jew by our behavior.

My parents also hosted social evenings with guests from foreign countries, frequently from Mexico and Guatemala, who came through the University. I remember visitors from Japan, India, France, and Italy. My doll cabinet from childhood holds gifts some brought me, along with "costume" dolls my parents added to foster my appreciation for other cultures.

My father truly had found the right calling as a teacher. But some time early on, he became discouraged over his effectiveness. He had set high standards for himself. His students in the University were, for the most part, of a different bent than what he had known. There were no admission requirements other than the equivalent of a high school diploma. He had a hard time pitching at the right level. Most of the students were part time, and many were not very motivated. Sociology wasn't a demanding discipline then, requiring layers of study, in the way history was. Yet he was enthusiastic about teaching night school, where the students typically were older and more focused.

US Ambassador to Guatemala Edwin J. Kyle, 1947

As scores of returning World War II veterans sought degrees through the G.I. Bill, the University perforce matured quickly and earned an incomparable place among Texas educational institutions. Joe was a popular teacher with these students, and many enrolled in his basic course, "Marriage and the Family" (or some variant of that name), which he offered time and again. He held an old-fashioned point of view with respect to the centrality of the family, with an emphasis on "family values" and "family responsibility." The nuclear family (which he did not define narrowly or burden with religious or nationalistic imperatives) was the basis of Western social order. Divorce was failure.

He acknowledged that veterans modified his thinking and taught him more about life than he could teach them. In particular, he learned about the very real struggles so many faced in re-adapting to "normal" life and reintegrating with their families: breakdowns from mental and physical disorders, estrangement leading to desertion and divorce. Many had witnessed horrors he had only read about. He was humbled by their experiences and honored to receive his highest commendations from these older students. One, a journalist named Bill Stalnaker, remembered him in the *Houston Chronicle* on June 8, 1964, as "a kind and understanding man . . . who could laugh uproariously at a funny joke." He recorded his former teacher's words during one of their occasional lunches:

There is a fine line that divides Hell from Heaven, love from hate, madness from sanity, color from color, despair from hope. In fact, there is a fine line that separates everything. Without it we could not distinguish darkness from light.

Joseph also initiated a course in criminology, I think in the 1950s. He was proud that every Houston police chief studied with him. He visited prisons and gave particular attention to students who had been incarcerated. I was a freshman at the University of Texas when he became greatly distressed over a prison visit with a married student (or maybe a university colleague) who had been arrested for homosexual activity. He offered to help, if this fine man would agree to change his behavior. The man's personal turmoil was beyond his comprehension. However, the great concern of his that stands out in my memory was over gun violence. Texas in those days was known as "the murder capital of the world." Joseph's lecture notes included comparative statistics with every European country; gun deaths in Texas outnumbered those of other countries by a wide mark.

My father began to shift his focus to Mexico in 1939, only five years after he started at the University. The chronology is out of order, but emotionally and intellectually, he had been searching for deeper soil in which to dig early on in his teaching career. He didn't have his own resources for pursuing this interest, and the University had no reason to subsidize him. Remarkably, he was encouraged by an acquaintance he first met through the Houston Good Neighbor Commission, M. M. Feld. The two men bonded over their common ideals. Informally, it also helped that the Felds' son and Dutchy were classmates and friends at public school and religious school. According to an article in the *Houston Press* (likely initiated by my mother), Mr. Feld, president of the Lone Star Bag and Bagging Company, was motivated by his sincere conviction that Texas and Mexico would be able to resolve their increasing problems if only they got to know one another. The article reports that my father and another faculty member, who specialized in government and economics, were provided support to "travel by auto to Mexico, where they will tour [for six weeks] practically every state, visiting small villages and large cities, talking to government executives and to farm laborers, inspecting manufacturing plants and college libraries." It was an incredible investment by M. M. Feld, which would give Joseph a new lease on life.

Everything about the new venture in Mexico fueled his imagination, drawing on his life experience, his education, and his philosophical probing into the causes of destructive social conditions. He shared a conviction with M. M. Feld that social progress required transcending cultural boundaries, but he was more skeptical of a reassuring outcome. As I remember his lessons, he recognized that to understand the problems and expectations of the indigenous peoples, principally Mayan, they could not all be lumped together under a monolithic heading. He made an effort to learn principal words of their languages and to identify their distinctive characteristics and histories. But his focus was on the cities, especially Mexico City, where there were staggering challenges: impoverished indigenous peoples overwhelmed by "New World conquerors," increasing Mestizo power uneasily bridging both worlds, North American penetration, oppressive authority of the Catholic church, popular uprisings, socialism, communism, revolutionary movements, and constitutional experiments.

The war years (of which I speak from childhood experience) brought new immigrants fleeing Europe into Mexico: Jews lucky to escape the horrors in their homelands, Germans who rejected and worked against Nazi ideology, and Nazis who were either in hiding or operating for nefarious ends in a loosely governed allied country. I recall occasional family suppers at a *Wurst Haus* near Hotel Geneva, where I learned to like wieners, sauerkraut, and potato salad with vinegar. Daddy spoke German with the friendly proprietor. But one evening the proprietor, or his waiters, engaged in animated conversation with a boisterous group of German men at a table nearby. Daddy, clearly upset, signaled us to leave, and we never went back. There was always an undercurrent of politics, which I couldn't fathom. Leon Trotsky, a figure in Dad's past who had escaped from Russia to Mexico for safe haven, was assassinated in Mexico City that summer of 1940 when Daddy made his first visit. Daddy pointed out for me the house in Mexico's artsy Coyoacán neighborhood where the murder took place.

US Ambassador to Mexico
William O'Dwyer, 1951

In the fall of 1940, Joseph began publishing observations on Mexico in the *Houston Chronicle* and speaking before influential audiences, and he continued to write articles on Mexico for numerous publications throughout the mid-1950s. He was particularly anxious to demonstrate that Mexico was a loyal ally of the United States in the war effort and warranted respect as an equal. In an article titled "Mexico's Unity," published in the *Yale Review*'s winter 1944 issue, he works through a tangle of different perspectives towards the US, not in any way underestimating conflicts or dangers. But he concludes:

> *It would be a mistake to put the friendship that now prevails for the American neighbor solely on an egotistical or material plane. . . . Most [influential] Mexicans want a continuation of this cordial relationship because they see clearly the folly of permitting the old era of dislike, distrust, rivalry, and non-cooperation to return. They, too, look forward to a world in which justice, humanitarianism, brotherliness, and equality will hold sway.*

In 1943, the family spent our first summer in Mexico, so Dad, with Mother's input, could work out the logistics for a study program for teachers and students. In the beginning, he visualized its principal appeal for prospective educators. The program was not about sightseeing and shopping, although opportunities were built into the experience. Among other requirements, participants for credit had to attend daily lectures given by faculty members of the University of Mexico or by government officials, social workers, artists, or a range of other specialists. He also prepared lectures in his areas of expertise, usually delivered to the students while traveling by bus to outlying regions. In subsequent summers, he offered two five-week sessions for two different groups, adding Guatemala and Cuba. In each of these countries, Dad would set up interactive programs with a major university. The University of Houston was the sponsoring partner.

I draw my prototype description mainly from reading brochures and articles in later years, but as a child, I participated in everything but the lectures. I loved those summers in Latin America, although retrospectively, I spent too much idle, unsupervised time on my own. I was, in my mother's words, "a rambunctious child." My mother planned some activities for me, most memorably, art lessons for three summers with Madame Grachine Nell Brodt, an American ex-pat who lived in Coyoacán and was often on the telephone with unhappy Frida Kahlo. Mother was creative and high-spirited, but her responsibilities for the students, sometimes groups of as many as 40, were exhausting and stressful. After my father added programs in Guatemala and Cuba, she came close to a breaking point. Yet she had an amazing ability to separate her professional and personal outlook. In 1947, an especially trying summer in Guatemala, she submitted and saw published a full-page newspaper article in the *Beaumont Journal* on the greatly admired American ambassador to Guatemala, Edwin J. Kyle, former dean and renowned agricultural scientist at Texas A&M University.

While the summer programs enriched our life experience, allowed us to escape the intolerable summer humidity, and enabled Dad to augment his pitiful salary at the University, Mother missed chances to do what she loved. She had an important part-time job: her former boss at the *Galveston Daily News*, Silas Ragsdale, had recommended her for the position of publicity director for the Galveston Chamber of Commerce. She was the first woman to be offered that opportunity, and she loved it. She didn't love the three-hour bus commute to and from Galveston at least twice a week, but even a small predictable income was worth it. She was also challenged to find day care for me, so I often went along with her, spending many afternoons at the *Galveston News* headquarters, provided crayons and newsprint for my distraction. Mother was expected to publicize Galveston as an exciting destination, to keep tourists coming in, no matter what problems, fears, or sadness the war engendered. Daddy took on a lot of responsibility in the household, including preparing breakfasts and taking Dutchy and me to a cafeteria for supper. Usually I couldn't wait to be with my daddy when he returned home from the University. However, he became impatient with me. The stresses took a toll on everyone in one way or another.

Mother gave up the Chamber job sometime before the birth of our baby brother Ernie in June 1944. This unplanned family addition truly was the joy of my parents' lives, and even I was excited and content to be displaced for a while. But the timing was not good. Daddy was in Mexico for the first advertised summer program, taking Dutchy with him. Mother was hospitalized for her third C-section. Although she was thrilled at almost age 42 to have a healthy, adorable little boy, letters she saved reveal that she was weak and resentful. The following summer our luggage for Mexico included two crates of PET milk, plus suitcases filled with glass bottles and cloth diapers and everything else needed for a baby. As careful as Mother was to have the maid she hired in Mexico boil water and sterilize everything the baby might touch, both she and Ernie developed serious dysentery. Then Grandfather Jacob died in June, and Daddy flew back

Ernie Pyle Werlin, c. January 1946

to Houston for the funeral. For five days Mother was left with full responsibility for the students, as well as for Ernie and me. It was a hard summer.

A six-month stretch in the fall of 1946 was worse. Ernie had a distended belly and screamed with pain. Doctors in Houston couldn't figure out what was causing the problem. Mother guessed something was wrong with his appendix, but there was no evidence for diagnosis ... until his appendix ruptured. He developed an infection that didn't respond to any known antibiotic. Mother sprang into action. She called Dr. Chauncey Leake, president of the University of Texas Medical School in Galveston, who previously had hired her for a publicity campaign. He arranged for an experimental antibiotic, Streptomycin, to be flown from Walter Reed Hospital to Houston's Hermann Hospital. Ernie was saved; he became known as "Miracle Baby." But there was no health insurance from the University in those years. My parents' debt had seriously mounted, in spite of significant write-offs by physicians and other health providers. Just about the point when they were beginning to regroup, in 1948, my father was hospitalized by his first heart attack. The cycle of illness, debt, and recovery began again.

In most ways, the mid- to late 1950s were the easiest, most successful years for my parents. Mother had been reminding her devoted Joe to make good on his promise in 1928 that he would show her Paris and the Swiss Alps, that they would see Rome and London together. They didn't have the resources, so the obvious solution was to set up an international study program in Europe, which they initiated in 1951. My father remained committed to the program in Mexico, however, where he had established strong ties between the University of Mexico and the University of Houston. That connection would strengthen over the next two years.

It drew major attention in Houston in June 1951, when, on the recommendation of the president of the University of Mexico, Dr. Rodolfo Brito Foucher, "Professor Joseph Sidney Werlin, Director of the University of Houston International Studies Center of Mexico" was awarded the Distinguished Visitor Diploma and Medal by the government of Mexico's Federal District (i.e., Mexico City). The citation noted "his distinguished contributions generally to the cause of Mexican-American friendship." There was an impressive ceremony, held in the Federal District's ceremonial headquarters in Mexico City. American ambassador William O'Dwyer (former Mayor of New York City), appointed by President Truman, attended. Both Dr. Brito Foucher and my father understood the importance of extending this recognition to four men who had been forces behind the scenes: Mr. M. M. Feld; Dr. E. E. Oberholzer, founding president of the University of Houston; Mr.

2340 Underwood Boulevard, 1960

Hugh Roy Cullen; and Mr. R. E. "Bob" Smith, a prominent Houston oil millionaire and civic leader. They were also honored at the ceremony. My father was interviewed afterwards by the radio station affiliated with the University of Mexico. He delivered his remarks in Spanish; it is the only clear recording our family has of his voice.

Innocently, I was the cause of trouble for my father in the spring of 1953, at the height of Joe McCarthy and the Red Scare hysteria. My father had little time for hobbies, but he enjoyed learning languages, in the same way others liked to work crossword puzzles. He subscribed to a large-format color magazine, *Soviet Union* (approved by the US State Department in exchange for circulation of *Life* magazine in the USSR). It gave him a chance to practice his Russian and gain insight into current Soviet society. The format was handsome, but the content so absurd, so bathed in propaganda, that I thought my friends would find it as laughable as I did. I toted a couple of copies in my bookbag on my usual morning bus ride — in a segregated public bus — across town to the private Episcopal school in "restricted" River Oaks (Jews not permitted to own residences), where I was a scholarship student. Among my fun-loving and popular classmates was a daughter of R. E. "Bob" Smith (who had been among the recipients of the Distinguished Visitor Award from Mexico). I don't know for sure who reported my actions, but the father of some girl in my small class notified the University of Houston about my alarming activity. My father was called before a University investigating committee to explain why his daughter was showing Communist propaganda in her school. Fortunately, he was highly respected enough that he wasn't censured, but he was told to cancel his subscription and to destroy copies on hand. He was in a quandary about what might be behind this action and had fears of losing his job.

My father harshly reprimanded me over my poor judgment in not asking permission to take his magazines to my school and not considering the consequences. The following morning, he acknowledged he had overreacted to a ridiculous accusation, but it was a painful experience for both of us. He was an extraordinary father, and I had let him down. School performance was important, but he cared more about my overall character development, my sense of curiosity and intellectual inquiry. I have some 20 full-page, typewritten letters he sent me from the time I went away to college until shortly before his death. He expected letters in return; he not only wanted to know what I was studying but wanted to learn about activities that interested me, my social life, and how I expressed myself. He encouraged my intellectual curiosity and writing skills. He counseled and comforted me during bad patches. That was true for my brothers as well, although he had different expectations for his daughter. He responded to the flattering encouragement I was given to continue in graduate school with "No, you are *not* the Margaret Mead type." (In truth, I agreed.) He always supported my mother's ambitions, but he regretted how hard she had to work to maintain a career, to supplement family finances, and to be a wife and mother.

The significant recognition my father's summer programs brought to the University of Houston — by now the third largest university in Texas, but not part of the state system — did not guarantee a safety net for the International Studies Center. In early 1956, a short-term president of the University who had been elevated to a new position as chancellor called my father into his office. Without inviting him to sit down, this former general announced with military coldness that the University was withdrawing all funding for the summer programs: "Study in other countries is not part of this university's mission." My father was baffled and devastated. The University had always endorsed his programs. What could have caused this change in attitude? Why the contempt for the value of foreign study? I never learned all my father's speculations, but in retrospect I connect the dots between my father's PhD focus on the Russian Revolution, McCarthy-era hysteria, the University's reprimand over my circulation of a Soviet Communist magazine at my respected Episcopal school, and my father's high appreciation for an "international" perspective, all of which made his American patriotism suspect to this uncharacteristically military-minded leader of the University.

There was a bright lining to the heavy cloud that my parents didn't foresee. They decided to carry on with the travel program under the moniker Werlin International Cultural Tours. The educational component — lectures by faculty of foreign universities, private meetings with public officials, a cultural focus — remained at the core. However, the program was no longer offered for university credit; participants would not be required to attend lectures or provide a validating essay and other evidence of compliance. As a consequence, they attracted a new clientele of older, more financially secure adults, in addition to the college students who sought a lighter summer experience. The demands on my father were easier. Mother was happier. And they were able to enjoy hard-earned profits for their own benefit.

I traveled with my parents to Europe for the first time in 1955, following my high school graduation. I was able to experience for myself their unique approach. My father prepared history lectures to augment guided tours. Among other memorable

Dr. Werlin lecturing at Supreme Headquarters Allied Powers Europe (SHAPE), Paris, c. 1954

opportunities, he procured a block of tickets for our group to hear the great Paul Robeson sing at the Royal Albert Hall. (We were Texans, Southerners, previously not exposed to an African American artist of world renown!) We attended a lecture on contemporary British politics at Exeter College, Oxford, where my brother Herb (Dutchy) was a graduate student. We sat in on a meeting at the Supreme Headquarters of the Allied Powers in Europe (SHAPE), outside Versailles. What stands out most for me, however, was being with my father in Madrid when he bought an illustrated copy of *Don Quixote* as a gift for the building custodian at the University of Houston, who had been helping him brush up on his Spanish.

In the fall of 1959, Mother found her dream house in Houston, in an older residential neighborhood near the University of Texas Medical Center. Wealthy Houstonians now preferred ranch-style houses in the Memorial area, so this grand lady on classy Underwood Boulevard was picked up at a bargain. Mother insisted that they pay off the house right away. Life was good, but she was taking no chances. Dad had had another heart attack in the mid-1950s. He dismissed increasing signs of heart trouble. She was worried about him.

Dad continued to teach, while working on his book manuscript, tentatively called "Mexico Today." In truth, he no longer had passion for this ambitious project and set it aside for reasons that had as much to do with an uncertain purpose as with obsolete research and changing attitudes. He was energized by a new passion, shared with his brothers: investing in the stock market. They enjoyed riding the bull, but in the spring of 1962 the bear brought them down hard. Daddy never financially recovered. His full-time salary at the University, as I recall Mother lamenting, was less than $10,000. Herb was in Kenya, doing research for his PhD thesis, and he had savings to carry him through. I was married, living in Seattle, raising his first grandchild. He was most unhappy about losing resources to send his young son, "his pal" Ernie, to the University of Pennsylvania the following fall. The old cycle of illness, debt, and recovery ceased this time at debt. He projected optimism, but he had warnings that he was not in good health. His heart stopped on Memorial Day 1964.

To speak of Mother's resilience and tenacity would require another long chapter. But her commitment to her husband's legacy brings Joseph Werlin of 1928 back into view. Mother arranged for a librarian friend from the University of Houston to inventory the groaning shelves of books in their home for possible sale. His library still held some 75 titles of Russian books, a number of which he had returned with in 1928; 50 titles in the German collection, some also of 1928 vintage; and over 600 books and articles of Mexicana. Mother offered other books to the University library. She sold the Mexicana collection to Brigham Young University, using the proceeds to endow the Joseph S. Werlin Memorial Scholarship in Sociology at the University of Houston.

Ferdinand Schevill's *History of Florence* was not among the titles for sale. The signed portrait he sent his younger friend Joe in 1936, "to help him remember our common work and our common distant goal," would remain on the wall behind his desk for all the years that Mother lived in this last home. She carried on with unbelievable vitality to the minute she collapsed from a stroke, which brought on her death, on April 1, 1985. She outlived her beloved Joe for 21 years.

• • •

Mother organized the unveiling of the Joseph S. Werlin Scholarship dedication and memorial plaque on June 8, 1968. Some of those who were in attendance have appeared in this account: Rabbi Robert Kahn gave the invocation;

Prof. Ferdinand Schevill
Dated August 14, 1936
Inscription reads, "*For Joe – To help him remember our common work and our common distant goal. This is the way I looked 25 years ago!*

Ferdinand Schevill"

Dr. Ray K. Daily, billed as Joe's "lifelong friend," gave the welcoming remarks; and Mr. Silas Ragsdale was the chairman of the Scholarship Fund Committee. The benediction was offered by another University of Chicago alumnus, nationally distinguished theologian Dr. Winfred E. Garrison, then serving as chairman of the Philosophy Department at the University of Houston.

Joe's most cherished professor at Rice University, Dr. Radoslav Tsanoff, was the featured speaker. Rice's legendary professor of philosophy was 81 years old in 1968. His three-and-a-half typewritten pages of prepared remarks carried the emotion he felt at being called upon to deliver a eulogy for the long-ago student he had so appreciated. He spoke of his student's high attributes, which he first recognized in his class on the history of philosophy, emphasizing his engagement with "ideas of political, economic, moral, that is to say broadly social significance." Professor Tsanoff's touching tribute is not easily condensed, but his concluding lines bring together teacher and student in words that move beyond words:

> *Long years, indeed centuries hence, University of Houston professors and students will read his name in this room. In doing honor to past achievement in the field of social studies, may they be moved to renewed endeavor, to productive activity in what has been called the Republic of Minds, the spiritual dynamic in the life of mankind.*

Joseph Sidney Werlin had earned his place in the Republic of Minds, where he aspired to be remembered.

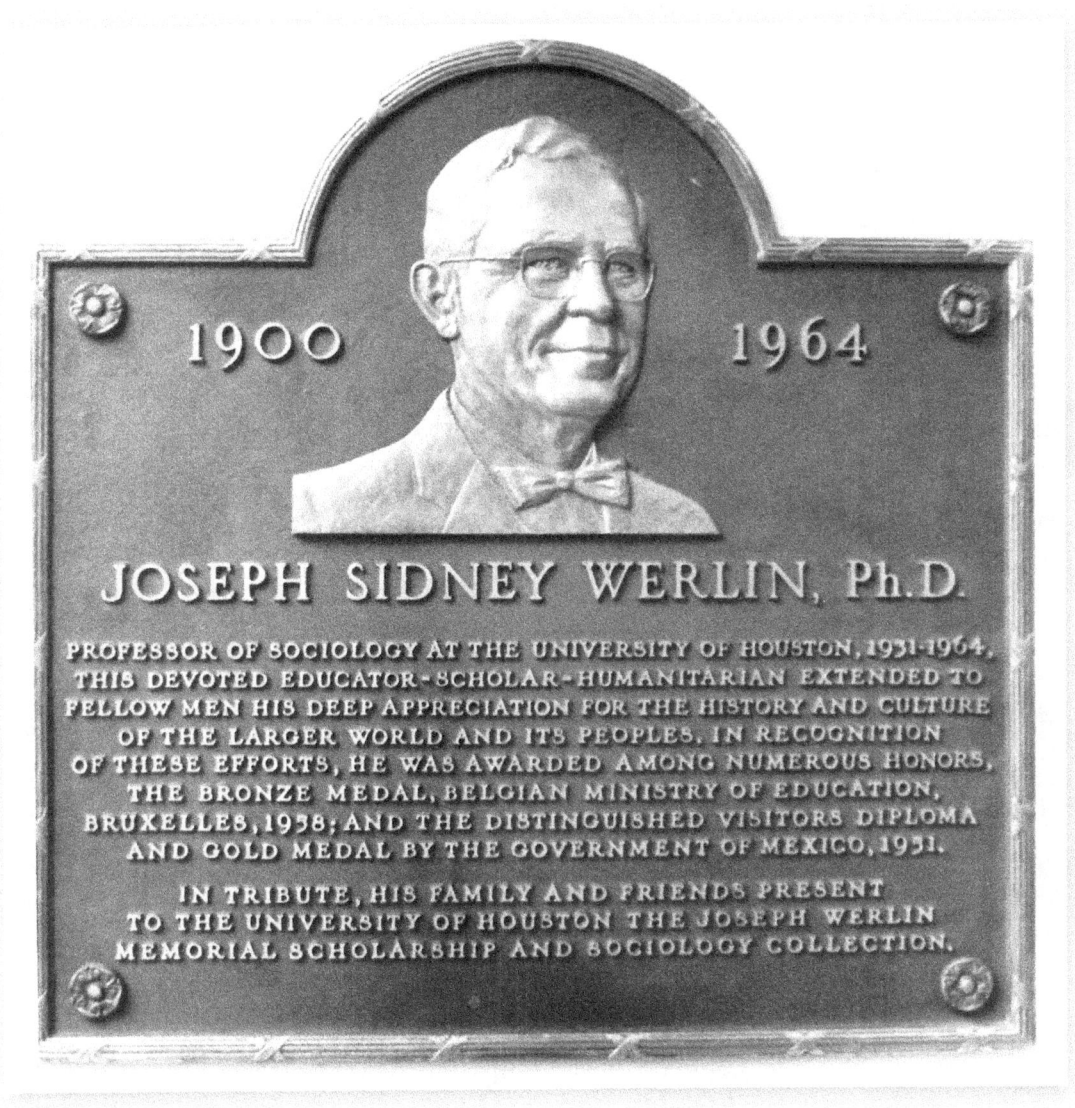

Memorial plaque in the Werlin Library,
Department of Sociology, University of Houston
Dedicated June 1968

As Life Turned Out | 253

Celebrating the establishment of the
Joseph S. Werlin Sociology Faculty Award
to Promote US–Latin American Cultural Understanding
University of Houston, November 5, 2004
(*L-R*) Joella Werlin (wearing Rosella's Guatemalan jacket
and Mexican jewelry), Ernest Werlin, Herbert Werlin

Biographical Notes

He was so much a part
Of all things Good:
Home . . . Family . . . Children
History . . . Languages . . . Countries . . .
Travel . . . boats and trains . . . skies and planes . . .
But oh . . . so much a part
Of all good books!

— Frances E. Heid
Poet and family friend

This biographical essay was originally written by Rosella Werlin in February 1967, for inclusion in a program booklet for guests attending a ceremony to establish the Joseph S. Werlin Memorial Scholarship in Sociology at the University of Houston. Some details have been modified or updated and other notes have been added by me.

Werlin boys at Pearland Farm, c. 1913
(Auto belonged to the town doctor)

JOSEPH SIDNEY WERLIN WAS BORN in Philadelphia, Pennsylvania, on December 5, 1900, the second child and first son of Sarah Chausky and Jacob Baer Werlin(sky). Both parents had emigrated with other family members from Tsarist Russia in 1890, when they were 15 years old, to escape pogroms threatening Jewish areas of settlement and to seek the promises of the New World. They were married in Philadelphia in 1895.

The lure of the West and the possibility of farming one's own land, which seemed the essence of the American dream to Jacob Werlin, induced him in 1910 to invest his meager savings, plus borrowed funds, in a small farm and home in Pearland, Texas. However, within three years, unyielding soil, unexpected drought, inexperience in agricultural techniques, and absence of other resources combined to leave the family, then totaling six children, in a state of total penury. The Werlins moved to Houston to begin life anew.

In spite of limited education and inability to find work to support his family until the early 1920s, when he was hired as bookkeeper for a midsize furniture company, Jacob Werlin was a man of books. He taught himself to write in polished English at a high grammatical level, enabling him to contribute articles to Houston-area publications. He even authored, at his own expense, a manual on bookkeeping for farmers. He embraced America in dress and outlook, but he remained deeply religious and a passionate Zionist. He owned the first Hebrew typewriter in the state of Texas and had completed two manuscripts on biblical subjects by the time of his death in 1945. His five living children designed a bookplate in his memory. The caption read, "His delight was in the Law of the Lord, and in His Law did he meditate day and night."

Jacob B. Werlin, 1928

Joseph developed ready eagerness for books and education, although he rejected his father's old-world religious attitudes. He fared well among other farm kids in the two-room schoolhouse in Pearland. However, when the family moved to Houston, Joseph, then age 12, as the eldest

Tennis break at Annapolis, 1919

son, had to contribute to family support and could not continue in school. Among other jobs, he worked as a stock boy and office clerk at the E. Alkemeyer Company, one of the leading wholesale-retail mercantile establishments of that era, earning approximately three dollars a week for a 12-hour day. Later, he worked for Radoff Brothers and other establishments under similar conditions and salary. Throughout this period, he turned over his wages to the family. However, he continued to study, using resources of the public library, and he prepared himself for higher education with the help of an occasional tutor.

After the outbreak of World War I, Joseph determined to compete in the entrance exams for the United States Naval Academy at Annapolis and so embarked on an intensive two-year preparation program during his spare time. He also took training at the YMCA in boxing, and he learned to play tennis. He received a coveted congressional appointment — but only as second alternate from his district in Texas; however, the other two candidates failed their examinations. Jacob, anticipating the religious discrimination his son might face, had his Russian patronymic legally changed to Werlin. With pride and anticipation, Joseph entered the Academy in the fall of 1919. However, he was soon disillusioned: this world was as foreign to him as that which his parents had experienced when they landed at Ellis Island. He was socially, emotionally, and academically unprepared to make his way among more privileged American sons, and he encountered his first brush with anti-Semitism. He withdrew from the Academy in the spring of his plebe year, but aspects of the discipline and at least one important friendship — with another Jewish midshipman, Morris Smellow, subsequently a rear admiral — endured for his lifetime. (He met but did not really know Hyman Rickover, from the class of 1922. However, Joseph remained acutely conscious of the tribulations and successes of the famous admiral, "father of the nuclear submarine.")

In the fall of 1920, Joseph gained admission to the Rice Institute (now Rice University), which, among its other advantages, was virtually tuition-free. He maintained a job

Werlin in Annapolis uniform, 1919

after classes every day at Holland-Amdur Furniture Company, where his father was now employed, and he continued to turn over most of his salary to the family coffers. His deep appreciation and affection for the co-proprietor, Herbert Holland, who died suddenly in 1931, resulted in the naming of the firstborn Werlin child, Herbert Holland Werlin, in his memory.

By the time Joseph graduated from Rice in June 1924, he was persuaded that an academic career would be his goal. He proceeded on to the University of Chicago for graduate studies in history. His family's origins and the then tumultuous political developments in Russia, dramatized by the Communist Revolution of 1917 and its consequences, spurred his curiosity about that enigmatic land. He completed his MA degree in 1926, with encouraging success, submitting a thesis titled "The Russian Bolshevik Party as a Revolutionary Marxist Party." The road to earning his PhD was more problematic, as his focus made him something of an amphibian, caught between history and political science. His thesis advisor recommended that he attend lectures and examine resources at the University of Berlin, which had become a major center for the study of the Russian Revolution. Without clear objectives, in late January 1928 he set out from Galveston for Europe, where he would remain until August. His possibility for obtaining a visa to visit or study in Moscow was understood to be very uncertain — a rare feat during that suspicious and turbulent epoch — but in April he finally succeeded in gaining entry into Russia for a brief period of 20 days.

Joseph returned to Texas from his eight months of travel in early September 1928. In December he married his sweetheart, whom he had met the previous summer — Rose Ella Horowitz, a newspaper reporter, daughter of Rabbi and Mrs. Henry J. Horowitz of Galveston. The couple then moved to Chicago, where he continued his studies towards his PhD, which was granted on June 16, 1931. His doctoral thesis, "Russian Social-Democracy in the Period of Its First Three Congresses (1898–1905)," was a unique investigation into the foundations of the Russian socialist experiment. So

December 23, 1928

far as is known, he was the first graduate student at the University of Chicago to be awarded a PhD for a thesis on the Russian Revolution.

The year 1931 drifted downward into the deepest period of the Great Depression. Russia was a distinctly unpopular subject in the hostile, xenophobic political and economic climate of the time, and university appointments were not easily come by under any circumstances. The road thereafter was even more difficult. A first child, Herbert Holland, was born May 23, 1932. Rosella Werlin had found limited job opportunities as a reporter for various newspapers in Chicago, but as a new mother, her options were even more limited. She returned to Houston for three months at the beginning of 1933. The young father remained in Chicago, tutoring and teaching part-time in a high school and instituting a course for the University of Chicago's home-study program in Russian twentieth-century history and social development. Concerned that widespread unemployment had destroyed hope for others to seek higher education, he helped establish the People's Junior College, a college-credit program at nominal cost. He was able to set up headquarters at the Jewish People's Institute, in the densely populated West Side of Chicago, where he served as registrar and director. He also found a part-time position as a social worker. All three jobs provided this new father with less than $125 a month. And the monthly rental bill extracted $50!

A turn in fortune finally came in 1934, when he was invited to join the first faculty of the University of Houston, then expanding from a junior college into a four-year institution. He helped establish the Department of Sociology and was conferred a full professorship in 1945. The transition from history to sociology presented no obstacle for this new faculty member, even though he lacked formal academic training in the latter discipline. He had attended open lectures and had been in the presence of some of the leading social scientists in the world at the University

University of Chicago, June 16, 1931

of Chicago. The focus of his interests had always been on the nature of societies and the study of forces — historical, racial, demographic, and cultural — that gave any group its social and political characteristics. It was this passion that not only inspired his earlier investigation into the genesis of the Russian Revolution but which contributed to a lifelong inquiry into the tragedies of Nazi Germany. His interest in other peoples also inspired the courses which he most enjoyed teaching, those on the cultures of contemporary Mexico and contemporary Europe. He also was deeply convinced of the validity of the ethical principles that ideally governed Western societies, and therefore found satisfaction in teaching more recognized sociology courses in criminology and "marriage and family life."

From 1934 until 1943, Dr. Werlin directed his energies primarily to the administration and development of the Department of Sociology. However, during this time he became increasingly concerned with the problems of Mexican-Americans in Texas and the serious misunderstandings between the two neighbors, Texas and Mexico. With the ending of World War II in view, Dr. Werlin conceived of a summer study center in Mexico for university credit. Through the cooperation of the National University of Mexico and other institutions in the region, lectures by native educators, government officials, and social welfare administrators were combined with sightseeing and local travel. Credit studies included classes in history, sociology, and Spanish. The concept, initiated in 1944 under the auspices of the University of Houston, continued successfully until 1953. In later years, it was broadened to include similar study centers in Guatemala and Cuba. The program in Guatemala was inaugurated in affiliation with the University of Guatemala (San Carlos) and the one in Cuba with the University of Havana. These programs set a precedent by being the first in those countries to establish college credit affiliation with an American university. In later years, the study program expanded to Europe, although no longer for college credit. Dr. Werlin arranged for lectures with faculty at the Sorbonne, Oxford, and other universities in countries where the group traveled.

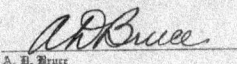

University of Houston Distinguished Service Award, 1959

Joseph Werlin maintained primary interest in Mexican-American relations even as he expanded study programs into other countries. He secured scholarships at the University of Houston for students from Mexico and other Latin American countries and participated on the Houston board of the Texas Good Neighbor Commission, delivering lectures before various public and professional groups and writing numerous articles for scholarly journals and local newspapers. In 1951, he was awarded the Distinguished Visitor's Medal and Diploma from the Government of the Federal District of Mexico, and he eventually made approximately thirty separate trips to Mexico, visiting almost every region. At the time of his death in 1964, he had made considerable progress on a book tentatively titled "Today's Mexico," which he hoped to be an exhaustive general work of sociological and historical interpretation covering the spectrum of contemporary Mexican life.

Joseph Werlin never tired of reminding his family that "the world is my oyster" (or "your oyster"), and he actively sought to open it through travel and linguistics. He believed that reading and speaking the language of a people were first requirements for honest evaluation of their literature, culture, and behavior. Consequently, he methodically acquired facility with all common European tongues — Spanish,

Werlin receives Distinguished Visitor's Medal
Federal District (Mexico City), 1951

French, German, Italian, and Russian — and learned, at least to some degree of competence, Portuguese, Greek, Dutch, and Danish. He also studied Sanskrit, and he spent more than a year investigating Indigenous dialects spoken in Mexico and Guatemala.

He was author of numerous articles, including "Mexico's Unity" in the *Yale Review* (Winter edition, 1944); "Mexico's Opinion of Us" in the *Southwestern Atlantic Quarterly* (Duke University Press, July 1944); "The Pathology of Hyper-Nationalism" in the *Southwestern Social Science Quarterly* (December 1939); and "Mexico: Twelve Years of Observation," a series in the *Houston Chronicle* (November 26–December 2, 1952). He also was continually sought out as a platform lecturer by civic, fraternal, and educational organizations, a pleasure he was forced to forego in later years for health reasons.

Among the professional associations to which Dr. Werlin belonged were Phi Kappa Phi, the Southwestern Sociological Society, the National Sociology Honorary Society, the American Sociological Association, and the World Sociological Congress. In addition to receiving the Distinguished Visitor's Medal and Diploma from the government of Mexico City in 1951, he was the recipient of a bronze medal from the Belgian Ministry of Education in 1958, presented at the Brussels World's Fair for his "work on behalf of international understanding." In 1959, he was conferred honorary citizenship of Vieux Montmartre (Paris) for "a quarter century of visiting, writing, and lecturing on Europe."

Joseph Werlin died of a heart attack, suddenly and without warning, on May 30, 1964. At the time of his death, he was survived by his wife of 35 years, Rosella Horowitz Werlin; sons Herbert Holland and Ernest Pyle; daughter Joella; grandson Adam Henry Zivin; brothers Reuben, Eugene, and Samuel; and sister Nadine (Mrs. George Cain).

Rosella Werlin died on April 1, 1985. Herbert Holland Werlin died on January 25, 2014.

Reuben, Sam, Nadine, Eugene, and Joseph
May 1964

Joseph Werlin and family
Leopold Street home, c. 1950

Last family portrait
Werlin family with grandson Adam Henry Zivin
Underwood Boulevard home, August 1963

A Daughter's Tribute

*The light of sanity, of peace, of understanding will
not come from the East; certainly not from Poland . . .*

— Diary, April 5, 1928

In October 1990, my husband Robert Autrey and I joined a University of Chicago travel program billed as "West Meets East." We set out one year after the Berlin Wall came down, one week after the formal reunification of East and West Germany. We were the first Americans whom many "on the other side" had ever met. The mood of hope, mixed with anxiety and distrust, was electrifying! We were taught a new word: *Mauerkopf*, meaning "wall-head." We encountered wall-heads on both sides.

I carried with me selected pages of the Diary, determined to follow my father's 1928 footsteps wherever our paths might cross. In Berlin, we walked along Unter den Linden, looked for the oldest buildings of Friedrich Wilhelm University, strolled in the Tiergarten, detoured to see what remained of the "New Synagogue" on Oranienburger Strasse (still undergoing postwar restoration), enjoyed cafes in chic Charlottenburg, spent a fascinating afternoon in Potsdam — all places my father had written about. But I was especially anxious to visit Leipzig, a short distance from Berlin.

I wasn't prepared for such a dreary city, blackened by soot, its historic cultural center overshadowed by hideous Soviet-era concrete buildings. Most in our group chose to travel on to Dresden. But we remained behind, determined to learn what we could about the "large statue" where an aggressive photographer had coerced my father into having his picture taken in 1928. I showed the postcard featuring the *Völkerschlachtdenkmal* to our city guide. Might that monument still stand? Perhaps be concealed around a corner nearby? My question elicited an amused response. Of course! This is a famous place. We must see it!

We taxied 20 minutes out of the city center to the site of the unimaginably colossal Monument to the Battle of the Nations, dedicated in 1913. It was strangely deserted; there were no other tourists in sight. Robert recorded that memorable experience for me, as I posed to mimic my father, seated on the same low wall surrounding a reflecting pool. My photo did not come out as well: the air was so badly polluted that the 300-foot-high Teutonic "temple" behind me is a nondescript gray block without any heroic detail. It was a monument to heroes without any heroes.

Joseph Werlin, June 24, 1928 Joella Werlin, October 16, 1990

Völkerschlachtdenkmal (Monument to the Battle of the Nations), Leipzig
Dedicated in 1913 to commemorate the 100th anniversary of Napoleon's defeat at Leipzig
No doubt in its day it was seen as a monument to a war that would end all wars.

A Daughter's Tribute | 267

Warsaw

Nowhere did I feel the ugliness of World War II linger more than in Warsaw. Consciousness of a society that had sunk to the nadir of civilized behavior depressed my interest in venturing out beyond the incongruous luxury of the Marriott Hotel where we were staying. We could see Soviet military conscripts selling off their shabby uniforms on the streets. I had underlined in Daddy's diary his disgust with the idle, "pampered" military soldiers and officers he saw, "with their ribbons and medals, their boots and spurs and swords." He wrote, "By their glitter and glamour they make war possible.... It makes war appear merely a parade, a beautiful pageant deceiving them along with the unhappy others." Looking ahead, he said, "The light of sanity, of peace, of understanding will not come from the East; certainly not from Poland." Then he added, "Mayhap this light will come from the Soviet; more likely still it will come from the West, for poor as its record has been, omnipresent as the old elements and features still are, the signs of a new and saner dawn are nevertheless on its horizon." (Oh, Daddy, how you misjudged!)

I had to bear witness! We walked (as I recall) to the site of the Monument to the Heroes of the Warsaw Ghetto Uprising. Few people were around. Guards stood as stone-cold as the monument itself. I held up my point-and-shoot camera, hanging off a lanyard, to take a picture, and realized as I snapped that a small Asian child was pushing her pink doll buggy in front of the fallen hero, now bloodied by autumn leaves. The mother rushed to pick up her child, but I stopped her by tightly crossing my hands over my heart and smiling. She smiled back. After that moment of hope, I was ready to see Warsaw with my daddy.

A child pushes her pink doll buggy across the steps of the
Monument to the Heroes of the Warsaw Ghetto Uprising
Warsaw, Poland, October 1990
(Photo credit: Joella Werlin)

Sources and Resources

Correspondence, Joseph S. Werlin–Samuel N. Harper, 1928, published by permission, Special Collections Research Center, the University of Chicago Library

Letters, Frederick L. Schuman to Joseph S. Werlin, 1933: Original letters are included in the Frederick Lewis Schuman Papers, Williams College Archives & Special Collections

Professor Joseph Werlin papers, University Archives of the University of Houston Libraries Special Collections (includes correspondence, speeches, notes, lecture materials, and extensive subject and press files; also specific materials pertaining to the International Cultural Studies programs, Department of Sociology)

Rosella Horowitz Werlin papers (MS 77-005), Rosenberg Library, Galveston, Texas (includes scrapbooks with articles and other materials pertaining to RHW's journalism career in Galveston)

Werlin Papers (Rosella Horowitz and Joseph Sidney Werlin), Dolph Briscoe Center for American History, the University of Texas at Austin

Note: All unsourced documents, letters, and photographs in this book are in possession of the Werlin family.

Joseph S. Werlin (1900–1964) was the first PhD candidate at the University of Chicago approved for a proposed thesis on the origins of the Russian Revolution. In January 1928, he set out from Galveston, Texas, to study in Berlin and Moscow. His travel diary shows his curiosity to understand foreign ways and cultures, foretelling an unanticipated career turn.

At age ten, Joe's immigrant parents moved their family from Philadelphia to Pearland, Texas. After a brief stint at Annapolis, he entered Rice Institute in the fall of 1920, completing a BA in European history. He earned an MA from the University of Chicago in 1926 and a PhD in 1931. The Great Depression, anti-Soviet fears, and anti-Semitism combined to dash opportunities in his chosen area of study. In 1934, he was offered a teaching appointment in sociology on the first faculty of the University of Houston, where he remained until his death.

"Greenhorn," a humorous, mildly derisive term, often was applied to Eastern European immigrants in the early twentieth century. Joseph Werlin, American-born, well-mannered, and university-educated, might not seem to fit the image. But on this journey, he referred to himself as a "greenhorn," an "innocent abroad."

Joe initially meant his diary only for family interest when he sent handwritten pages to his fiancée — an aspiring journalist — in Texas. Later, he recognized wider appeal. He interviewed Moscovites for their responses to the new Red order and offered insights into the 1928 German elections, noting the weak showing of "the famous (or infamous) Hitler." Related correspondence, documents, and photos illuminate dimly lit places and stirrings in 1928. He senses no gathering winds of war, but he reveals tensions in this precarious post–World War I period, which a decade later will erupt with unimagined calamity.

Joella Werlin, his daughter, develops this story and reveals his life as it turned out.

JOELLA WERLIN was born and raised in Houston. Her Texas upbringing and outlook was differentiated from her peer group's by summer travels with her professor father and journalist mother to Mexico, Guatemala, and Cuba, where her father led international studies programs. She attended the University of Texas at Austin for one year before transferring to Connecticut College (New London), where she received a BA in European history. She holds a graduate diploma in anthropology from the University of Oxford. After marriage and living for several years on the East Coast, her family — with two young children, Adam Zivin and Joselyn Zivin — relocated to Portland, Oregon.

For 15 years, she served as director of public affairs and community relations for the Portland ABC-TV affiliate. She later became a professional personal historian, helping individuals, families, and family-owned businesses preserve a permanent record of their life and career stories. Now that she is retired, living in Seattle, Washington, *A Texas Greenhorn* emerges from that most valued career experience.

www.ingramcontent.com/pod-product-compliance
Lightning Source LLC
Chambersburg PA
CBHW081831170426
43199CB00017B/2698